ALSO BY DAVE BARRY

CLASS CLOWN

THE MEMOIRS OF A PROFESSIONAL WISEASS:
HOW I WENT 77 YEARS WITHOUT GROWING UP

DAVE BARRY

SIMON & SCHUSTER

New York   Amsterdam/Antwerp   London
Toronto   Sydney/Melbourne   New Delhi

Simon & Schuster
1230 Avenue of the Americas
New York, NY 10020

First Simon & Schuster hardcover edition May 2025

SIMON & SCHUSTER and colophon are registered trademarks of Simon & Schuster, LLC

Simon & Schuster strongly believes in freedom of expression and stands against censorship in all its forms. For more information, visit BooksBelong.com.

For information about special discounts for bulk purchases, please contact Simon & Schuster Special Sales at 1-866-506-1949 or business@simonandschuster.com.

The Simon & Schuster Speakers Bureau can bring authors to your live event. For more information or to book an event, contact the Simon & Schuster Speakers Bureau at 1-866-248-3049 or visit our website at www.simonspeakers.com.

Interior design by Wendy Blum

Manufactured in the United States of America

1   3   7   9   10   8   6   4   2

Library of Congress Cataloging-in-Publication Data has been applied for.

ISBN 978-1-6680-2178-1
ISBN 978-1-6680-2180-4 (ebook)

For Mom and Dad, the two best parents I ever had.[*]

---

[*]   They would have approved of this joke.

CONTENTS

INTRODUCTION

SO I'M IN A ROCK BAND WITH STEPHEN KING.
(I'm not name-dropping here; I have a point.)

It's an all-author band called the Rock Bottom Remainders. If I had to identify our biggest weakness, as a band, I would say it's performing music. We suck at that. What we're good at is endurance. We have endured, as a band, for more than thirty years, something you cannot say about, for example, the Beatles.

I met Steve (I call him Steve) at our first rehearsal, in 1992. When I arrived, the other authors were already "jamming," which is what musicians call it when everybody is playing something on an instrument, but nobody knows for sure what anyone else is playing. At least that's how the Remainders jam.

So I shouldered my guitar and joined in. After we spent maybe a half hour trying, with only sporadic success, to play the same chord at the same time, we took a break. As I was unshouldering my guitar, Steve, whom I'd never met, came over to me, leaned his face down to mine (he's a big guy) and said, in a booming voice, "So, Dave Barry, WHERE DO YOU GET YOUR IDEAS?"

Then he laughed a maniacal horror-master laugh. We all laughed, because "Where do you get your ideas?" is the cliché question authors get asked all the time, to the point where many of us have a joke response, such as "Costco."

The truth is, there's no simple answer to the question of where ideas come from. Sure, sometimes it's obvious. If you're a humor columnist, and your dog manages to snag your uncooked Thanksgiving turkey off the kitchen counter and eat a bunch of it raw, then vomit it back up, then, shortly thereafter, notice the mess on the floor and decide for some dog reason to eat it *again*, your initial reaction is going to be "Dammit! The dog has ruined Thanksgiving!" But your immediate next reaction is going to be, "Hey! That's an idea for a humor column!"

But most of the time you have no idea where you got an idea: It just appears in your brain. Of course it had to have been inspired by *something*—your childhood, your education, your social environment, your fourth vodka gimlet, or some combination of these and other factors, swirling around in your subconscious mind until an idea burbles up to where you can grab hold of it and turn it into words, and thus survive for another day as a writer, instead of having to get a real job.

So it's complicated, the ideas question. You could write a whole book about it. And that, basically, is what this memoir is: my attempt to give a non-Costco explanation of how, over the decades, I was able to pull enough jokes out of my butt, or wherever they came from, to achieve fame and fortune in the field of humor writing.

Although I hesitate to use the word "fame." I have achieved a certain level of celebrity, but it's a pretty low level. I mean, people do sometimes recognize me in public, but it turns out, upon further review, that a substantial number of these people think I'm Carl Hiaasen. Carl is my good friend—I love Carl—but he's a completely separate human being.

So I worry that I'm not famous enough to write a memoir. I'm nervous about venturing into a genre dominated by mega-celebrities such as Barbra Streisand, who wrote a 970-page memoir teeming with anecdotes about all the famous people she has known. For example, in her book she describes the time she got a phone call from Warren Beatty, then writes: "I hung up and asked myself, Did I sleep with Warren? I kind of remember. I guess I did. Probably once."

Think about that: Barbra Streisand has had so many celebrity encounters that *she doesn't even know for sure whether she slept with Warren Beatty.* I can't compete with that. Warren Beatty has never even texted me, let alone called. Sure, I've had some noteworthy experiences. I once used a Barbie doll to set fire to a pair of men's underpants on national television (more on this later). Also I'm in a rock band—did I mention this already?—with Stephen King. But I'm nowhere near Barbra's league.

So when I started this memoir project, I was genuinely unsure about whether it was a good idea. Throughout the writing process, I was nagged by nagging questions, such as: "Why would anybody want to read this?" And: "Who's going to care?"

And those questions were coming from my *wife.*

No, that's a joke. My wife has been very supportive. But I'm hoping to reach a wider audience. So to you, the person reading these words who, ideally, is not one of my close relatives who got the book for free, I say: Thanks. I hope you enjoy this memoir. It's not all jokes—there are some serious parts, especially in the early chapters—but I hope you'll be entertained.

I also hope I succeed in answering the question of where my ideas come from. I'll start by talking about two people who were major influences on me, especially in my early life—two people without whom I would literally not exist.

I refer, of course, to Barbra Streisand and Warren Beatty.

But seriously, it's time to meet my parents.

CHAPTER ONE

MOM AND DAD

LIKE SO MANY MEMBERS OF THE BABY BOOM GENER-
ation, I started out as a baby.

> Mr. and Mrs. David W. Barry
>
> announce
>
>
>
>
> DAVID MCALISTER BARRY
>
> JULY 3rd, 1947

This happened in 1947, in Armonk, New York, a hamlet (yes, a hamlet; Google it) about thirty miles north of New York City.

Today Armonk is a prestigious address. IBM has its world head-quarters there. It's a tony little town, a power hamlet, with high-priced real estate and an affluent population. Today you can't throw a rock in Armonk without hitting a hedge-fund manager.

It wasn't like that when I was growing up. My friends and I threw a great many rocks (we didn't have video games) but to the best of my recollection we never hit anybody affluent.

Back then Armonk was a village of around two thousand people, pretty much all of whom knew each other. There were some well-to-do residents and some who commuted to corporate jobs in the city. But there were also working-class families and tradespeople. Among our neighbors were two carpenters and two plumbers. This was fortunate for my father, who needed a lot of advice on carpentry and plumbing, because he was building our house.

My father wasn't in construction; he was a Presbyterian minister. The reason he was building our house was that he didn't have the money to hire somebody else to do it. So he did it himself, starting with the foundation, which he dug by hand.

My sister, Kate, and me in 1948, next to the house our dad was building

Dad learned house-building as he went along, and it did not always go smoothly. I remember once he was trying, unsuccessfully, to hang a door for the better part of an afternoon. He finally gave up and sent me to our neighbors, the Petersons, to see if Henry Peterson might be available for a consult. Henry, an older Swedish gentleman, was a friend of my father and a master carpenter.

When Henry saw what Dad had done to the door, he shook his head and said, "Dave, Dave, Dave," which, with his Swedish accent, came out as "Dafe, Dafe, Dafe." Then he grabbed some tools and hung the door expertly in a few minutes. Which I imagine is what my father was hoping would happen.

(The Petersons were great neighbors. When I had to sell candy for Little League, I always went to them first, because Mrs. Peterson was really nice. I *hated* having to sell things. My sales pitch was "You don't want to buy any Little League candy, do you?" But Mrs. Peterson always insisted that I sell her some.)

So throughout my childhood, the Barry house was basically a working construction site, with unfinished walls and ceilings, building materials lying around and the occasional random electrical wire sticking out from somewhere. Dad spent many, many weekends and evenings working on the house, and although it improved over the years, it was never really 100 percent finished, at least not while I lived there.

Our house had quirks. We got our water from a well, and from time to time the water would stop running, which meant somebody had to prime the pump. This was usually my job, especially if Dad was at work. I'd grab a flashlight and go out to the pump house, which was a dank, low-ceilinged subterranean shack containing the pump and approximately four hundred trillion spiders. I'd climb down in there, unscrew the plug, pucker up and blow air into the pump[1] until it was primed, and we had running water again, at least temporarily. Over the years I

---

1. That's right, you had to blow into the pump. I still don't understand the mechanics of it, but it worked.

primed the pump many, many times. The spiders would be like, "Oh, YOU again."

We lived on a one-lane dirt road, maybe a half mile long, with three other families. The town didn't maintain our road, so when it snowed, it was up to the families—the dads, really—to clear off the snow. For years the system they used was to put tire chains on somebody's car and use it to tow a homemade V-shaped wooden plow, which theoretically would push the snow off to the sides of the road. This was not a great system. The rope that pulled the plow was always breaking, and the car was always getting stuck. So the dads spent a lot of time pushing the car, shouting instructions to each other, getting red-faced, sometimes saying bad words, sometimes stopping to catch their breath and—as dads did back then whenever they had a spare moment—fire up cigarettes.[2]

I don't mean to suggest, in describing the Barry homestead, that I grew up in some kind of underprivileged, hardship childhood environment. Not at all. Not even close. Spiders aside, I had a wonderful childhood. We didn't have a lot of material things, but we had a LOT of fun. And we had freedom. Behind our house were several large tracts of undeveloped land, which we called the Woods. That land has long since been subdivided into manicured McMansion estates, but back then it was one big sprawling nature preserve, many unoccupied acres of trees and meadows and brooks and ponds.

The landowners didn't mind if we local kids ventured onto their property,[3] and venture we did. We spent countless happy hours roaming the Woods, exploring, climbing trees, swinging on vines, damming creeks, swimming in and skating on lakes and ponds, catching deeply unfortunate frogs, shouting, burping, farting and of course throwing rocks, many rocks.

When we weren't in the Woods, we were riding our bikes all over

---

2. Everybody smoked back then. Our family doctor was Mortimer "Monty" Cohn, a close friend of my parents. When my father went in for a physical, Monty would always tell him he needed to quit. Then the two of them would light up. Dr. Cohn smoked unfiltered Camels.

3. At least that was our assumption.

Armonk, pedaling for miles, looking for adventures to have and other kids to play with and/or annoy. We played red rover, hide and seek, capture the flag, running bases and various mutant forms of baseball involving as many as fourteen and as few as two players per team. We sometimes got into fights. We shot many, many things, including each other, with BB guns. When we got a little older we hitchhiked to Mount Kisco or White Plains to go to the movies. We experimented with cigarettes[4] and engaged in what I will euphemistically describe as "mischief."

Needless to say we did most of these things without parental supervision. You've heard this ad nauseam from us Boomers, but it's true: Parents back then often had no idea where their kids were or what they were doing.[5] The prevailing parental philosophy was that if the kids got home by suppertime without major injuries, all was well. It wasn't that our parents didn't care about us; I think it was mainly that they didn't view the world as a fundamentally dangerous place. They grew up in the Depression and had recently been through a world war. To them, the 1950s weren't so scary.

Also parents back then were pretty busy. At least mine were. My dad, when he wasn't building our house, was commuting to New York City to do his real job, which was being executive director of the New York City Mission Society, a nonprofit organization that ran programs for inner-city kids. He was active in New York's antipoverty community and the

---

4. For a brief period, when I was twelve or thirteen, my friends and I also experimented with corncob pipes, which we bought at the Armonk Stationery Store, which sold a variety of things—candy, cigarettes, sodas, newspapers, comic books—but not stationery. We'd go out in the woods and stuff the pipes with "cherry blend" tobacco, which was like peat moss drenched in cough syrup. Then we'd fire up our pipes with a Zippo lighter—we LOVED Zippo lighters—and puff away like maniacs. We must have looked utterly ridiculous, but we thought we were cool.

5. I regularly see Facebook posts by my fellow Boomers waxing nostalgic—we Boomers love our nostalgia—about how great our free-roaming childhoods were; how the lack of parental oversight made us happier, more self-reliant, and just all-around better than These Kids Today, whose parents supervise their every living moment from birth through approximately age thirty-seven. I basically agree with these posts, but I wonder: If we Boomers truly believe free-range childhoods are so wonderful, why didn't we let our own kids have them? Because we didn't. We Boomers invented helicopter parenting. When my kids were young I would never have let them do half the stuff I did. *Hitchhiking,* for God's sake.

civil rights movement. He often worked late and on weekends, going to meetings and community events, sometimes giving guest sermons in churches in Harlem, the Bronx, Bedford-Stuyvesant.

My dad was born in Minneapolis, Kansas, where his dad was a pastor. When Dad was two, his father was assigned to a church in Cleveland, where Dad grew up. He went to Oberlin College and then to Chicago Theological Seminary. In Chicago he met my mom; they got married and moved to New York City, where Dad had gotten a job at the Presbyterian Board of National Missions. Seeking room to raise a family, they moved to Armonk—in those days, Armonk land was cheap—and bravely embarked on their do-it-yourself house project.

My dad was not a good carpenter, but he was a very good man. He was wise and kind and caring, and he devoted his life to making other people's lives better. People just naturally saw the goodness in my dad; they loved him, trusted him, confided in him, counted on him.

He wasn't a pastor, so he didn't have a congregation, but he was a person people turned to when they had trouble. Many times our phone would ring,[6] and it would be someone in tears, someone sick, someone with family problems, someone whose child was in trouble, someone talking suicide.

"Is Dave there?" they'd say.

Dad would get on the line and sit there in the living room, smoking his Kent cigarettes, listening—he was a great listener—for however long it took, talking quietly, calmly, always calmly, offering what comfort he could, never judging. If they needed Dad to be there, he'd put on his hat and coat and head out, day or night. He was always there for people who needed him.

Dad was a devout Christian, but he didn't judge others by their beliefs.

---

6. We had one phone, in the living room. Everybody had one phone, usually in the living room. It was a heavy black metal thing with a rotary dial, attached to the wall by a wire, and when it rang the entire household responded. Whoever was closest to the phone would hasten to answer it, then announce, loudly, who the call was for. The announcer's voice would be even louder, and more urgent, if it was a long-distance call. *LONG DISTANCE!!*

Over the years he officiated at many weddings, and quite a few were for people who didn't consider themselves religious or whose churches didn't permit them to marry each other. He'd marry Jews to Catholics, Baptists to atheists. If two people loved each other, he'd marry them.

I'm making my father sound saintly, but he wasn't the least bit holier-than-thou. He was down-to-earth, never pompous or pretentious or smug. People felt comfortable around him. He didn't wear a clerical collar. He loved parties, loved to drink and dance and sing, loved to write song parodies. He loved humor of almost any kind. He was a fan of the great humorist Robert Benchley and owned several books of Benchley's collected columns. When I was somewhere around eleven or twelve I read those books and became obsessed with them; they definitely influenced my writing style, and I still read them today.

Dad was self-deprecatingly funny. He had a running joke involving the fact that he didn't have a PhD degree because he took a job and never got around to finishing his thesis. He'd be doing some menial household task, and he'd announce: "If only I had finished my PhD thesis! Instead here I am, cleaning this toilet."

He loved to laugh, my dad. Which is one reason he married my mom.

Over the years the question I've been asked by interviewers more than any other is "Where did you get your sense of humor?" I always answer: my mom.

Mom had a harder childhood than Dad. While his family was spared the worst of the Depression, hers struggled. She was born near Longmont, Colorado, to parents with little money; she spent her early years in a small house with a sod roof. When she was around ten her family moved to Minatare, Nebraska, near Scottsbluff, where her father got a job as a mechanic in a sugar-beet factory.

She didn't have a happy home life. She didn't get along with her mother, whom she seldom spoke of, and saw even more rarely, later in life. She didn't have fond memories of Depression-era Nebraska, which she found bleak and boring. My brother Phil—our family historian—recalls: "She missed Longmont and Colorado terribly because it was in the foothills of the Rockies and beautiful, but the Minatare and Scotts-bluff area was flat plains and drab, and the wind whistled and howled at night, which she hated. She made fun of life in Minatare, like saying going to funerals with her friend Gwen was the entertainment."

Gwen was my mom's friend and co-conspirator. They were not respectful of authority. My mom would tell us about the time they got into trouble in high school—as they often did—and a teacher told them, sternly, that they were going to stay after school for detention. Gwen turned to my mom and, in a voice radiant with joyful anticipation, said, "Oh, Marion, *shall* we?"

Mom loved that memory.

As soon as she was old enough to leave home, she did, and she never went back. She went to the University of Nebraska, working to pay her way. After she graduated she moved to Chicago, where she got a job as a secretary for what turned out to be the Manhattan Project, although as a low-level clerical worker she had no idea what that

Dad and Mom, newlyweds

meant. Her most memorable experience from that job was that she once took dictation from Enrico Fermi, though she couldn't recall anything specific about it.

It was in Chicago that she met my dad. They made each other laugh, and in time they married, two funny people in love.

They had four children: my big sister, Kate; me; my little brother Phil; and my even littler brother Sam. My mom was, in many ways, a typical fifties suburban housewife dealing with a houseful of kids. She spent her days—long days—cleaning, cooking a zillion meals, packing school lunches, shopping for groceries, and schlepping us around to Little League games, scout meetings, school functions, parties, etc., in the station wagon, telling us that if we didn't stop punching each other she was going to turn the station wagon around. On the surface, she was a normal mom of the times.

But she was not like the other moms. She had an edge—a sharp, dark sense of humor coiled inside her, always ready to strike.

An example: There was a pond in the Woods behind our house, and we Barry kids spent a lot of time there—ice-skating in the winter, general pond tomfoolery the rest of the year. I have a distinct memory of a summer day when I was maybe seven or eight years old, heading to

The Barry kids, Easter 1956: Kate, baby Sam, Phil and me

the pond with my sister, Kate. My mom, who was (as she often was) in the kitchen, shouted out the window to ask us where we were going.

We answered that we were going to the pond, and Mom, in the cheerful voice of a fifties TV-commercial housewife, shouted, "Don't drown, kids!"

"We won't!" we cheerfully shouted back. We thought it was funny. But it's a joke most moms would never have made.

One of her favorite expressions, when something went wrong, was "Oh well, someday we'll all be dead." This always made everyone feel better. Seriously, it did.

Mom would sometimes take us along when she ran errands around Armonk—going to the drugstore, picking up the dry cleaning, buying groceries. The tradesmen of the town were always happy to see her. I remember once we walked into Briccetti's market, where Ray Briccetti was, as usual, behind the meat counter, working the slicer, and when he saw Mom he called out, "Marion!" (They all called her Marion.) "How ya doing?"

Mom answered brightly: "Just shitty, Ray!"

Which Ray loved. She was not like the other shoppers.

If one of us Barry kids was having a problem—say, with a teacher— Mom would declare, "I'm going to put on my bathrobe and pink curlers and drive right down to the school and give that teacher a PIECE OF MY MIND."

Which of course she would never have actually done. But it helped anyway, because it was funny. Even when we were adults, when we had problems, Mom would threaten to solve them by donning her bathrobe and curlers and going to see whoever was causing the problems. And it always helped, at least a little.

My friends loved my mom. When I was in college, my roommate Rob Stavis visited our house during a break, and he told Mom that he'd just been dumped by his girlfriend and he was feeling really depressed. Mom, who loved Rob, listened with a thoughtful, sympathetic expression. When Rob was done, Mom put her hand on his arm and said, "Rob, she was a little snot." And Rob burst out laughing, because he knew deep down inside that she was right.

Another example: Every Christmas, an acquaintance of my parents used to send us a home-baked fruitcake. I assume it goes without saying that nobody in our family actually liked fruitcake. Nevertheless this dense wad of holiday thoughtfulness arrived at our house every year, and at some point it became part of a cherished tradition involving me, my mom and the kitchen door.

"Look, Davey!"[7] she'd exclaim. "The fruitcake has arrived!"

"Hurrah!" I'd say. "I hope we don't accidentally leave it in the kitchen doorway, like last year!" Then I'd open the kitchen door and place the fruitcake on the sill.

"UH-oh!" my mom would say. "It's getting drafty! I had best close the kitchen door!"

And she'd slam the door on the fruitcake. Sometimes she had to slam it several times to put it completely out of its misery. Then we'd throw it into the garbage can. We carried on this tradition for at least ten years; it's still one of my fondest Christmas memories.

One last example: One of our Armonk neighbors was a man named Tom Schroth, who was the editor of a now-defunct newspaper, the *Brooklyn Eagle*. Tom was a funny, fun-loving guy and became a close friend of my parents. At some point my dad, who, as I have noted, was always trying with limited success to build our house, borrowed Tom's Skilsaw.

In 1955 the *Eagle* folded, and eventually Tom moved to Washington, DC, to take a job as the editor of *Congressional Quarterly*. But the Skilsaw remained at our house. This became a running joke between Tom and my parents, with Tom pretending to be outraged and demanding that his Skilsaw be returned. Over the years they exchanged a series of letters on this subject, culminating in this one, which Tom sent to my dad in 1962:

7.　She called me Davey to distinguish me from my dad, whom she called Dave. As I grew older I came to dislike being called Davey, but that did not stop my mom.

Congressional Quarterly

Editorial Research Reports
1156 19TH STREET, N.W.   FEDERAL 8-4660
WASHINGTON 6, D. C.

THOMAS N. SCHROTH
EXECUTIVE EDITOR

Jan. 12, 1962

Dear Dave,

Do you have my skilsaw? I want my skilsaw.
And, dammit, if you do have my skilsaw, what are you doing
with it? Why are you keeping my skilsaw from me?

We're thinking of moving to another house, see.
And if we move to another house, see, I'll need that
G -- D --- skilsaw, see. So please send it to me.

Send it to me right away, Dave. I want my
skilsaw. I want my skilsaw.

Your friend,

Tom

Shortly after my parents received that letter, Mom—who had been threatening to do something about the Skilsaw situation for some time—took action. She loaded the Skilsaw and my brother, Sam, who was five years old, into our car, and, without telling Tom she was coming, drove from Armonk to Washington, DC, a trip of a little more than 250 miles. She did this solely so that she could ring Tom's doorbell that evening and—when he opened the door, utterly shocked to see her standing on his doorstep—hand him the saw and say: "*Here's* your goddamned Skilsaw."

Nobody else's mom that I knew of ever did anything like that.

So those were my parents: a dad who was very good, but also funny; a mom who was very funny, but also good. They gave us Barry kids a wonderful childhood.

Which is not to say they were perfect. They had their issues, as people do, and in later years, they both struggled.

Dad developed an alcohol problem. This happened after I'd left home, when I was in my early twenties. He had always enjoyed drinking, which

Dad and me at a New York City Mission Society benefit event around 1970.
Yes, I had sideburns.

was a major component of the Armonk social scene that my parents were part of in the fifties and sixties.[8] They and their friends hosted or went to cocktail parties, sometimes pretty wild ones, virtually every weekend. But Dad always seemed under control. I never saw him drunk, at least not observably drunk.

But by the seventies he was drinking more, a lot more, and in time he spiraled down into full-blown alcoholism. His drinking was affecting his work, and people were noticing. He was missing appointments, disappearing for long periods. He crashed his car, and though he insisted he wasn't drunk, Mom knew he was. She was terrified that he'd hurt somebody, or himself.

Somewhere in there she called me—I was working at the *Daily Local News*, a newspaper in West Chester, Pennsylvania—and asked if I could come up to New York City to talk to Dad about his drinking. I didn't want to, but I went. When I got to the City Mission offices, I stopped outside Dad's door to talk with his secretary of many years, who loved

---

8. Alcohol was a big part of Armonk's identity in those days. Armonk is right on the border between New York—where back then the drinking age was eighteen—and Connecticut, where the drinking age was twenty-one. So a lot of Connecticut people between the ages of eighteen and twenty-one—and, to be honest, younger than that—came across the state line to drink. At one point our little village of two thousand people had something like twenty bars; everyone called it "Barmonk."

him, as everybody who worked with him did. She was crying, telling me how hard it was to see him this way, sometimes slurring his words, sometimes falling asleep at his desk.

I was nervous when I went in to see Dad, not knowing what I'd find, but he didn't look or sound drunk. He knew why I was there, but he acted like it was just a friendly visit, no big deal. He took me to lunch at a nearby restaurant; he didn't have any alcohol. We had an uncomfortable meal. I tried to confront him about his drinking, but he fended me off, insisting, in his calm and reasonable-sounding way, that people were overreacting, that he didn't have a drinking problem.

I didn't believe him. He didn't seem right to me; he seemed evasive, which was not like the dad I knew. I told him what I thought, tried to challenge him, but he kept insisting, calmly, that he was OK, there was nothing to worry about. In the end I gave up. He was my father, the wise man, the rock of the family, the beloved and respected Rev. Dr. Barry; I was his son, a twenty-something kid. That was our dynamic, and it wasn't going to change over lunch. We went back to his office and hugged each other goodbye, but it wasn't a good hug.

Things got even worse after that. Dad got into another car crash. Mom was getting desperate, worrying about him, worrying about herself, sometimes even wondering if she should leave him, which was unthinkable to me, but she was thinking it.

Then one day she called me with good news: Dad was getting help. He'd hit bottom and called a friend who was in Alcoholics Anonymous. The friend came to the house, told Dad to pack, and took him to some kind of drying-out retreat, where he stayed for a couple of weeks. When he came home, Mom told me, "I have Dave back."

A few months later I got a letter from Dad. I no longer have it, so this is paraphrasing, but it was something like *I dimly remember, through my alcoholic haze, my son coming to see me, and trying to talk to me. I'm sorry you had to do that, and I'm sorry I didn't listen.*

That was Dad working AA's twelve-step program, specifically steps eight and nine, the ones about making amends. Dad was fully committed to AA; he faithfully attended meetings and remained sober for the rest of his life.

But he did more than that. Through AA, he met a man named Buford Peterson, a former prisoner and recovering alcoholic. Buford had founded an organization called Fellowship Center, which provided alcoholism counseling to prison inmates. In those days, most prisons offered drug-addiction counseling, but often there were no programs for inmates—there were many—who were incarcerated because of crimes related to drinking. Dad and Buford became close friends and allies; Dad eventually became president of Fellowship Center, and he spent his remaining years working to expand its programs throughout the New York State prison system.

That was my dad: not just dealing with his own problems, not just trying to right whatever wrongs he'd done, but also finding a way to use his experience to help other people, and devoting the rest of his life to that purpose. He was a good man. He was the best man I ever knew.

Unfortunately he wasn't a healthy man. He was a heavy smoker for most of his life, even after he'd given up alcohol (he always said that nicotine was the tougher addiction to beat). He had heart issues, and when he reached his midsixties they caught up with him. He was hospitalized, but the doctors said there was nothing more to be done; he came home, to the house he built, to die.

Mom called me, told me to come to come to Armonk, told me Dad didn't have much time left. This was in 1984; I'd recently been hired by the *Miami Herald* to write a humor column for its Sunday magazine, *Tropic*, but I was still living in the Philadelphia suburbs. So I drove home to see my dad.

Afterward I called my editor at *Tropic*, Gene Weingarten, to ask if it would be OK if I wrote a nonhumor column about that last visit.[9] Gene

---

9. This is something I've learned about myself over the years. I'm a humor writer; I've never wanted to be a serious writer. But sometimes when something bad happens in my life, I have to write about it before I can get back to writing humor. These essays have usually been well received; people sometimes say, "You should write more serious pieces." But I don't *want* to write serious pieces, because they're almost always the result of something bad happening.

said yes, and I wrote a column titled "A Million Words." Here's how it ended:

> So I go in for my last words, because I have to go back home, and my mother and I agree I probably won't see him again. I sit next to him on the bed, hoping he can't see that I'm crying. "I love you, Dad," I say. He says: "I love you, too. I'd like some oatmeal."
>
> So I go back out to the living room, where my mother and my wife and my son are sitting on the sofa, in a line, waiting for the outcome, and I say, "He wants some oatmeal." I am laughing and crying about this. My mother thinks maybe I should go back in and try to have a more meaningful last talk, but I don't.
>
> Driving home, I'm glad I didn't. I think: He and I have been talking ever since I learned how. A million words. All of them final, now. I don't need to make him give me any more, like souvenirs. I think: Let me not define his death on my terms. Let him have his oatmeal. I can hardly see the road.

We had two memorial services for Dad, one in New York City, one in Armonk, both overflowing with people and tears. So many people loved him. After the Armonk service, just the immediate family—Mom, Kate, Phil, Sam and I—went to the little rural cemetery to bury his ashes, which were in a cardboard box. We put the box into the hole the cemetery people had dug. We said some words, hugged each other, cried.

Then we walked away from the hole. It was raining, and we were still crying. Mom, holding my arm, was reading the names on the nearby gravestones. Suddenly she stopped.

"So *that's* why we don't see him around anymore!" she exclaimed. Now we were all laughing while we cried.

Nobody would have laughed harder at that than Dad.

So even then, moments after burying her husband of forty-two years, Mom was funny. She could always be funny.

But funny isn't the same thing as happy.

Mom and me in 1974. Yes, I had a mustache.

Mom had long struggled with depression, a bleak, hopeless mood that would envelop her like a storm cloud, sometimes lingering for days. She saw psychiatrists for years and took prescription antidepressants, but the darkness was always lurking. More than once she talked about suicide, which she considered, unapologetically, to be her right.

When we were growing up, we knew when Mom was having these moods, but she could usually fight through them, soldiering on with her mom duties, trying hard not to let her problems become our problems. Over the years, she was able, most of the time, to manage her depression, or at least live with it.

Then Dad died. He hadn't been a perfect husband; his alcoholism years were hard for her. But for most of their marriage, he was a steadying, supportive force in her life. He loved her, and he *got* her. When she lost him, she lost her anchor. She wasn't sure where she wanted to live or what she wanted to do. I assumed—I think we all assumed—that she would eventually figure it out, find her way to a new life. She still had friends, and she had her health.

And she still had her sense of humor. For a while, after Dad's death, she worked as a secretary/legal assistant to Joe DiGiacinto, who had a law practice in White Plains, New York. Joe is my oldest and closest Armonk friend; we were born a few days apart in Mount Kisco Hospital and were schoolmates from kindergarten through high school. Joe knows my family well, and over the years he became the unofficial Barry family legal counsel, although we can never get him to bill us. He loved my mom, and he was happy to hire her because she was smart, she was a good typist, and she was an extremely non-boring person to work with. She wrote wonderful letters. At one point while she was working for him, Joe handled a minor legal issue involving my newspaper column. When it was concluded, Mom sent me this:

JOSEPH W. DiGIACINTO
ATTORNEY AT LAW
235 MAIN STREET
INTERNATIONAL TELEX: 236000 ETLX UR   WHITE PLAINS, NEW YORK 10601-2495   NO. WESTCHESTER OFFICE
DOMESTIC USA TELEX: 12041 XAS NYK   TEL.(914) 428-8500   96 SMITH AVENUE
MT. KISCO, N.Y. 10549
(914) 666-2409

July 24, 1986

David M. Barry
Coral Gables, Florida 33156

Re: BARRY V.

Dear Mr. Barry:

Attached hereto are copies of two letters both dated July 12, 1986 written by [redacted] and addressed to Joseph W. DiGiacinto. The letters are self explanatory. However, if you have any intelligent questions concerning the same I assume you will contact me. I would appreciate it if you would communicate by writing since I do not have time to entertain frivolous phone calls.

It is the policy of this firm to inform our clients of our hourly rates. Mr. DiGiacinto's time is billed at $350.00 per hour and all legal assistance is billed at $249.00 per hour. A total of 21 minutes of billable time was spent on this matter. A bill will be sent to you at the end of the month.

Very truly yours,

Mom

Marion McA. Barry
Legal Assistant

MMB:sp

enclosures

cc: [redacted] File
Joseph W. DiGiacinto

22

She wrote that more than two years after Dad died; at that point she seemed, to me anyway, to be doing OK.

But she wasn't.

She decided to sell the house, and she thought maybe it was time to leave Armonk. But she didn't know where she wanted to go. For a few months she moved around the country, living briefly with my brothers, Sam and Phil, who were both in California, and with me, in Florida. But she couldn't settle on a place, couldn't find what she was looking for. At one point she thought she might want to live in Connecticut, so I flew up from Florida to look at some places with her. A few months later I wrote an essay about that trip, titled "Lost in America." Here it is:

My mother and I are driving through Hartford, Conn., on the way to a town called Essex. Neither of us has ever been to Essex, but we're both desperately hoping that my mother will want to live there.

She has been rootless for several months now, moving from son to son around the country, ever since she sold the house she had lived in for 40 years, the house she raised us in, the house my father built. The house where he died, April 4, 1984. She would note the date each year on the calendar in the kitchen.

"Dave died, 1984," the note would say. "Come back, Dave."

The note for July 5, their anniversary, said: "Married Dave, 1942. Best thing that ever happened to me."

The house was too big for my mother to handle alone, and we all advised her to sell it. Finally she did, and she shipped all her furniture to Sunnyvale, Calif., where my brother Phil lived. Her plan was to stay with him until she found a place of her own out there.

Only she hated Sunnyvale. At first this seemed almost funny, even to her. "All my worldly goods," she would say, marveling at it, "are in a warehouse in Sunnyvale, Calif., which I hate." She always had a wonderful sense of absurdity.

After a while it didn't seem so funny. My mother left Sunnyvale to live for a while with my brother Sam, in San Francisco, and then with me, in Florida; but she didn't want to stay with us. What she wanted was a home.

What she really wanted was her old house back.

With my father in it.

Of course she knew she couldn't have that, but when she tried to think of what else she wanted, her mind would just lock up. She started to spend a lot of time watching soap operas.

"You have to get on with your life," I would tell her, in this new, parental voice I was developing when I talked to her. Dutifully, she would turn off the TV and get out a map of the United States, which I bought her to help her think.

"Maybe Boulder would be nice," she would say, looking at Colorado. "I was born near Boulder."

"Mom," I would say in my new voice. "We've talked about Boulder 50 times, and you always end up saying you don't really want to live there."

Chastened, she would look back at her map, but I could tell she wasn't really seeing it.

"You have to be realistic," I would say. The voice of wisdom.

When she and I had driven each other just about crazy, she went back out to California, and repeated the process with both of my brothers. Then one night she called to ask, very apologetically, if I would go with her to look at Essex, Conn., which she had heard was nice. It was a bad time for me, but of course I said yes, because your mom is your mom. I met her in Hartford and rented a car.

I'm driving; my mother is looking out the window.

"I came through Hartford last year with Frank and Mil, on the way to Maine," she says. Frank was my father's brother; he has just died. My mother loved to see him. He reminded her of my father.

"We were singing," my mother says. She starts to sing.

I'm forever blowing bubbles
Pretty bubbles in the air.

I can tell she wants me to sing, too. I know the words; we sang this song when I was little.

First they fly so high, nearly reach the sky
Then like my dreams, they fade and die.

But I don't sing. I am all business.

"I miss Frank," says my mother.

Essex turns out to be a beautiful little town, and we look at two nice, affordable apartments. But I can tell right away that my mother doesn't want to be there. She doesn't want to say so, after asking me to fly up from Miami, but we both know.

The next morning, in the motel coffee shop, we have a very tense breakfast.

"Look, Mom," I say, "you have to make some kind of decision." Sounding very reasonable.

She looks down at her map. She starts talking about Boulder again. This sets me off. I lecture her, tell her she's being childish. She's looking down at her map, gripping it. I drive her back to Hartford, neither of us saying much. I put her on a plane; she's going to Milwaukee, to visit my dad's sister, then back to my brother in Sunnyvale, Calif. Which she hates.

The truth is, I'm relieved that she's leaving.

"You can't help her," I tell myself, "until she decides what she wants." It is a sound position.

About a week later, my wife and I get a card from my mother.

"This is to say happy birthday this very special year," it says. "And to thank you for everything."

Our birthdays are weeks away.

About two days later, my brother Phil calls, crying, from a hospital. My mother has taken a massive overdose of Valium and alcohol. The doctors want permission to turn off the machines. They say there's no hope.

We talk about it, but there really isn't much to say. We give the permission.

It's the only logical choice.

The last thing I saw my mother do, just before she went down the tunnel to her plane, was turn and give me a big smile. It wasn't a smile of happiness; it was the same smile I give my son when he gets upset listening to the news, and I tell him don't worry, we're never going to have a nuclear war.

I can still see that smile any time I want. Close my eyes, and there it is. A mom, trying to reassure her boy that everything's going to be OK.

To this day I feel guilty about that last visit with Mom—how selfish I was, how cluelessly arrogant, thinking I knew what she needed to do, when I had no idea, none, what she was going through. She was in unbearable pain, and she didn't see any other way to end it. Also I think she didn't want to inflict her misery on her children. I think that, in her mind, removing herself from our lives was an act of love, a mother's love.

I didn't see that coming, didn't see how much she was suffering, didn't do anything meaningful to help her. Instead, I bought her a stupid map. And I will never stop feeling guilty about that.

But the dominant emotion I feel when I remember my mom isn't guilt: It's gratitude. She was the sharpest and funniest person I knew; I owe much of my personality, and all of my career, to her. I wouldn't reduce her life to a struggle with depression any more than I'd reduce my dad's life to a struggle with alcoholism. They were both good people—smart, funny, decent people—and although they definitely weren't Ozzie and Harriet, they were excellent parents and role models. They gave us Barry kids a wonderful childhood, and they taught us, by the way they treated others, how they believed a person should act. Mostly it was your basic, old-school Midwestern values:

Don't act like you're better than other people. Be polite to everybody, not just people you want to impress.

Be modest; don't toot your own horn. If you're something special, people will figure it out for themselves.

Above all, never take anything too seriously. Especially not yourself.

These are good values; I still try to live up to them. And I've tried, in my half-assed way, to pass them along to my own kids. The older I get, the more I understand that this is the most valuable thing I have, the wisdom I got from my parents.

Thanks, Mom and Dad.

CHAPTER TWO

SCHOOL

I BEGAN MY EDUCATION AT WAMPUS ELEMENTARY, A public school that is still in operation, educating the youth of Armonk. ("Wampus" comes from the Native American word "wampus," which means, as far as I have been able to determine, "Wampus.")

I started kindergarten in 1952. Harry Truman was the president; we were deep into the Cold War with the Russians; the nuclear arms race was on. Not long after the 1952 school year began, the United States tested the first hydrogen bomb, which was such big news that we even heard about it on the Wampus Elementary playground; I remember older kids, more excited than scared, running around shouting, "H-bomb!"

Atomic war was part of the school curriculum in the fifties, most notably in the form of the famous "duck and cover" drills, in which we students would practice crawling under our desks to protect ourselves in the event of a nuclear blast. We really did that. It seems pretty stupid now, but back then—when the threat of nuclear attack felt very real— it also seemed pretty stupid. I think we all knew, deep in our hearts, that school desks did not provide meaningful protection against atomic bombs; if they did, why not erect giant school desks over major cities? But we didn't really mind the duck-and-cover drills. They were more entertaining than, for example, school.

Some people built home fallout shelters, which were a thing for a while in the fifties and early sixties. I didn't know anybody who had one. My family certainly didn't; my dad had his hands full just providing us with a regular shelter.

But I did, briefly, have a survival kit. This was a collection of items that would theoretically help keep you alive in the event of a nuclear war. I don't remember where I got the idea for it, but I definitely remember, when I was maybe ten or eleven, putting a bunch of stuff into one of my dad's old toolboxes and lugging it around. (I also remember that my mom found this amusing.) I believe my survival kit included a flashlight, some matches and a penknife. But the items I definitely remember were two Hershey bars, which I apparently thought would provide me with vital sustenance in the radioactive hellscape that Armonk would be reduced to following an exchange of nuclear missiles with the Russians.

As it happened—and whether or not this was a direct result of my assembling a survival kit, we may never know—the Russians failed to attack Armonk. So after a day or two of lugging my toolbox around, I ate the Hershey bars—they were just sitting there, going to waste—and that was pretty much the end of my organized efforts to survive.

The other scary thing I remember from my early school days was polio, or poliomyelitis, an incurable, highly contagious disease that attacked children and could cause paralysis and death. There was a polio epidemic in the early fifties, and the grown-ups were terrified. Our parents tried to hide their fears from us, but we heard them talking about it—about families they knew that had been stricken, about what they should do to protect us. They worried about whether and where to let us play; worried if our playmates caught colds; worried, a *lot*, if we caught colds. We were just kids, but we felt their worry.

Then in 1952 Dr. Jonas Salk created a vaccine that prevented polio. That was the good news. The bad news—for me, it was very bad news indeed—was the way this vaccine was administered.

A shot.

On a warm and sunny day in May of 1954—I was in first grade—all the students of Wampus Elementary were lined up on the playground. One by one, we were taken into the cafeteria, where Dr. Mortimer "Monty" Cohn was waiting with a needle the size of a harpoon. Or so it seemed to me.

I hate needles. I have hated them all my life; over the years I have, following a shot or blood draw, wound up unconscious on the floor of more than one medical facility. And while today I am deeply grateful to Dr. Salk for creating the vaccine, and Dr. Cohn for injecting it into me, my experience that May day on the Wampus Elementary playground—standing in that long line, moving forward one grim step at a time toward a fate that I viewed as WAY worse than either polio or death—will forever be a big wad of scar tissue in the Bad Memories lobe of my brain.

The polio shots were big news all over the country. The North Castle *Villager*, a newspaper that covered Armonk, ran a story on May 6, 1954, about the vaccinations at Wampus Elementary. The headline reads:

"A Lark," Say Kids, as Polio Shots Begin

I imagine whoever wrote that headline is dead, but if he or she or they are still alive, and he or she or they happen to be reading this, let me just say to him or her or them, with all due respect: YOU LYING LIAR. Perhaps not every child getting a shot that day was as big a baby as I was, but *nobody* thought it was "a lark." And even if we *had* enjoyed it, none of us—I speak for my generation here—would ever have used the term "lark."

The *Villager* article begins as follows:

Hesitation gave way to curiosity and then to pride this week as hundreds of Northern Westchester school children found there's really nothing to taking the Salk anti-polio shots.

A few lips may have quivered at first, and there was a little doubt here and there as to just what the needle would feel like. But afterward it was all smiles.

Again, with all due respect: IT WAS NOT "ALL SMILES," YOU LYING NEWSPAPER LIAR WHO CLEARLY WAS NOT THERE.

The *Villager* article continues:

> The second round of shots will be given next week, and the final set four weeks later.
>
> Half of the children receive the vaccine, the other half a harmless control fluid. Study after the polio season will show the effectiveness of the vaccine. Only children in grades one through three are receiving the shots.

Almost a year later, the *Villager* printed the names of the students who got the vaccine. My sister's name was among them, as were the names of many of my classmates. But my name was missing. I had been given the "harmless control fluid," which meant that I had to get *more shots*. I had to get *twice as many shots as my sister*.

I think this at least partly explains why I ended up being an atheist.

Anyway, aside from polio and nuclear war, elementary school was a pretty good experience. I learned to read and write, useful skills that I still sometimes employ. My first reading textbooks were the famous *Dick and Jane* series, starring two wholesome-looking youngsters afflicted with some kind of nervous tic that caused them to speak like actors in the climactic scene of a porn movie:

> *Dick said, "Oh, Jane. Oh, oh, oh."*
> *Jane said, "Yes, Dick. Yes, yes, yes."*
> *Dick said, "Ohmigod, Jane."*

I also learned to add and subtract, which turned out to be the only math skills I have ever really needed in adult life (and to be honest I have done very little subtracting). I made art projects out of construction paper and this white paste—you Boomers remember this paste—that turned out to be delicious. I enjoyed eating that paste WAY more than I enjoyed eating the Wampus Elementary cafeteria food, which came from giant government cans left over from some previous war, possibly the French and Indian.

The best part of elementary school was recess, which is when we students were released onto the playground to swing on the swings, slide on the slides, chase each other around, throw things and pretend to be Davy Crockett. That was the first big fad I remember. Davy Crockett was a rifle-totin', bear-shootin', coonskin-cap-wearin', Alamo-dyin', franchise-anchorin' frontiersperson who was the subject of a 1954 miniseries on the *Walt Disney's Disneyland* TV show. We all watched that show, and we all knew the Davy Crockett song:

> *Davy, Davy Crockett*
> *King of the wild frontier!*

I had a Davy Crockett T-shirt, which I wore whenever possible. On the Wampus Elementary playground, at recess, we boys reenacted the scene from the final episode of the TV series wherein Davy Crockett makes his courageous last stand, fighting off the Mexican attackers at the Alamo. (Disney didn't show him actually dying; the episode fades out with actor Fess Parker, having run out of bullets, swinging his rifle at the Mexicans, looking like a man practicing with a nine iron.)

In our playground reenactment, the part of the Alamo was played by a largish boulder that had a flat top so you could stand on it. The problem was that everybody wanted to play the part of Davy Crockett. I certainly did: After all, I had the name AND the T-shirt. Nobody wanted to be the Mexicans. So basically our reenactment consisted of a group of small boys standing around on a rock, trying to look heroic in the face of an attacking horde of invisible Mexicans.

In the interest of not getting bogged down in a Boomer fifties-TV nos-

My second-grade school photo

talgia wallow (*Howdy Doody*! *Lassie*! *Winky Dink*!) I will fast-forward to fifth grade, which I spent at Whippoorwill School, a stately 1924 red-brick building that once was Armonk's only public school and is now a condominium where, according to Zillow, a two-bedroom unit will run you north of $700,000. It amuses me, thinking that people have paid that kind of money to inhabit spaces where my classmates and I once sat at uncomfortable, graffiti-scarred desks staring at mimeographed[10] test pages in Mrs. DeLucia's class, desperately trying to remember the capital of Vermont.[11]

The Big News Thing that happened while I was in fifth grade was

---

10. All you Boomers who, to this very day, vividly remember the smell of a freshly made mimeograph, raise your hands. Yes! I see you.

11. Montpelier.

Sputnik.[12] That was the Earth's first man-made satellite, which the Russians launched into orbit in October of 1957, and hoo boy, did it ever upset the grown-ups. Until Sputnik, we Americans just assumed we were technologically superior to the Russians. Why not? We had nicer cars! We had way more television sets! Some Americans even had color TV! Granted, the color rendering was terrible, so the people on TV all appeared to have fatal skin disorders. But still! The Russians didn't even *have* color TV! So HOW COULD THEY SEND UP A WORKING SATELLITE BEFORE WE DID?

Yes, Sputnik was a major blow to America's self-esteem. But we are not a nation of quitters. Just as Davy Crockett did not quit whacking Mexicans at the Alamo until he was dead, the United States of America did not quit the Space Race. On December 6, 1957, less than two months after the Sputnik launch, a team of American scientists, engineers, military personnel and civilian officials gathered in Cape Canaveral to watch the launch of America's first satellite. Here's the Wikipedia account of what happened:

> The booster ignited and began to rise, but about two seconds after liftoff, after rising about 1.2 m (four feet), the rocket lost thrust and fell back to the launch pad. As it settled, the fuel tanks ruptured and exploded, destroying the rocket and severely damaging the launch pad. The Vanguard 1A satellite was thrown clear and landed on the ground a short distance away with its transmitters still sending out a beacon signal.

That's right: While Sputnik was hundreds of miles overhead, hurtling along at eighteen thousand miles an hour, broadcasting cheerful futuristic beeps as it zipped all the way around the Earth once every ninety-six minutes, our rocket soared to approximately the height of a mailbox, then blew up. On the plus side, our satellite courageously con-

---

12. "Sputnik" is Russian for "Little Sput."

tinued transmitting a beacon signal, thereby making itself easy to locate as it lay there on the ground.

So all of a sudden the United States didn't look so superior. And as I said, the grown-ups of 1957 were totally freaked out by this. Something had gone terribly wrong; somebody had completely dropped the ball. And our nation's leaders felt it was time to put the blame where it belonged: on the fifth graders of Whippoorwill School.

At least that's how it felt. Suddenly we students were hearing a LOT from our teachers—who were hearing it from the politicians—about how America's young people needed to improve in math and science. Never mind the fact that it wasn't *our* fault the Russians were winning the Space Race: WE were the ones who were going to receive additional math and science instruction; WE were the ones who would be given more homework; WE were the ones who would be expected to understand algebra and trigonometry, including something called the "cosine," which none of us—I speak for my generation here—have ever really understood the purpose of. Did our nation's leaders—the people who were actually in charge when we fell behind in the Space Race—did THEY get saddled with trying to understand the "cosine"? They did not. They dumped that impossible task onto the fifth graders of Whippoorwill School.

And as you can tell, we are still bitter.

After Whippoorwill I attended grades six through nine at Harold C. Crittenden Junior High School, which is still educating the youth of Armonk, now as H. C. Crittenden Middle School. Junior high was an exciting time for me, and by "exciting," I mean "deeply disturbing." This was because of an experience I had there—an experience I am reluctant to talk about even to this day; an experience I would not wish on anyone else.

Puberty.

The worst thing about puberty, for me, was how long it took to arrive. I was a late bloomer. While one after another of my male classmates started growing taller, speaking in a deeper voice and sprouting hair in new locations, I was stuck with a slightly larger version of the puny hairless body I'd been sporting since my Davy Crockett days.

And it wasn't just my male classmates who were changing. The girls were undergoing an even more dramatic transformation, which was starkly evident when we returned from summer vacation at the beginning of seventh grade. The girls were no longer girls: They were definitely young women. It was as if they had all attended Summer Bosom Camp. The boys definitely noticed this, and were feeling powerful new biological stirrings in the form of semipermanent boners. A Category 5 puberty storm had hit Harold C. Crittenden Junior High; waves of hormones were sloshing through the halls.

Our social lives were also changing. We were no longer having adult-supervised parties with cake and ice cream and balloons and pin the tail on the donkey. Instead we were having grown-up-free parties with slow dancing and holding hands and spin the bottle and kissing and making out and sometimes, according to rumor, reaching bases. We were passing notes in class. We were going on dates. We were going steady.

And when I say "we," I mean "not me." Here's what I looked like in junior high:

I was still awaiting a visit from the Puberty Fairy. I wore thick glasses, and my dad cut my hair using electric clippers he bought at a drugstore. I have already established that my dad was a truly fine human being, but he was not a professional barber any more than he was a professional house-builder. He cut my hair the way a person might mow a lawn, quickly and efficiently, cutting everything to the same length, namely, short. The result was a hairstyle that left me with an expanse of bare forehead that appeared to be the size of a regulation volleyball court.

So I was not one of the Cute Boys. I was not a hit with the girls. I did attempt one serious date, in eighth grade, and it was such a hideously awkward experience that thirty-two years later it was still vivid enough in my memory that I wrote a column about it. I'll excerpt that column here, because although it's meant to be humorous, it's actually quite accurate:

The first rule of dating is: Never risk direct contact with the girl in question. Your role model should be the nuclear submarine, gliding silently beneath the ocean surface, tracking an enemy target that does not even begin to suspect that the submarine would like to date it. I spent the vast majority of 1960 keeping a girl named Judy under surveillance, maintaining a minimum distance of 50 lockers to avoid the danger that I might somehow get into a conversation with her, which could have led to disaster:

Judy: Hi.
Me: Hi.
Judy: *Just in case you have ever thought about having a date with me, the answer is no.*

The only problem with the nuclear-submarine technique is that it's difficult to get a date with a girl who has never, technically, been asked. This is why you need Phil Grant. Phil was a friend of mine who had the ability to talk to girls. It was a mysterious superhuman power he had, comparable to X-ray vision.

So, after several thousand hours of intense discussion and planning with me, Phil approached a girl he knew named Nancy, who approached a girl named Sandy, who was a direct personal friend of Judy's and who passed the word back to Phil via Nancy that Judy would be willing to go on a date with me. This procedure protected me from direct humiliation, similar to the way President Reagan was protected from direct involvement in the Iran-contra scandal by a complex White House chain of command that at one point, investigators now believe, included his horse.

Thus it was that, finally, Judy and I went on an actual date, to see a movie in White Plains, New York. If I were to sum up the romantic ambience of this date in four words, those words would be: "My mother was driving." This made for an extremely quiet drive, because my mother, realizing that her presence was hideously embarrassing, had to pretend she wasn't there. If it had been legal, I think she would have got out and sprinted alongside the car, steering through the window.

Judy and I, sitting in the back seat about 75 feet apart, were also silent, unable to communicate without the assistance of Phil, Nancy and Sandy. After what seemed like several years we got to the movie theater, where my mother went off to sit in the Parents and Lepers Section.

The movie was called *North to Alaska*, but I can tell you nothing else about it because I spent the whole time wondering whether it would be necessary to amputate my right arm, which was not getting any blood flow as a result of being perched for two hours like a petrified snake on the back of Judy's seat exactly one molecule away from physical contact. So it was definitely a fun first date, featuring all the relaxed spontaneity of a real-estate closing, and in later years I did regain some feeling in my arm.

Other than that extremely painful experience, I had little one-on-one interaction with girls in junior high. At parties, when other boys were slow-dancing with girls and attempting to reach bases in dark corners, I was the person operating the record player[13] and amusing the other puberty-impaired loser boys by making hand farts. This was the genesis of my career in humor.

The big organized youth social event in Armonk back then was Canteen, which was held on Friday nights at Crittenden Junior High. I believe the idea was to give us youths a wholesome, supervised activity so that we wouldn't spend the weekend nights committing acts of vandalism. And it worked! At least it worked on Friday nights. There was still vandalism on Saturday nights.

There were two main elements to Canteen: the gym, where the boys played basketball, and the cafeteria, where the girls danced to 45 r.p.m. records with each other until the gym was closed, at which point the boys went to the cafeteria and either danced with girls or (this was me) stood around wishing they had the confidence to dance with girls.

One record that got a lot of play in the Crittenden cafeteria, and on the planet in general, was "The Twist." This was the Chubby Checker song that was a huge hit, reaching number one in 1960 and again in 1962 and inspiring a monster dance craze. Why was the Twist so popular? The answer is simple: White people could do it. *Anybody* could do it. *Our parents* could do it. It was an easily replicated mechanical movement requiring no natural dancing ability whatsoever to execute. Even I sometimes did the Twist. I *still* do the Twist, at weddings.[14] That is the impact it had on me.

Aside from the Twist, the other major world event I remember from

13. For you youngsters: I'm not talking about a "turntable" here. I'm talking about a boxy machine that played 45 r.p.m. records, the kind that had a big hole in the middle and many scratches. You'd stack a bunch of 45s on the spindle, and the record player would plop them down one on top of the other and play them at a level of fidelity so low that it was not always possible to determine what the specific song was. You youngsters have NO IDEA what you missed.

14. Usually not during the actual ceremony; it's more polite to refrain from twisting until the reception.

my junior-high years is the presidential election of 1960, John F. Kennedy vs. Richard M. Nixon. This was the first election I paid attention to. It was a big deal for my parents, who were still sad about the fact that in the 1952 and 1956 elections, their candidate, Adlai Stevenson, had lost to Dwight Eisenhower, because the American people were simply not ready—will probably never be ready—for a president named "Adlai."

My parents were ardent Democrats. But they had friends—good friends—who were equally ardent Republicans. I remember hearing them argue about politics at cocktail parties. Cocktail parties were big in that era: People routinely got dressed up and went to each other's houses to drink liquor and smoke cigarettes and sing and dance and act up and just generally have fun, and they didn't feel the least bit guilty about it.

My parents hosted or attended cocktail parties almost every weekend in Armonk. When they were the hosts, our house would fill with people and noise; we Barry kids thought this was very exciting, and we'd eavesdrop on the festivities. During the Kennedy-Nixon campaign we heard some major arguments between Democrats and Republicans— heated, emotional, sometimes angry. But never nasty. At the end of the night everybody hugged everybody, because they were friends, and they understood that they could disagree about politics without believing the other side was evil. Mistaken, maybe. Evil, no.

They had their flaws, the Armonk adults of 1960: Their drinking was excessive, their smoking was foolish, and they looked ridiculous doing the Twist. But when it came to politics, they were a lot saner than we are today. They understood that most people want basically the same things— peace, justice, a decent life for themselves and their kids—and that politics is basically an argument about how best to achieve those things. So they didn't automatically assume that anybody who disagreed with them was vermin scum, which is pretty much how we do politics now.

Another thing that was different back then was the relationship between teachers and students. My junior-high teachers routinely used disciplinary techniques that would probably get them arrested today. For example, we had a math teacher, Mr. Schofield, who would throw chalk at you—he had excellent aim—if you weren't paying attention. Mr. Friedman, who taught social studies and was somewhat less accurate, threw erasers. Mr. Fletcher, who taught history, would, if you were a misbehaving or inattentive boy (girls were exempt from this), whack you on the head with the hand on which he wore an Iona College class ring that felt like it weighed eleven pounds. Some of us still have dents in our skulls from Mr. Fletcher's class.

We didn't consider these disciplinary measures unusual or cruel. It never would have occurred to us to tell our parents that a teacher had thrown something at or struck us; if we had, our parents would have asked us what we did to deserve it. I'm not saying that corporal punishment is an ideal way to discipline students. I am saying that we tended to pay attention in Mr. Schofield's, Mr. Friedman's and—above all—Mr. Fletcher's classes.

Another aspect of our Harold C. Crittenden education that absolutely would not fly today was the sex-based curriculum: Boys took shop, and girls took home economics. No exceptions, no options. At certain points of the week we boys would troop off to the shop, where we would learn, over the course of several months, how to use tools to turn pieces of wood into slightly smaller pieces of wood stained brown. Meanwhile the girls were in the home ec room wearing aprons and baking cookies, in preparation for future careers in which they would stay at home, raising the kids and baking things for us males to eat when we came home from our breadwinner jobs making brown-stained wooden things.

As it turned out, most of us boys did not use our carpentry training in later life, and most of the girls ended up with careers outside the home. One of the girls who definitely did was Glenn Close, who attended Harold C. Crittenden Junior High for several years. Really. She was in my eighth-grade homeroom, and I will always remember a conversation I had with her one morning while we were waiting for school to start.

"Forget about baking cookies," I told her. "You should become a famous actress."

No, I'm kidding. I mean, Glenn Close really was in my homeroom, and I'm sure we exchanged words, but I don't recall any of them. I do recall that she was nice.[15]

Back in 1962 Armonk public schools only went through ninth grade, so in 1962 my class started tenth grade a few miles away at Pleasantville High School. Pleasantville was, as its name suggests, a nice all-American town; in fact it was the home of *Reader's Digest*. Pleasantville High looked—still looks—like a high school in a movie, a big red-brick building with a classic white-columned portico out front.

Most of the student body entered through that portico, which meant we passed under the watchful gaze of the assistant principal, Anthony Sabella, a large, stocky man universally known as Tough Tony, though nobody called him that to his face. Mr. Sabella—who also refereed high school sports—stood by the front door every morning inspecting the incoming students for violations of the dress code. If he saw a girl whose skirt was too short, or a boy whose hair was too long or pants were too tight (skinny white Levi's were a popular look), he would bellow the student's name (he seemed to know everybody's name) and send her or him home to correct the problem.

During the school day Mr. Sabella patrolled the halls, referee-style, looking for infractions, and if he caught you committing one, he did not hesitate to grasp you firmly by the neck—I speak from experience—and inform you of your punishment, which was usually detention. Technically, the highest authority at Pleasantville High was the principal, Mr. McCreary, a small, gray formal man who had been principal since the dawn of time. But the guy who ran the school was Tough Tony.

I ended up loving my time at Pleasantville, but I started out deeply intimidated, and not just by Mr. Sabella. I didn't know most of the students, and a lot of them seemed really *old* to me, like actual grown-ups with cars. As in every high school, there was a hierarchy, with

---

15. Another Armonk public-school student who went on to become famous was Laura Branigan, who was five years behind me. I knew her brother Jim but can't remember anything at all about her, though I'm sure she was also nice.

upperclassmen at the top, and cliques—the jocks, the cheerleaders, the nerds, the student-government go-getters, the arty kids, the hoods, the tough girls with giant beehive hairdos that according to urban legend had been rigidly hair-sprayed in place so long that they housed spider colonies. The Pleasantville football team was a big deal; there were pep rallies on Friday, and most of the school went to the games on Saturday. There were clubs and organizations and dances and traditions and an alma mater. There was a whole complex society at Pleasantville High, and for a while I didn't feel as though I was a part of any of it.

But gradually, as one does, I found my niche, my high school persona, which was, basically, wiseass. Joining me in this role was Lanny Watts, a very smart, funny guy I met in tenth grade who became my best friend and co-conspirator in numerous acts of wiseassery.

Lanny and I prided ourselves on taking nothing seriously; we made fun of everything. We *lived* to make fun of things. To pick one example: We joined the Pleasantville High fencing club. We had absolutely no interest in competitive fencing; we just thought that the idea of the fencing club was hilarious.

Our club membership did not survive the first meeting. The fencers received some basic instruction from the club's faculty adviser—I think he was a French teacher—then we paired off to practice lunging at each other. Many years later I wrote a column about what happened next:

> Lanny was paired against one of the veteran club members, who had assumed his fighting stance, holding his fencing sword in the ready position; suddenly Lanny ran from the room, only to return a moment later holding: a trombone. Even though I was lying on the floor and trying not to wet my pants, I still have a vivid motion picture in my mind of the scene that followed: Lanny charging forward, blowing into the trombone and thrusting boldly with the sliding part, as his opponent retreated in confusion and—yes—fear. Lanny and I were immediately kicked out of the fencing club. But I think they knew who won.

To this day, that remains one of my fondest high school memories. You may be thinking: But wasn't that kind of obnoxious? Disrupting the fencing practice, when the other students were serious about it?

The answer is yes, it was obnoxious. Looking back from my old-person perspective, I realize that Lanny and I were, at times, complete assholes, and I hereby apologize to any former members of the Pleasantville High fencing club who are reading this. What we did was wrong.

But still: a *trombone*.

Lanny Watts and me, a pair of wiseasses clearly up to no good.

When Lanny and I were seniors, there was a big school dance, and we volunteered to be on the publicity committee. Actually, we were the entire committee. Needless to say, we did not volunteer out of a sincere interest in publicizing the dance. We volunteered because we had come up with what we considered to be a brilliant plan for incorporating an obscene reference into the dance posters. The key to this plan was the fact that we seniors were the class of 1965. So we made a bunch of posters that said:

WHEN YOU'RE IN THE COLLEGE CLASS OF

69

YOU'LL STILL REMEMBER THIS DANCE

The "69" was much bigger than everything else. Basically each poster was a giant "69" with some words around it. As I say, Lanny and I thought this was brilliant. The thing was, all posters had to be approved by the school authorities. So one morning before school Lanny and I found Principal McCreary—we figured he was our best shot—in the hall outside his office and showed him our posters. He read them and—in his defense, he was something like 285 years old—said they were OK. He got out his pen and was about to initial the posters to indicate his approval when up walked Mr. Sabella.

Uh-oh.

Mr. Sabella, who was much more street-savvy than Mr. McCreary, took one look at the posters and declared that they were unacceptable. Mr. McCreary asked why, and Mr. Sabella, glaring at Lanny and me, said, "Because they have *obscene implications.*" Mr. McCreary, red-faced and befuddled, said, "Oh." Mr. Sabella ordered Lanny and me to stuff our posters into a trash can, and that was the end of our brilliant scheme.

Incredibly, we did not get detention for that incident. I think Mr. Sabella viewed what we did as hijinks, as opposed to a serious rule violation. Scary as he could be, he was a reasonable man. He could even be funny, as I learned when I had him as a teacher. In addition to being assistant principal, he taught American history, and it was one of the best classes I had in high school. He was an entertaining speaker, and he encouraged freewheeling discussion. He didn't mind if you argued with him; in fact he liked it. In the end Mr. Sabella turned out to be one of the Pleasantville people I remember most fondly, which is amusing considering how many times he basically lifted me off the floor by my neck.

Another teacher I remember fondly is Regina Adams, who taught

English composition. We did a lot of essays in her class, and at some point I started trying to make mine funny, and she encouraged me. I wrote one essay—something about being excited for the school year to end—that she liked so much she wanted me to read it to the class. I definitely did *not* want to do that, as my carefully cultivated image was wiseass, not teacher's pet. Mrs. Adams asked if she could read the essay to the class, keeping the author anonymous. I was OK with that. So Mrs. Adams read my essay, and my classmates laughed in the right places. It felt good, hearing people laugh at my words. It still does. So thanks, Mrs. Adams.[16]

In my senior year I wrote my first published humor piece, which appeared in the school newspaper, the *Green Lantern* (Pleasantville's colors were green and white). My friend Tom Parker was coeditor, not because he was interested in journalism but because he wanted to be able to write "Editor of School Newspaper" on his application to Yale.[17] The other coeditor was Philomène Dursin, who, following the ancient custom of women in organizations with men, did the actual work.

But as I say, Tom was my friend, and thus the *Green Lantern* published a story I wrote about an unofficial Pleasantville tradition: the senior boys' loadball game. This was a tackle football game played on a muddy field by senior boys who were simultaneously consuming a large quantity of beer. Nobody kept score, and there were no rules. There could be forty or fifty players involved at any given moment, and sometimes more than one football. It was chaotic and violent and very stupid. It was a LOT of fun.

Needless to say the loadball game was not a school-sanctioned event. Under no circumstances would the school newspaper cover it, which was of course why I wanted to get it into the school newspaper. I did this by

---

16. There's one other high school teacher I want to acknowledge, but he doesn't fit into the narrative, so I'll mention him here: Jerry Solin, who taught advanced math. He was so good at it that for a brief period—maybe thirty-five minutes, but long enough to pass the exam—I sort of understood calculus.

17. It worked; he was accepted.

writing about it as if it were a legitimate sporting event, with subtle references to, but no actual mention of, beer. I don't have the original column, and the only joke I recall is something about players being sidelined with cut thumbs.[18] I don't remember whether my fellow students thought my story was funny. But I do remember enjoying seeing it in print.

As I said, I wound up loving high school, which for me was mostly a fun and—the occasional zit notwithstanding—stress-free time. My world was small and comfortable. I was vaguely aware that there was a larger world out beyond Armonk and Pleasantville, but it didn't affect me much.

Although that was changing. The comfortable blandness of the fifties had faded, and my little cocoon was about to be punctured by the sixties, in all its manifestations—some good, some bad, some weird.

My first true sixties experience was decidedly good: The August 28, 1963, March on Washington, where Martin Luther King gave his "I Have a Dream" speech. I was there. I rode down on a bus from New York City with a group of staff members from Camp Sharparoon.

Sharparoon was one of the summer camps for inner-city kids—the other one was Camp Minisink—operated by my dad's organization, the New York City Mission Society. Growing up, we Barry kids were campers at both of these camps, which was a mind-expanding experience for us—going from Armonk, where everybody was white, to environments where we were a racial minority. I remember a couple of summers at Camp Minisink when I believe my sister, Kate, and I were the only white campers. Those were good summers: I made friends, had fun, learned a LOT of new slang and never felt, even for a moment, less than completely accepted by the other kids. I seriously doubt that a Black kid would have been accepted the same way in Armonk back then.

Anyway, by 1963 I was too old to be a camper, so I worked that summer on the maintenance crew at Camp Sharparoon. At the end of the

---

18. Explanation for young people: Back then we opened beer and soda cans by pulling off pop tabs, which had sharp edges.

summer the City Mission Society organized a trip for staff—mostly college students—who wanted to attend the March on Washington. The night before the march we went to a big candlelight rally in Harlem, where we all held hands, Black and white together, and sang "We Shall Overcome." Which we sincerely believed we would.

Early the next day we piled into buses and rode to DC, where we joined the largest crowd I'd ever been part of, miles and miles of people, hundreds of thousands of us, hot and happy and hopeful. We gathered around the reflecting pool in front of the Lincoln Memorial to listen to the speeches. I was maybe one hundred yards from the speakers' platform. My parents were closer; Dad was a guest of his friend Whitney Young Jr., head of the Urban League, who was one of the speakers that day.

We were excited to hear Dr. King speak; he was the star. But I don't think most of us realized—I certainly didn't—how famous that speech would become. I mainly remember the feeling of being part of something really big, and of being absolutely certain that I was on the good side. This is a feeling I would have less and less often as the years went by, and the sixties receded, and I grew old.

A little less than three months after the euphoria of the March on Washington came the gut punch of Dallas. I was at Pleasantville High, in Spanish class. The teacher, Miss Nauman, arrived late, crying, and told us that President Kennedy had been shot. We all sat there, stunned; there was obviously going to be no Spanish that day. A few minutes later another teacher came in to tell us that the TV newspeople were saying the president was dead.

School ended early; everything was canceled. As we waited for our buses I was in the milling crowd of students across from the high school on what was known as the Corner, where students often gathered to smoke and joke around and generally carry on as teenagers do when they form into clots.

But we were a subdued group that day. It was the first time I remember experiencing an uneasy feeling that would become familiar in the sixties—the feeling that huge things were happening, things that nobody had seen coming, things that nobody fully understood. Until Dallas, it felt, at least to me, as though somebody—somebody important, some older person wearing a suit, somebody with all the requisite information—was in control. After Dallas, more and more, it felt as though nobody was in control. That was a big part of the vibe of the sixties.

Another event that happened in the fall of 1963—which I in no way mean to compare with the Kennedy assassination, although it was huge for me—was that the New York State Department of Motor Vehicles issued me a driver's license. The day it arrived I got into my mom's car and put at least a hundred miles on it, driving randomly all over the greater Armonk area in a state of pure automotive rapture.

My mom's car at the time was a 1961 Plymouth Valiant station wagon, possibly the least exciting car ever manufactured, the soybean curd of cars. It was ugly, and it went from zero to sixty in roughly a fortnight. In other words it was a typical Barry family car. My dad, who never had a lot of money, always bought used cars, but they usually weren't *normal* used cars, like Fords or Chevys. Mostly they were mutant cars that nobody else had, and for good reason.

For example, for a brief but exciting time we had a British car called a Hillman Minx. This was a boxy black vehicle that had a mechanical defect—at least ours did—such that the steering wheel would sometimes, without warning, become completely disconnected from the front wheels. Really. When this happened you could spin the steering wheel a full 360 degrees, but the Minx would keep right on going in the same direction, while the driver stomped frantically on the brakes and—at least in my dad's case—said non-Presbyterian words. I'm guessing there are no Minxes left in England because they were all driven into the sea.

After the Minx we got a Nash Metropolitan, a tiny vehicle with hilariously cartoonish styling. It looked like the main character in a comic called *Carl the Car's Big Adventure*. The good news was, the steering worked. The bad news was, the motor—which turns out to be a key component—frequently did not work. This made the Metropolitan a lot safer than the Minx, but not as suited to getting from Point A to Point B. It was more suited to remaining motionless at Point A with the hood propped open.

So compared to the Minx and the Metropolitan, my mom's Plymouth Valiant, slow and ugly as it was, was a Ferrari, and when I got my driver's license I drove it every chance I could. Driving was a huge thing for us, the Boomer suburban kids of the sixties—the freedom to cruise around unsupervised, picking up our friends, honking at other kids, listening to Top 40 tunes on the low-fi a.m. radio.

I listened to the big New York stations, and their fast-talking hepcat deejays—epitomized by Murray the K and his *Swingin' Soiree* on WINS, and Bruce "Cousin Brucie" Morrow on WABC. In late 1963 they were playing hits like "My Boyfriend's Back" by the Angels, a touching, romantic song in which a young lady informs an unwanted suitor that her true love has returned home and is going to beat the crap out of him. At the end of the year the number one song in the country was "Dominique," sung in French in an irritatingly shrieky voice by somebody called the Singing Nun. The number two song, by the Kingsmen, was "Louie Louie," which was allegedly in English but nobody understood the words, so we assumed they were dirty, which is one reason why we liked it.

That was the music we were listening to as 1964 dawned.

Then, in January, we heard it—it seemed like we all heard it at once—a sound from England that was genuinely different, starting with those driving power chords, propelling you into the song—C to D, C to D, C to DEEEEEEEEE . . .

Oh yeah I'll tell you somethin' . . .

And BOOM, the Beatles exploded, all over the radio, all over everywhere.

We—I speak for my generation here—loved them immediately, and not just because of their music. We loved that they were smart, and funny, and they didn't take themselves seriously. We loved that older people hated their haircuts. We wanted to grow our own hair long and start a band and have screaming girls swoon over us. At least I did, although the hair had to wait until my appearance was no longer being monitored by Mr. Sabella.

I graduated from Pleasantville in 1965. My classmates, in recognition of my contributions to the intellectual and cultural legacy of the Class of '65, elected me Male Class Clown.[19] They also chose me to be one of the commencement speakers, which was an honor that I did not deserve and totally failed to take seriously.[20] I have mercifully forgotten the specifics of what I said, but I do remember that it was a lot of vacuous bullshit about the Future, with a Bob Dylan quote about blowin' in the wind thrown in. I'm still embarrassed by that speech and hereby apologize to any of my classmates who happened to be paying attention.

Then it was on to college. I went to Haverford, a small, all-male (it's now coed) school in suburban Philadelphia, founded by Quakers. Academically Haverford is a highly rated school, but it's not particularly well-known; I've long said that the official motto should be "We Never Heard of You, Either."

I applied to Haverford because Lanny Watts's big brother, Dave, went there. That was the sole reason. One weekend Lanny and I went down to visit, and it seemed like a cool place, so I decided to apply. I didn't apply anywhere else; I don't know what I'd have done if Haverford hadn't accepted me. I realize now that my approach to this decision was overly casual, bordering on stupid, but back then choosing a college was not the insane, endless high-pressure ordeal it is today, when parents start obsessing about college while their children are still in the womb.

In any event, Haverford turned out to be a good place for me, though at first I was seriously intimidated by the other students. Up until then I'd always thought of myself as one of the smart kids, and I'd always gotten good grades. But at Haverford *everybody* had always gotten good grades, and they all seemed to be accomplished in other ways, like being thes-

---

19. The Female Class Clown was Toni Flood. Hi, Toni!

20. The other student speaker was our valedictorian, Diane Bloch, a smart and thoughtful person whose speech was way better than mine.

pians or chess masters or debate champions, or throwing the javelin, or playing the French horn. Also the professors all seemed terrifyingly intelligent.

Eventually, as I had at Pleasantville High, I found my way at Haverford. I made friends—really good friends, guys who are still my friends today—and I had many memorable and sometimes highly entertaining experiences. I also got something of an education, although I have to admit that this was not my highest priority.

I was an English major, which meant I read roughly a third of the way through many great literary works. Technically I was supposed to read all the way through these works, but most of them—*The Brothers Karamazov* comes to mind—contained vast quantities of words, and I frankly did not have time to read them all, what with my busy schedule.

What occupied much of my time at Haverford was playing in rock bands. This may be a pathetic thing to admit, but: The thing I remember most vividly about the four years I spent at a top-notch college, being exposed to iconic literature and distinguished academic minds, was playing "Hang On Sloopy" to crowds of gyrating college students in widely varying states of consciousness. That was my true passion, my identity: *I'm in a band.*

I was in bands all four years at Haverford. Really it was just one band that went through various names and combinations of personnel. We started out, in my freshman year, as the Stomp Jackson Quintet. Nobody in the band was named Jackson, and I'm not 100 percent certain—my memory is hazy—that there were five of us. But we liked the name because, hey, why not.

Next, in an effort to be more hip, we became, briefly, the Guides. We had heard somewhere that "guide" was a slang term for a person who helped other people get through LSD trips, so we thought the Guides would be a psychedelic name. The problem was, nobody but us had ever heard of this term. People kept mishearing our name and thinking we were the Guys, which would have been a stupid name for a band (although in retrospect not as stupid as the Guides).

So we finally, somewhere in my sophomore year, came up with the name we used the longest: the Federal Duck. This idea came to us one night when a group of us were sitting on the grassy bank of Haverford's scenic little duck pond, enjoying the evening air. And by "enjoying the evening air," I mean "smoking pot."

We had enjoyed quite a bit of the evening air when we noticed that some ducks had exited the pond and were waddling in our direction. As we watched them approach, my roommate, Bob Stern, expressed the concern that these ducks might be part of some kind of government anti-narcotics operation. He was joking, of course (I think), but we nevertheless grew concerned as the ducks kept coming, because (a) we were very stoned, and (b) those were different times. It's not like today, when grandparents are doing edibles, and in cities like New York—to judge from the weed aroma wafting everywhere—marijuana isn't just legal, it's mandatory. Back then you could get into serious trouble, like prison trouble, for possessing a single joint. So we tended to be paranoid.

Which is why, as the Haverford pond ducks approached, we got up and moved away. We laughed, because we knew our concerns were silly. *Ha ha! Clearly these ducks do not pose a threat to us! They're ducks!* But we did move.

We also came up with a new band name. And from then on we were the Federal Duck—or just the Duck, as we were familiarly called by our approximately three hard-core fans. We were cheap and fairly reliable, so we played lot of gigs, on some weekends both Friday and Saturday nights. We played at Haverford, of course, but we also played for mixers and fraternity parties at colleges all over the Philadelphia area—Bryn Mawr (our sister college), Villanova, Penn, Ursinus, Drexel, Temple, Harcum, Beaver[21] and others. We even played at Swarthmore, despite

---

21. Yes, Virginia, there really was a Beaver College, and it was an all-women institution. In 2000 it changed its name to Arcadia University, explaining that "the time had come for this institution to have a name that emphasized the achievements of its students, alumni, faculty, staff and programs." It is not clear, to me anyway, how "Arcadia" accomplishes this; a more honest explanation would be "We wanted a name that didn't make people laugh."

the fact they were Haverford's archrivals, since both were nerdy schools founded by Quakers and generally not great at sports.[22]

We were a party band, not an arty band. We played a lot of simple bulletproof three-chord garage-band standards—songs like "Sloopy," "Louie Louie," "Gloria," "Money" and "Land of 1,000 Dances," which actually has only one chord and can go on for weeks if necessary. We played "Satisfaction," "Get Off of My Cloud" and "Under My Thumb" by the Stones, and "Purple Haze" by Jimi Hendrix. We played "96 Tears," by ? and the Mysterians. We played "Got My Mojo Working," the Butterfield Blues Band version, and "Knock on Wood," the James Cotton version. We played "I Can't Keep from Crying," the Blues Project version. We had no particular genre beyond Songs People Dance To. Sometimes we'd get requests, and we'd say, "Sure! We can do that!" Then we'd play "Land of 1,000 Dances."

Musically we were never anything special, though some of my bandmates were genuinely talented, particularly bassist Bob Stern and keyboardist Ken Stover, who both went on to play professionally.[23] I was a ploddingly mediocre rhythm guitarist and singer. But as I say, we played a lot, and over time we became at least halfway decent.

We played under a wide variety of conditions, not always hospitable. I remember playing an event for some college organization at a restaurant, and one of the waitresses—at the time I thought of her as an old lady, though she was probably in her thirties—stood directly in front of us for a few seconds, staring at us, then slowly, deliberately, raised her hands and stuck her forefingers into her ears. Not a fan of our sound.

We got used to playing through adversity. One time we played in a Penn frat house, in a room with a big window looking out onto the front porch.

---

22. If I recall correctly, in my four years at Haverford our football team won only two games, and both were against Swarthmore. Not long after I graduated, Haverford dropped the football program. A few years ago, visiting the campus for a reunion, I bought a T-shirt that says "HAVERFORD COLLEGE FOOTBALL—UNDEFEATED SINCE 1972."

23. Bob was a classically trained violinist when he got to Haverford. When the Duck needed somebody to play bass, he learned how in roughly ten minutes, and he got to be really good. In later years he returned to the violin and became a superb jazz violinist; he now plays regularly in venues like Birdland with the Gil Gutiérrez Trio.

While we were performing there was a loud crash, and a sofa, which had been outside on the porch, came flying through the window into the room. The frat bros and their dates avoided the scattering glass, but they continued dancing; evidently this kind of occurrence was not that unusual. So we kept right on playing. As I recall the song was "Louie Louie."

Frat parties were the trickiest, especially when the brothers decided they wanted to grab our microphones and sing, or, worse, play our instruments. More than once I found myself wrestling with some drunk bro midsong for possession of my guitar. As the evening wore on, there occasionally were beer-fueled fights; sometimes there would be fighting, dancing and vomiting going on simultaneously. At some parties we'd line up our amps in front of us, forming a barrier for us to play behind. This was suboptimal from an acoustic standpoint, but we felt safer.

Notwithstanding the occasional hazardous gig, I loved being in the Federal Duck. The sixties were raging, and it was cool to be in a rock band, and I was in one. In the escalating culture war between old and young, squares and hippies, I was definitely on Team Hippie. I grew my hair long, which meant that when I left the Haverford campus, I was sometimes the target of anti-hippie remarks, especially when I happened to walk past groups of older men.

"Can't tell if that's a boy or a girl!" one of them would say—this was considered the height of wit—and the others would laugh, and depending on how likely it seemed that I might get the crap beat out of me, I'd either give them the finger or just keep walking.

I should note here that I did not spend my entire college career playing in a rock band and smoking pot. I also, time permitting, attended classes, and I wrote a lot of words. Many of these words were in the form of papers about great works of literature of which, as an English major, I had read roughly one-third. But some of the words were in the form of humor columns for the student newspaper, the *Haverford News*.

I got started when the editor, my classmate Dennis Stern—who went on to have a distinguished career at the *New York Times*—assigned me to do an actual news story. If I recall correctly, the assignment was to cover the opening of the Nixon for President office in Ardmore, a town next to Haverford. As a long-haired pot-smoking hippie, I had no desire whatsoever to talk to a bunch of Nixon people, so instead I remained in my dorm room and wrote a humor piece—at least I thought it was funny—about the arrival of the Nixon campaign. I don't remember if Dennis published it. But from then on he wisely used me as a humor columnist, not a reporter.

I wrote maybe a couple dozen humor columns for the *Haverford News*. Years later, at the Class of 1969's thirtieth reunion, we had an event in the Haverford gym, and somebody posted enlargements of some of my columns on the walls. The older me didn't find them particularly funny, although back when I wrote them, I thought they were hilarious. Maybe it was the pot.

I did get some serious journalism experience during my college years: For two summers, 1967 and '68, I worked as an intern at *Congressional Quarterly* in Washington, DC. I got the internship because the editor was my old next-door neighbor and family friend Tom Schroth, the man to whom my mom returned the legendary Skilsaw.

Congressional Quarterly, or *CQ*, was a magazine that covered the workings of Congress for its subscribers, mostly institutions such as newspapers and libraries. It was a serious publication staffed by serious professional journalists in a serious town. But my job—lowly intern gofer—was actually fun.

I had a press pass, and every day I'd go to Capitol Hill to fetch documents that the *CQ* reporters wanted, mostly copies of testimony given by witnesses in congressional hearings. There was little security back then, and with my pass I could roam all over the Capitol and the congressional office buildings. This was exciting, as sometimes there were famous and powerful people in those hallways. Once, in 1967, while looking down at the list of documents I was supposed to fetch, I literally bumped into Ted Kennedy; as I backed away, apologizing, I bumped into the person he was talking to, who turned out to be Bobby Kennedy.

That same summer I was collecting press releases one afternoon in the Senate Press Gallery, and I saw Art Buchwald joking with some reporters.

I was in awe; he was a beloved celebrity, the dean of American humor columnists and my mom's favorite writer. In twenty-five years he would also be my friend, but nineteen-year-old me could not have imagined that.

My senior year at Haverford began in 1968, a truly shitty time for America. The year started with the Tet Offensive, a major setback in a war that the public had grown sick of. In March, Lyndon Johnson, realizing he'd probably lose if he ran again, announced that he wouldn't. In April Martin Luther King was assassinated, and there were bad riots in a bunch of cities, and it was clear that it would be a long time before Dr. King's dream came true. In June Bobby Kennedy was assassinated. In August the Republicans nominated Richard Nixon for president, and the Democrats, amid clouds of tear gas, nominated poor old Hubert Humphrey. In November Nixon won. He claimed to have a Secret Plan to end the war. But not, as it turned out, any time soon.

For me, 1969 was all about Vietnam. Despite the fact that the nation wanted out, and the new president had promised to get us out, we weren't out. Which meant that as soon as I graduated from college, I'd be drafted.

Like many people, I was opposed to the war. I thought—I still think—that it was a horrendous mistake, an unforgivable waste of lives, American and Vietnamese. I thought it was insane that, at a time when the country had come to see the war as futile—and had elected a president who promised to end it—we were still sending people over there to keep it going.

So I didn't want to go. But I didn't have any basis for a medical or psychological deferment, and I didn't want to pretend that I did. I also didn't want to go to Canada. So I applied to my draft board for conscientious objector (CO) status.

I probably didn't deserve to get it. A true CO is morally opposed to all violence, which I wasn't. My moral opposition was specifically to Vietnam; if I'd been around during World War II, I'd have gone. But my draft board granted me CO status, I think because my father was a clergyman and because I went to a college with a Quaker tradition. I was lucky.

So I spent the two years after my graduation doing alternative service—that is, working in a civilian job deemed by my draft board to be in the national interest. The job I ended up with was in New York City, as a bookkeeper in the finance department of the national headquarters of the Episcopal Church. Really. My contribution to the nation's welfare was two years of running an adding machine and making journal entries.

All these years later, I still feel guilty about Vietnam, because I was able to avoid it, and so many guys, including guys I knew, were not. I think the real guilt belongs to the people who got us into that terrible war, and lied about how it was going, and took way too long to get us out. But I still feel guilty. As I say, it was a shitty time.

I graduated from Haverford in June of 1969. It was a hot day, and my roommates—Bob Stern, Ken Stover and Rob Stavis—and I elected, in the interest of comfort, not to wear pants under our graduation robes. Here's a photo of us taken before the commencement ceremony, preparing to make our way in the world:

Future leaders boldly facing the future: Rob Stavis, me, Bob Stern, Ken Stover.

I love this blurry, stupid photo. For me it captures the end of the first major phase of my life, the juvenile wiseass years, the era when, as far as I was concerned, nothing was really *that* important, and my main goal in life was to amuse myself.

This is not to say I stopped being a wiseass, or trying to amuse myself, or being stupid. These remained—they still remain—basic components of my personality. But after I left school I had to temper them as I tried to adjust to the Real World and its requirements—making a living, acting like an adult, wearing pants.

One of the first grown-up things I did, right after I graduated, was get married. For the record, I've been married three times. My first two marriages ended in divorce. Out of respect for the privacy of the people involved, I'm not going to talk about those marriages, other than to say that both of the women to whom I was married are good people, and I bear full responsibility for the fact that things didn't work out. In 1996 I married Michelle Kaufman, and we've been very happily together ever since, except for the time she made me take her to see Barry Manilow.

But getting back to 1969: When I graduated from college, I had no plan for the future, beyond the two years I was about to spend book-keeping. I had a BA degree in English but no idea what I was going to do with it. I had no career goal, no real ambition. The rest of this book will be about how, despite my utter lack of direction, I wound up with the best job any English major ever had.

CHAPTER THREE

MORPHING INTO A HUMOR COLUMNIST

IN THE FALL OF 1971 I WAS FINISHING MY TWO YEARS IN New York City. During that time I had become a moderately competent bookkeeper[24] and a veteran New Yorker.

I'd mastered the subway system, having spent hundreds of fun hours riding the IRT line between Nereid Avenue in the far north Bronx and Grand Central Terminal during rush hour. I understood the rules of subway etiquette, the main one being that you must never make eye contact with another rider, even when you're mashed together so tightly that you're involuntarily exchanging bodily fluids.

I had learned that, on the sidewalks of Manhattan, even if you're in no hurry, you must always walk with brisk urgency, as though you have reason to believe that somewhere, not too far behind you, is a lunatic with an ax.

I'd become a fan of New York bagels, New York pizza and the New York Mets, who, impossibly, won the 1969 World Series, triggering a wondrous celebration during which I saw at least a hundred people dancing the hora in the intersection of Second Avenue and Forty-Third Street while a blizzard of computer-printout paper swirled down from

---

24. It's mainly adding and subtracting. You do not need the cosine.

the surrounding office buildings. On my subway ride home that night, the motorman—I was pretty sure he was not sober—announced the stops in this way: "Next stop Allerton Avenue and THE METS WON THE WORLD SERIES."

So I had figured out New York. But I had not figured out my career plan. I had no definite goal other than not remaining a bookkeeper. I had a vague notion that I wanted to do something that involved writing, but I didn't know what kind of writing. I spent a couple of weeks reading the want ads in the New York papers, which listed many openings for bookkeepers but zero for writers. I even went to an employment agency, where a condescending man told me he couldn't do anything for me until I got a haircut.

I was seriously considering this when some friends from my Haverford days, Buzz and Libby Burger, told me that a friend of theirs, Hannah Gardner, had told them that there was an opening for a reporter job at the paper where she worked, the *Daily Local News* in West Chester, Pennsylvania. So I traveled down there and applied. I interviewed with the editor, Bill Dean, and the number-two guy, Bob Shoemaker, stressing my experience as an intern at *Congressional Quarterly*, which was pretty much all I had to stress. Apparently it was enough, because they hired me, and suddenly I was a newspaperman, raking in a cool $98 a week, before taxes.

The *Daily Local News* was an afternoon paper with a circulation of around thirty thousand. It came out six days a week, Monday through Saturday, and it covered Chester County in suburban Philadelphia. There were a dozen reporters, a two-man sports staff, two photographers and—this being 1971—a Women's Page editor. We all sat at gray metal desks in the newsroom, talking on telephones with clunky headsets and pounding out stories on big old heavy typewriters, keeping carbon copies that we impaled on spikes on our desks and never referred to again. We drank shitty coffee from a vending machine that also dispensed soup and hot chocolate, all from the same tube. (I don't think anybody ever got the soup.)

We were very, very local at the *Daily Local News*. We covered the police, traffic accidents, fires, courts, county commissioner meetings, township board of supervisors meetings, borough council meetings, school board meetings, zoning meetings, sewer authority meetings and many other varieties of meetings, endless meetings, virtually all of them hideously boring. We wrote many obituaries, so many that I sometimes wondered how there was anybody still alive in Chester County. We wrote items about school events, church events, Girl Scouts, Boy Scouts, women's clubs, theater groups, the American Legion, the VFW, the Rotary Club, the Masons, the Elks, the Eagles and the Loyal Order of Moose.

We often received phone calls from local residents with news items they wanted us to print. Sometimes these items were beneath even our standards, such as when people took their kids to Disney World and thought this event should be reported in the newspaper. But often these items were deemed newsworthy. If, for example, a Chester County resident called in to report that they had grown an unusually large zucchini, and it happened to be a slow day, there was a decent chance that one of our photographers, Larry McDevitt or Bill Stoneback, would be dispatched to the scene to take a picture, and if it was a *really* slow day the zucchini might end up on the front page. That was how local we were at the *Daily Local News*.

I loved it. I loved it immediately, and I loved almost everything about it. I also learned a LOT. Pretty much everything I know about journalism, I learned in the first few months at the *Daily Local News*. I learned, for example, that if you interview somebody, and he tells you his name is John Smith, you need to ask him how he spells "John" and how he spells "Smith," because it might turn out to be "Jon Smyth." I learned that robbery is not the same thing as burglary. I learned that a grand jury hands an indictment up, not down. I learned that if a house is burning down, and the homeowners are standing there, watching, and you walk up to them and ask them basic reporter questions such as what their names are and how they think the fire may have started, sometimes they will answer politely, and sometimes they will hate you and yell at you to leave them alone, but you have to walk up and ask them anyway because that's your job.

Sometimes I learned the hard way. When you get a phone call from a very upset widow who tells you that her late husband's name was "Stewart," not "Stuart," which is how you spelled it in his obituary, you definitely remember from then on to check the spelling of every name, every time.

I also learned a lot about what readers of a local newspaper are, and are not, interested in. You could make a major mistake in a story about a meeting of a zoning board and never hear a peep from the readers about it. But if you, in writing a photo caption, misidentified a goose as a duck (I did this), you would hear from literally dozens of readers, some of them quite irate. And if the newspaper should ever—God forbid—leave out the daily horoscope, the phones would not stop ringing.[25]

But I loved it all. I loved the chaotic noise of the newsroom as deadline approached—typewriters clattering; police and fire radios sporadically blaring out staticky transmissions; editors calling out "Who's up for an obit?"; reporters occasionally, for a wide variety of reasons, yelling "Fuck!" I loved when at the end of the day—or even, if I'm being honest, sometimes during the day—I'd go with some of the other younger reporters to a nearby bar called Joe's Sportsman's Lounge, where we'd drink twenty-five-cent draft beers, and pretty much all we ever talked about was our jobs, because our jobs were (to us anyway) fascinating.

I never knew for sure what I'd be doing when I got to work, where I'd be sent that day—maybe to a fire, and maybe to a speech by John Kenneth Galbraith. I covered shootings, parades, charity canoe races, a smokestack demolition, a campaign stop by presidential candidate George McGovern, and the grand opening of a regional sewage treatment facility, an event at which the guests drank champagne from plastic stemware while overlooking the aeration tank. I covered an armed hostage situation, a major train derailment and chemical spill, a local Nazi group and a gas-station

---

25. Some callers would want us to read them their horoscopes for that day. Usually we read them straight, although sometimes, to amuse ourselves, we took liberties ("You say you're a Sagittarius? UH-oh").

giveaway campaign in which the station was giving away free gas to streakers (streaking was big in the early seventies).

I covered these things and many, many more things, especially things involving meetings. But even counting all the meetings, it was WAY more interesting than bookkeeping.

Sometimes it was pretty exciting. In June of 1972 Chester County—along with much of the East Coast—was nailed by a tropical cyclone, Agnes, which had started out as Hurricane Agnes. It rained torrentially for days. The rivers and creeks rose quickly, overwhelming their banks, and there was bad flooding everywhere—massive damage, chaos, people having to flee their homes, people trapped, deaths.

For several days I basically didn't sleep. I spent most of that time riding along with photographer Larry McDevitt, looking for flood stories. Larry had grown up in the news business; his father had been the editor of the *Daily Local News*, and Larry started working there as a teenager. He knew every politician, cop and firefighter in Chester County, every creek, every bridge, every back road. He drove us from disaster to disaster, listening to his police scanner, frowning, puffing on his cigar, figuring out where the action was and how he could get us to it.

At one point we found ourselves in Downingtown, where the Brandywine Creek, normally a placid stream, was no longer flowing quietly under the bridge across Route 30. It was now a raging river flowing *over* the bridge, cutting the town in half. Larry wanted to get closer—newspaper photographers always want to get closer—so he started wading out into the water, and like an idiot I followed him, and suddenly water was surging around our waists and we had to grab on to a traffic-sign pole to keep from getting swept downstream, both of us laughing, although at least one of us was also terrified.

When we got back to the *Daily Local News* that night the newsroom was deserted. Larry went into the darkroom and started developing the many photos he'd taken; I went to my desk, pulled out my damp notebook and started typing. We were still both soaking wet. A few hours later, when we were done creating what would basically be the front page of the next day's paper, Larry came out of the darkroom with a bottle of scotch. We rinsed out some cardboard cups from the vending machine that dispensed shitty coffee, and we filled them with scotch, and we drank a toast to surviving Agnes. I'd had little sleep for days, and I've never liked scotch. But sitting there in the newsroom at two thirty a.m., exhausted, in my soggy shoes and pants, I thought: *I love this job.*

The *Daily Local News* was where I learned journalism, and where I found my identity as a newspaper guy, which deep down inside I will always be. It was also where I started regularly doing the thing that eventually would change my life: writing humor columns.

The paper had a feature on the op-ed page called Ad Lib, which was a space for columns written by reporters. Anybody could submit an Ad Lib. Some people wrote about serious issues; some wrote slice-of-life observations; some wrote personal essays.

After just a few weeks at the paper, I submitted a column, and Bill Dean, the editor, published it. It ran on November 18, 1971, my first humor column in a real commercial newspaper. Here's how it started (I've cut it some):

I've been a reporter for the *Daily Local News* for about one month, so I figure it's about time I wrote a comprehensive article about what it's like to be a reporter. Just in case there's anybody out there in newspaper land who thinks, as I once did, that exciting things go on all the time when you work for a newspaper.

This is not the case.

Since I've been here, not one person has come bursting into the newsroom screaming: "The thirty-foot man-eating iguana has escaped from the zoo and just ate the Civil Defense Office!"

What does happen is the Editor says, "Dave, we got a picture here of the contestants in the Miss Plastic Dishrack Contest. Get on the phone and see if you can find out their names. Plastic Dishracks are big in this area, Dave."

Or someone tells me to rewrite the minutes of last week's meeting of the Society for the Renaming of the Grand Canyon, the high point of which appears to be the opening prayer.

And so on. It wasn't great. But it was a start.

Bill Dean, a genuinely nice person and a fine newspaperman who taught me a lot, encouraged me to keep submitting Ad Libs. And I did, every week; I wrote dozens and dozens of them. Rereading them all these years later, I find myself cringing, but I also see the rudiments of what would become my humor style. For example, I often assumed the voice of Wildly Incorrect Authority—the supremely confident expert spouting nonsense, a technique I learned from the great Robert Benchley. In a column about surviving in the wilderness, I wrote:

> If you or one of your companions gets bit by a snake, don't panic. Take a razor blade and make a cut shaped like an "X," then suck out all the blood. Snakes just hate this, and after you've done it to them one or two times they stop biting people altogether.

This is from a column about how to play chess:

> First the two players take their men into the locker room and give them a pep talk.
>
> "Let's get out there and get that king," they say. They never explain why.

I also attempted political satire. This is from a 1972 column about the Democratic presidential primaries, with me writing in the voice of a father explaining the situation to his son:

> After the Florida primary, it turned out that Hubert Humphrey was the front runner.
>
> "Why, Dad, because he got the most votes?"
>
> No, Humphrey only got 18 percent of the votes in Florida. George Wallace got the most votes, 42 percent.

"Then why isn't George Wallace the front runner?"

Because the other candidates don't like him. They say he's a demagogue.

"What's that, Dad?"

A demagogue is somebody who gets more votes than the front runners. He did this by using a sneaky, underhanded, immoral technique.

"What technique?"

He started saying he was opposed to busing before the front runners thought of it.

"But what is busing, Dad?"

Busing is one method used to achieve racial integration in the schools. It started out in the South, and now the courts are saying it has to be used in the North. Most of the candidates are against it.

"But, Dad, if most of the candidates are against it, how did the idea get started in the first place?"

Well, son, back in the old days, most of the candidates were for it. That was when civil rights was a good thing to be in favor of.

"Isn't anybody in favor of civil rights anymore?"

Oh, yes, indeed they are. All of the candidates are solidly in favor of civil rights. But they'd like to keep them down South, where they belong.

In that column I was definitely copying the style of Art Buchwald.

I enjoyed writing Ad Libs, and I loved it when people—this happened sometimes—told me they enjoyed reading them. But the *Daily Local News* wasn't paying me to be a columnist. I was still primarily a reporter, although my job description was expanding. After a year Bill Dean named me city editor, which meant that in addition to my reporting duties, I was responsible for supervising the dozen or so stringers—part-timers who were paid pitiful sums to cover meetings in Chester Country's outlying municipalities.[26]

---

26. One of these stringers was Signe Wilkinson, who went on to win a Pulitzer Prize at the *Philadelphia Daily News*. I can't claim any credit for that: She won it for cartooning.

A year or so later I got a bigger promotion, this time to news editor, which meant I was supervising the full-time reporters, some of whom were quite a bit older than I was. I was assigning stories, evaluating people, hiring and firing people, writing headlines ("East Goshen Board Airs Zoning Change") and laying out the front page, a high-stress activity that was like having to solve a jigsaw puzzle on a tight deadline with the phone ringing a lot and completely unexpected pieces sometimes showing up at the last second.

So I was pretty busy being news editor, and I wasn't writing many Ad Libs anymore. But I was enjoying what I was doing, and I'd come to believe that I'd found my life's work.

Then in 1975 I made a huge mistake, or so it seemed at the time. I decided that, after four years at a small-town paper—much as I enjoyed it—I needed to make a career move to Big Time Journalism. So I applied for a job at the Philadelphia bureau of the Associated Press, and I got hired. I gave my notice at the *Daily Local News*, had a goodbye party and left for what I thought was a better job.

I regretted it almost immediately. I want to stress that the AP is a venerable organization that provides an invaluable service and has produced many fine journalists. But it wasn't for me.

Philadelphia was a hub bureau, a sort of central clearinghouse, which meant there was a lot of clerical work to do—sorting and routing stories on the various wires, responding to requests from member newspapers, making sure the sports and weather stories got formatted correctly and sent out when and where they were supposed to, that kind of thing. We also did a lot of recycling—taking stories that had been printed in AP member newspapers and rewriting them to go out on our wires so other members could use them.

I once picked up a story about a tragic canoeing accident from the *Philadelphia Bulletin* and rewrote it for the wire. Then somebody at the *Bulletin*, apparently unaware that they had already run the story, ran our version. Then somebody in our bureau, apparently unaware that we had already run it, rewrote it and put it on the wire *again*. For all I know this story is still out there somewhere, staggering around zombie-like, the Canoe Tragedy That Will Not Die.

So instead of writing my own stories, I was spending a lot of time processing other people's stories. And when I was allowed to write, I had to conform strictly to AP style, which tended to be bland and generic, and which did not (at least not in the Philadelphia bureau) allow much room for humor. There was no Ad Lib at the AP.

Also, because I was the new guy, I got a lot of overnight shifts, which consisted mostly of doing clerical stuff in an empty newsroom at three a.m. It was like being a bookkeeper all over again, but lonelier and with worse hours.

I hated it. I went to work with a pit in my stomach, and I couldn't wait for my shift to end. I wanted to quit, but I didn't know where to go; I was too embarrassed to go crawling back to the comfort of the *Daily Local News*.

So I stuck it out at the AP for a little over a year. And then one day my friend Buzz Burger called me to say his dad had suffered a heart attack and he needed to hire somebody immediately. Bob Burger was the founder and owner of Burger Associates, a consulting firm that taught an effective-writing course to business clients. It had two employees, Bob and his number-two guy, Chuck Meyers. Bob, under doctor's orders to quit traveling, needed somebody to replace himself pronto.

I knew nothing about teaching effective writing to businesspeople. But I hated working at the AP. So I gave my notice and took the job with Bob, and just like that I had quit journalism. This may seem like a rash decision, which it definitely was, but (a) I was really, *really* unhappy at the AP, and (b) it ultimately turned out, in a convoluted way, to be the main reason I ended up becoming a humor columnist.

I bought a briefcase and two suits and spent the next few weeks in training, which meant watching Chuck teach a course at Con Edison in New York and a couple more courses at DuPont in Wilmington, Delaware.

Then it was time for me to teach a course. My first client was Rohm and Haas, a chemical company. I got to the building in downtown Philadelphia two hours early. This allowed me plenty of time to prepare by sitting in a men's-room stall trying not to puke. I was seriously questioning my recent life decisions. A little over a year earlier I'd had a job I loved, which I'd left for a job I hated, which I had now left for a job—a job requiring a suit *and* a briefcase—that I might also hate, plus I didn't even know whether I could do it.

So I was terrified as I walked into a conference room containing thirty-two people, mostly chemical engineers (a job I knew absolutely nothing about), most of whom were older than me, and all of whom *looked* older than me, because I looked like I was thirteen years old, although in an effort to look older I had grown a mustache, which made me look like a thirteen-year-old with a mustache. I had to somehow keep the attention of these people for five days, during which I was supposed to convince them that I had some useful knowledge to impart.

I got through it. At times I felt like a fraud, but I got through it. And thus I became a business-writing consultant, which was my job for the next seven years. I traveled around the country giving the Burger course for Colgate-Palmolive, Sperry UNIVAC, Air Products & Chemicals, Union Carbide, DuPont, Arthur Andersen, SmithKline and a bunch of other companies. I got better at it as time went on. I may even have helped some people improve their writing, although it was almost always a battle.

Bob Burger, who designed the course, was a brilliant, quirky man with an unusual set of skills. He was a child-prodigy pianist and a math whiz, one of those people who can do big calculations in their heads.

"Bob," I'd say to him. "What's three hundred ninety-seven times forty-three?" He'd frown into the distance for maybe two seconds, then say, "Seventeen thousand seventy-one." He was always right.

He invented a word game called Skink, which he tried to market, but it never caught on, possibly because you had to be as smart as Bob to play it. He was an excellent table tennis player and a terrible driver. He also could be absent-minded. One time he was upset about two things: (1) He couldn't find his pipe, and (2) his car wasn't running right. After listening to Bob complain about these things for several days, his wife,

Beth—a saintly woman—had an idea, and was able to locate Bob's missing pipe.

It was under the accelerator pedal.

Bob came up with the idea for a business-writing course while he was teaching at the Tuck School of Business at Dartmouth. He decided to strike out on his own and wrote a book—*How to Write So People Can Understand You*—that was the basis of the course. It was essentially a collection of rules, some of which were old standards—beware of the passive voice; don't use a big word ("utilize") when a smaller one ("use") will do; strike out words that add no information ("You need wheat ~~in order~~ to make bread"); etc.

But some of Bob's rules were less conventional. He was emphatic about avoiding what he called "verb mutilation"—turning verb ideas into other parts of speech, usually nouns. Take this sentence:

It was our conclusion that the explosion of the tank was due to the failure of the relief valve.

The sentence is grammatical, but its three verb ideas have been mutilated into nouns: "conclusion," "explosion" and "failure." As a result, a weaker verb—"was"—has been pressed into service twice to make the sentence work. With the verbs unmutilated, it reads:

We concluded that the tank exploded because the relief valve failed.

Much better.

Bob believed verb mutilation was the biggest single cause of clumsy, turgid writing; I believe he was right.

I spent many hours trying to convince my students that they had mutilated their verbs. But my biggest challenge was getting them to accept another of Bob's rules, which to my mind was the most important one: Always start with a "lead."

The lead is an opening that gets straight to the point, telling the reader immediately the most important thing the writer has to say. This is, of course, a fundamental tenet of journalism, but it definitely had not caught on in the business world when I was teaching.

My students almost never started with their most important message. Sometimes they put it last; often they hid it somewhere in the middle. For example, if they were writing a report for upper management about a research project, they almost always organized it chronologically. They'd start with an explanation of why the project was done, followed by a detailed discussion of how the research was conducted, followed by a mass of data, followed by some conclusions, maybe followed by some recommendations, and then sometimes some other stuff. Their reasoning was: *My project was complicated, so to understand it, my bosses need to slog through it the way I did, starting at the beginning.*

In the second part of the course, the students would bring in actual reports or memos they'd written, and we'd edit them together. I had many conversations like this:

ME (*after reading a twenty-page, single-spaced report*): If you had to reduce this report to one sentence, what would it be?

STUDENT (*after some thought*): If we substitute Compound B for Compound A in this manufacturing process, we can make the same product at a significantly lower energy cost.

ME: Where do you say that in your report?

STUDENT: Partly in the conclusions, and partly in the recommendations.

ME: Why don't you start with it?

STUDENT: How would my bosses understand it?

ME: I understand it, and I never even took chemistry.

I had variations of this conversation hundreds of times. My argument was: Before you start explaining, you should tell your readers *what* you're explaining. I did not always persuade my students. I found that many people in the corporate world were reluctant to get to the point, possibly because nobody else in the corporate world seemed to be getting to the point. But I tried.

I taught the Burger course for seven years, traveling all around the country. I didn't always love it, but I got better at it. And it turned out to be good for me, for three reasons:

First, I learned to speak in front of groups. Every time I started a course, I was facing a tough crowd—a roomful of skeptical corporate employees expecting to be bored. To keep their attention, I used a lot of humor—jokes about dangling participles, jokes mocking the ridiculously stilted language people used in business correspondence ("Enclosed please find the enclosed enclosure"). In time I became comfortable entertaining audiences; this skill was invaluable when I started doing book tours, which are much more about talking than about writing.

Second, it broadened my perspective. In my newspaper years I had a government-centric view of the world. I spent a lot of time talking to elected officials and other government people. I rarely talked with businesspeople, unless their businesses happened to be burning down. I assumed that business was boring and monolithic, and that the employees were mostly drones doing mindless jobs, unlike us English majors in journalism keeping democracy alive by covering the regional sewage authority.

What I learned, in the belly of the corporate beast, is that the business world, although it can be boring, is also fantastically varied and complex, and it's inhabited by all kinds of people, including smart, funny, creative and subversive ones. I think this new perspective helped me when I went back to column-writing; I had more respect for my readers, and a better understanding of the world they live in.

Third, teaching the course improved my own writing, because I had to pay more attention to the nuts and bolts of how writing works. When I was critiquing my students' reports, I often faced resistance: People with highly specialized technical expertise or years of business experience can be reluctant to accept writing advice from an English major who looks thirteen. I couldn't just say "Hey, I'm a good writer, and my way sounds better." I had to convince them I knew what I was talking about.

I once got into an argument with a group of research chemists, people with PhDs, about the wording of a sentence. To convince them I knew what I was talking about, I ultimately had to go to the whiteboard and diagram the sentence, which satisfied them (scientists respect a whiteboard). I don't think I could do that today, but back then I knew how, because, in an effort to bolster my credibility as an authority, I had read every book on grammar and usage I could get my hands on.[27] And I think that ultimately made me a better humor writer. I became more conscious of details, of how even minor changes in vocabulary and structure affect the tone of a sentence—to make it sound more pompous, or more stupid, or whatever effect I'm going for. To this day I can spend an hour wrestling with a question like which word would be funnier in a given sentence, "squirrel" or "armadillo."[28]

By the late seventies I was comfortable teaching the Burger course. It was reasonably satisfying work, and the pay was good. I'd hit my thirties, and I figured this was going to be my future: I was a business-writing consultant.

But I had a little side gig.

I was on the road a lot, which meant I spent a lot of time in hotels and airports, during which I had nothing to do. So I started writing humor columns again. I wrote them longhand on a yellow legal pad, and when I got back from trips I typed them up and brought them to my old paper, the *Daily Local News*, where I still had friends, who graciously published them. Pretty soon it was a weekly feature, essentially the column I would write for the next thirty years. The topics were pretty random, as these excerpts demonstrate:

---

27. The most useful reference I found was *A Dictionary of Contemporary American Usage*, by Bergen Evans and Cornelia Evans. It's an excellent resource, clear, comprehensive, wise and often quite entertaining. Unfortunately, it's also out of print. It's a bit dated now, but I still use my 1957 edition.

28. The answer is "weasel."

What could be more fun than an outdoor barbecue? I can think of several things offhand, such as watching the secretary of state fall into a vat of untreated sewage.

For more than a year now, President Reagan and the Congress have been working very hard on reducing government spending, so it should come as no surprise to anybody that they have managed to increase it.

Let's look at the positive side of nuclear war. One big plus is that the Postal Service says it has a plan to deliver the mail after the war, which is considerably more than it is doing now.

The main freshwater fish are bass, bream, guppy, carp, frog, muskellunge, piccolo and crappie. Some people claim there are also trout, but this is a mythical fish, like the Loch Ness Monster. Nobody in recorded history has ever even seen a trout, let alone caught one.

I fly a lot, because of the nature of my job. I'm a gnat.

Without question, the greatest invention in the history of mankind is beer. Oh, I grant you that the wheel was also a fine invention, but the wheel does not go nearly as well with pizza.

My family had a system for car travel. My father would drive; my mother would periodically offer to drive, knowing that my father would not let her drive unless he went blind in both eyes and lapsed into a coma; and my sister and I would sit in the back seat and read Archie comic books for the first 11 miles, then punch each other and scream for the remaining 970.

The *Daily Local News* paid me $22 per column, so this was definitely not my livelihood; I was still a full-time business-writing consultant. But I was seeing reader reactions to my columns, mostly in the form of letters. Some letters were critical; usually these were from a type of reader I would come to know well, the Humor-Impaired ("For your information, Mr. Barry, a piccolo is NOT A FISH"). But most of the letters were nice.

After a year or so, I decided to see if I could get my column into other newspapers. I made copies of a batch of my *Daily Local News* columns and sent them to some big newspaper syndicates, but nobody was interested. So I started sending them directly to newspapers, mostly small- and medium-sized papers in the Northeast. Most of them weren't interested either, but a few were; every now and then one would print a column and pay me $10 or $20.

Then a small California newspaper syndicate connected with me and began sending my column out. By the early eighties it was starting to feel more and more like a real thing, this column gig.

One of my columns caught the attention of Dave Boldt, the editor of the *Philadelphia Inquirer's* Sunday magazine, who invited me to submit something to him. This was a big deal for me, because the *Inquirer* was then building a reputation as one of the best big-city papers in the country, making waves and winning Pulitzers. I wrote an essay for Dave about my experience with junior high shop class, which he published under the headline "How to Make a Board." He encouraged me to submit more essays, so I wrote a few—as I recall, one was about playing bridge, and another one was about hunting.

Then I sent him one that I definitely remember, because it turned out to be my big break. It was about the birth of my son, Rob. I actually submitted it twice: The first time, Dave gave it back and said, "Make it longer. And funnier." So I rewrote it, and this time Dave liked it; he paid me $350 for it, by far the most money I'd ever gotten for writing something. It focused on the "natural childbirth" movement that had pretty much taken over the birthing process, at least in Baby Boomer America.

As I described it in the essay, under the old system of having babies, fathers were not directly involved: "They remained in waiting rooms reading old copies of *Field and Stream*." I noted that "many fine people were born under this system." With natural childbirth, however, not only were the fathers expected to watch the baby get born, but also both parents were expected to attend classes. My essay continued:

The classes consisted of sitting in a brightly lit room and openly discussing, among other things, the uterus. Now I can remember a time, in high school, when I would have killed for reliable information about the uterus. But having discussed it at length, having seen actual full-color diagrams, I must say, in all honesty, that although I respect it a great deal as an organ, it has lost much of its charm.

When we weren't looking at pictures or discussing the uterus, we practiced breathing . . . What happens is that when the baby gets ready to leave the uterus, the woman goes through what the medical community laughingly refers to as contractions; if it referred to them as "horrible pains that make you wonder why the hell you ever decided to get pregnant," people might stop having babies and the medical community would have to go into the major-appliance business.

In the old days, under President Eisenhower, doctors avoided the contraction problem by giving lots of drugs to women who were having babies. They'd knock them out during the delivery, and the women would wake up when their kids were entering the fourth grade . . .

The most important thing to the natural-childbirth people is for the woman to breathe deeply. Really. The theory is that if she breathes deeply, she'll get all relaxed and won't notice that she's in a hospital delivery room wearing a truly perverted garment and having a baby. I'm not sure who came up with this theory. Whoever it was evidently believed that women have very small brains . . .

One evening, we saw a movie of a woman we didn't even know having a baby. I am serious. Some woman actually let some moviemakers film the whole thing. In color. She was from California. Another time, the instructor announced, in the tone of voice you might use to tell people that they had just won free trips to the Bahamas, that we were going to see color slides of a Caesarean section.

The first slides showed a pregnant woman cheerfully entering the hospital. The last slides showed her cheerfully holding a baby. The middle slides showed how they got the baby out of the cheerful woman, but I can't give you a lot of detail here because I had to go out for fifteen or twenty drinks of water. I do remember that at one point our instructor cheerfully observed that there was "surprisingly little blood, really." She evidently felt this was a real selling point.

And so on. The *Inquirer* magazine published my essay in the summer of 1981. This turned out to be excellent timing, because many members of my generation, the Boomers, were rising through the ranks of the newspaper business, and a lot of them were having babies. My essay struck a chord, and almost immediately after it ran I started getting calls from editors of other papers, some of them big-city papers. The first call I got was from an editor at the *Chicago Tribune* (I've forgotten his name) who said he wanted to reprint the essay and asked me what my price was. I figured I'd already been paid $350 by the *Inquirer*, so anything else I got was gravy. So I said, "How about fifty dollars?"

There was a pause. Then he said, "We pay five hundred dollars."

That was the end of our negotiations, although it later occurred to me that if I had countered with $25, he might have come back with $1,000.

A bunch of newspaper Sunday magazines reprinted the childbirth essay, and some of them picked up my weekly column. A few magazines asked me to do freelance pieces. Rodale Press, a small publishing house in Pennsylvania, contacted me about writing a humor book. I was still teaching the Burger course, still wearing a suit and scouring corporate memos for mutilated verbs. But doors were opening.

One of them opened when I got a call from Gene Weingarten, who had recently been hired as associate editor at the *Miami Herald*'s Sunday magazine, *Tropic*. (Gene claims that the first thing I said to him, after he introduced himself, was "Can you hang on a minute? My kid just threw up on my shoes.") Gene told me he liked my childbirth essay and wanted to run more of my writing.

So *Tropic* started printing my stuff, and I got to know Gene, who is—I mean this in a good way—insane (more on this later). In 1982 the *Her-*

ald flew me down to meet Gene and his boss, Kevin Hall, and to write about my impressions of Miami.

At the time the city was going through a very rough patch. Race relations were bad; there had been major riots in 1980 when an all-white jury acquitted four police officers in the beating death of a Black man after a traffic stop. The city was struggling to accommodate the massive influx of refugees from the Mariel boatlift. Crime was up, and there was cocaine everywhere.

Miami's sun-'n'-fun image was taking a savage beating. In November 1981 *Time* ran a cover story on Miami headlined "PARADISE LOST?" It began: "An epidemic of violent crime, a plague of illicit drugs and a tidal wave of refugees have slammed into South Florida with the destructive power of a hurricane."

This was the Miami I flew down to write about. I rented a car at the airport and immediately got lost in an area where, as far as I could tell, nobody spoke English.[29] Eventually I found the *Herald*, a big ugly building with a spectacular view of Biscayne Bay. I met Kevin and Gene, whose editorial guidance consisted of taking me to lunch, then sending me off to wander around Miami.

My essay ran as a *Tropic* cover story. It began:

> It was the kind of assignment that journalists dream about if they lead fairly limited lives: The editors at *Tropic* wanted me to fly down to Miami and become intimately familiar with every aspect of the city—its culture, its history, its people, its joys, its sorrows—in short, its very soul. They figured I would need three days.
>
> I had never been to Miami, so before I left Philadelphia I did extensive research in the form of talking to several of my friends. None of them had ever been to Miami either. I recalled reading somewhere that one-quarter of the murders in Miami are committed with automatic weapons, which is an indication of a highly technological society, but that was really all I knew.

---

29. This is still pretty much true.

Now before the Chamber of Commerce gets angry at me for mentioning murder so early in this story, let me stress that in the entire time I was in Miami I never saw anybody murdered in any way. So I want all you potential tourists out there to ignore what you've heard about the murder problem, although you might want to give some thought to the killer toads. But more on them later.

I wrote the story in the format of a standard journalist-explores-a-city piece, except I flagrantly violated the norms of journalism, such as the norm that says you should conduct interviews:

But Miami is more than just weather, businesses and dangerous reptiles. Miami is also people, and the only way to get to know the people of a city is to get out of the safety of the air-conditioned rental car and rub shoulders with them as they lead their everyday lives. I think my findings on the people of Miami are best summarized by this conversation on the street:

ME: Tell me, what are Miamians really like?

MIAMIAN: Well, I would say they are a juxtaposition of many peoples, really—people of many ages, many races, many cultures. True, this juxtaposition creates great tensions at times yet, paradoxically, it is also what gives the city its great vitality.

ME: Hey, that's terrific. What's your name?

MIAMIAN: I don't have one. You just made me up so you could get a good quote without having to get out of your rental car and talk to a bunch of people who carry open umbrellas when it's not raining and might try to shoot you with an automatic weapon.

It was a wildly unserious piece, making fun of some sensitive topics. It was generally well received by the readers, although Gene told me some important people hated it. He didn't give a shit; in fact, he thought that was great. As I was to learn, gleefully not giving a shit is a fundamental component of Gene's personality.

At this point I was writing freelance pieces for Gene at the *Herald* and Dave Boldt at the *Inquirer*, and both of them were talking to me about a full-time columnist job. Both papers were part of the Knight Ridder chain, and (as I understood it) upper management decreed that, to avoid a bidding war, each paper would make me a job offer at the same salary, $60,000, and that would be that.

The *Inquirer*'s offer was made by the editor, Gene Roberts, even then a newspaper legend, the man who presided over what would become known as the Golden Age of the *Inquirer*—seventeen Pulitzer Prizes in eighteen years. Gene and Dave Boldt took me to an upscale Philadelphia restaurant, where we ate steak and drank a lot of wine but did not talk business.

Then we went to Gene's house, where we drank scotch and—I swear—watched a VHS tape of a John Wayne movie, during which we continued to not talk business. When the movie ended, well after midnight, Gene walked me to the front door, and as we stood in the open doorway—me unsteadily—Gene offered me the job. It was to write three columns a week, focusing on local themes.

The *Herald*'s offer came from the other Gene, Weingarten, and it was: Come to *Tropic* and write a weekly column about whatever you want. The problem with that offer was, I didn't want to move to Miami. On my lone visit there, to write the cover story, Miami had struck me as a crowded, crazy, sometimes-scary place, not a place to raise a family. I expressed this concern to Gene, who, after consulting upper management, told me I didn't have to move to Miami.

So I had to choose between the *Inquirer* and the *Herald*. I asked a bunch of people where they thought I should go, and they were unanimous: the *Inquirer*. They saw it as a no-brainer—go with the more prestigious newspaper, the Pulitzer factory with the legendary editor, the paper that covered the area where I lived. Not one person thought it made any sense for me to go with the *Herald*.

I went with the *Herald*. One reason was the actual job. At the *Inquirer*, I'd be writing essentially every other day, mostly on local topics. That was an excellent job, no question. But at the *Herald* I'd be writing just once a week, and I could write about anything.

The other reason was Gene Weingarten. He was going to be my editor, and it had already become abundantly clear to me that he was (a) brilliant, and (b) a wild man. He loved to take chances, to blast past boundaries, to spit the revered conventions of Professional Journalism right in the eyeball. He was willing to try anything, as long as it wasn't boring. He had no fear of offending people, including people he worked for; in fact he *enjoyed* offending people. In a way he reminded me of my high school best buddy, Lanny Watts: a fellow wiseass, a partner in crime. Except now there was no Assistant Principal Sabella around to tell us we couldn't put up our dance poster.

And so in the spring of 1983 I gave my notice to Bob Burger, who was very gracious about it, and I left the business world. In fact I left the working world altogether, because almost everything I did from that point on was way too much fun to be called work. I was still living in tiny, bucolic Glen Mills, Pennsylvania. But I was now the humor correspondent for the *Miami Herald*, and my beat was any topic that caught my attention.

Which turned out, as we will see, to be some pretty weird topics.

CHAPTER FOUR

TROPIC

WHEN I JOINED THE *MIAMI HERALD*, THE US NEWSPA-per industry was flying high. There was no Internet (imagine!) so newspapers had little competition for daily in-depth coverage of news and sports, and virtually no daily competition for classified ads, cross-word puzzles, book and movie reviews, the comics, and the horoscope.

So everybody read newspapers, which meant newspapers attracted lots of advertisers, which meant they made big profits. Newspapers were rich, influential, respected, feared. They were also trusted, still basking in the afterglow of the Watergate scandal, when journalists were per-ceived by the public as (imagine!) the good guys.

The *Herald* was a big deal. It was the largest newspaper in the South, with a daily circulation of half a million in winter and more than four hundred reporters, editors and photographers. Most of the editorial staff worked on the fifth floor of the big ugly building with the spectacular view of Biscayne Bay. It was a classic big-city newsroom—crowded, chaotic; people in meet-ings, people smoking cigarettes, people who were trying to quit smoking bumming cigarettes, people talking on and sometimes yelling into phones, people staring at screens, people pounding furiously on keyboards and typewriters. Serious Daily Journalists practicing Serious Daily Journalism.

And then there was the Sunday magazine. It was located in a small suite of offices down a hallway, separated from the newsroom by a few yards physically, but by many miles philosophically.

Tropic. What a special place it was.

Start with the management. Or, rather, the "management." Not long after I began working there, the editor, Kevin Hall, left, and Gene Weingarten became the top guy. He hired Tom Shroder as his second in command. Tom and Gene are both superb editors, in part because they're both excellent writers: Tom has written critically acclaimed books; Gene, after he left the *Herald*, went to the *Washington Post*, where he won *two* Pulitzer Prizes for feature writing.

So they definitely were good at words. They were not so good at organization.

Especially not Gene. His desktop was basically a landfill, only more disgusting, because a landfill would have a lower saliva content. Gene is a chewer. Interspersed throughout the vast random pile of things on his desk—letters, memos, manuscripts, books, plates, cutlery, food wrappers, actual food, the late Jimmy Hoffa—were the mutilated corpses of Bic pens, dozens of them, each seemingly having been attacked by some kind of small, vicious pen-hating creature—perhaps a shrew—that had a medical condition—perhaps rabies—that caused it to produce copious amounts of drool. Every now and then, somebody would absentmindedly pick up one of Gene's pens and—YEEP—fling it violently away as one would an irate scorpion.

So Gene was not strong on keeping track of paperwork, or for that matter performing the other duties associated with a management position in a large organization. One time—this is a legendary Gene story—*Tropic* was visited by a group of executives of Knight Ridder, the corporation that owned the *Herald*. This was a planned visit: A memo had been sent to all department heads informing them that these executives would be touring the newspaper, and that each department head was expected to give a brief presentation on the operation of the department.

Of course Gene had not read the memo. The memo was undoubtedly somewhere in the desk landfill, drenched in spit. So when the suits arrived in the *Tropic* conference room, Gene was utterly unprepared. He decided, on the spur of the moment, to tell them about the forthcoming cover story, which was about a hurricane researcher. To illustrate this story, we'd photographed the researcher hanging by his hands from a tree branch; the plan was to run this photograph sideways, so it would look as though the man was clinging to a tree, his body horizontal, as if he were about to be carried away by the wind.

Gene was struggling to explain this to the suits, so he decided to ask *Tropic*'s art director, Philip Brooker, to show them the photo.

"Hey, Philip," he called. "Can you find the picture of the guy getting blown?"

So, OK, this was an awkward moment, but also mildly amusing. Everyone in the *Tropic* offices, even the suits, got a chuckle out of it. Everyone but Gene, that is. Gene was far, FAR beyond chuckling. He thought this was the single funniest thing that had ever happened since the invention of humor. He collapsed onto the conference table, snorting and slobbering, literally crying from laughter. He stayed there, facedown, quaking, for quite a while. Everybody else, having gotten over it, waited for him to finish.

Finally Gene pulled himself together enough to resume his presentation. But upon rising up and catching sight of the suits—still waiting—he was once again struck by the life-threatening hilarity of the situation, and down he went again. And this time, when he finally came up for air, the suits were . . . gone.

Thank you for visiting *Tropic* magazine! We hope you enjoyed your management briefing!

So *Tropic* was not a well-oiled machine. It was more like the laboratory of a mad scientist in an old black-and-white movie, with strange contraptions spewing sparks and smoke, and in the middle of it all a wild-haired lunatic cackling as he prepares to throw a giant switch and launch an experiment that will, if it goes according to plan, produce some wondrous benefit to humanity, but there's a chance that it will go catastrophically wrong and unleash some unspeakable horror and THERE IS ONLY ONE WAY TO FIND OUT *MUAHAHAHAHA*!

That was the *Tropic* philosophy: What the hell, let's try it. Gene and Tom were not interested in conventional stories. They wanted to surprise readers, move them, shock them, scare them, delight them . . . anything but bore them. Anything but be predictable. They were always trying for something new, always pushing the envelope. Sometimes they succeeded. Sometimes they failed. Sometimes—fairly often, in fact—they pissed people off, including *Herald* management, with whom they fought many battles. But sometimes it was worth it.

To pick one example: In 1989, when Orlando got its NBA team, the Magic, *Tropic* decided that we should foment a rivalry between Orlando and Miami's new team, the Heat, since both teams were going to suck for a while. So Gene and Tom dispatched me and photographer Bill Wax to Orlando, and I wrote a cover essay presenting my thoughtful, fair and balanced observations of the city. It began:

> This has gone far enough. I'm talking about the ugly, bitter feud that has erupted between Miami and Orlando. There has been too much hostility; too much vindictiveness; too much childish name-calling. There's no point in arguing over who started it. The point is that things have gotten way out of hand, and it does no good to dwell on whether the blame belongs to the good people of Miami, or to the low-forehead nosepicking yahoos of Orlando.

And so on. The essay was a vicious assault on Orlando, and it concluded by inviting *Tropic* readers to enter a contest by submitting anti-Orlando cheers.[30] The winners—about two dozen people—accompanied Gene and me on a bus to Orlando,[31] where we attended the first

---

30. Sample cheer:
    We may have drugs and we may have crime;
    We may have riots from time to time;
    We may be loud-mouthed rude city slickers;
    But at least we're not low-forehead yahoo nosepickers!

31. That was one fun bus ride. We had to stop halfway up to buy more beer.

regular-season game between the Magic and the Heat. It was wild: The Orlando management, led by its team president, the late Pat Williams, who was a madman, played along with the feud, putting us in a special seating area surrounded by yellow crime scene tape, with baking soda sprinkled around to simulate cocaine.

All of this was fun. It was definitely pushing the boundaries of journalism, edging into performance-art territory. But most people, even the Orlando people, enjoyed it.

What bothered people—what *really* bothered some people—was the *Tropic* cover that ran with my essay. It was a photo of me posing with a basketball. It was 110 percent Gene's idea. Both Tom and I told him there was no way it would be approved, but somehow he convinced the executive editor, Janet Chusmir, to let him run it. Which meant that the image on the cover of the Sunday magazine that the *Herald* delivered to a half million households, including those with impressionable youngsters, was this:

As you might imagine, some readers were upset. The *Herald* got angry calls and letters; one Miami radio-show host went on a multiday crusade to get Gene fired, get me fired, get people to cancel their subscriptions, get advertisers to dump the *Herald*. Janet Chusmir later told Gene that approving the photo was her biggest mistake as editor. Gene, of course, thought it was great.

So that was *Tropic*'s management: smart, even brilliant, but also sometimes juvenile, prone to wiseassery and snark. Under this leadership *Tropic* produced a remarkable amount of excellent journalism. Gene and Tom were one big reason. Another one was the writers they were working with.

Miami has long had a reputation as a great news town, and the *Herald* had a history of attracting ambitious and talented young journalists. It didn't always keep them; dozens, if not hundreds, of *Herald* reporters and photographers went on to distinguished careers at the *New York Times* and, especially, the *Washington Post*. But between the young hotshots and the veterans, there was a lot talent at the *Herald*. There were also some terrific freelancers in South Florida. This was the pool of talented people *Tropic* drew on.

Among those who produced words, photos and art for the magazine were Joel Achenbach, John Barry, Madeleine Blais, Philip Brooker, Michael Browning, Edna Buchanan, Michael Carlebach, Pete Collins, Bill Cosford, Brian Dickerson, John Dorschner, Michel du Cille, Tananarive Due, Chuck Fadely, Marc Fisher, Sydney Freedberg, C. W. Griffin, Carol Guzy, James Hall, Vicki Hendricks, Ran Henry, Carl Hiaasen, John Katzenbach, Marjorie Klein, Meg Laughlin, Jeff Leen, Elmore Leonard, Paul Levine, Linda Robertson, Bill Rose, Leon Rosenblatt, T. M. Shine, Maggie Evans Silverstein, Les Standiford, David Von Drehle, Mike Wilson and more.

So many smart people; so many great writers. And so much for them to write about. That was the third element that made *Tropic* special: Miami, this wild, exotic place, this beautiful, unpredictable, dangerous, brash, crazy, tumultuous town. It was fertile ground for storytelling, and for a few miraculous, wonderful years, *Tropic* flourished in it. I could not have landed in a better place, or at a better time.

My role in this enterprise was twofold. My main obligation was to write a weekly column, which could be on whatever topic I thought would be amusing. Sometimes it was my dogs, sometimes it was the news, sometimes it was about a news item some reader had sent me concerning an exploding toilet, sometimes it was really about nothing at all. Sometimes I actually left my house and went to events to write about them, almost like a real reporter, except I didn't care about being accurate or fair or tasteful. I was doing investigative humor. I was granted an amazing degree of freedom and resources: Gene and Tom would cheerfully approve my travel expenses to pretty much anywhere for pretty much anything that seemed like it might be entertaining.

For example, in 1984 I learned that the French wine industry was holding the First Annual French Wine Sommelier Contest in America at the Waldorf-Astoria. So I rented a tuxedo and went to New York, where I spent an evening in a vast ballroom filled with hundreds of Serious Wine People, seated at a table with Serious Wine Journalists. We were served many courses of fine French food and many, many glasses of fine French wine. Here's an excerpt from the column I wrote:

We in the audience got to drink just gallons of wine. At least I did. My policy with wine is very similar to my policy with beer, which is I just pretty much drink it and look around for more. The people at my table, on the other hand, leaned more toward the slosh-and-sniff approach, where you don't so much drink the wine as you frown and then make a thoughtful remark about it such as you might make about a job applicant. ("I find it ambitious, but somewhat strident." Or: "It's lucid, yes, but almost Episcopalian in its predictability.") As it happened, I was sitting next to a French person named Mary, and I asked her if people in France carry on this way about wine. "No," she said, "they just drink it. They're more used to it."

There were 12 sommeliers from around the country in the contest; they got there by winning regional competitions, and earlier in the day they had taken a written exam with questions like: "Which of the following appellations belong in the Savoie region? (a) Crepy; (b) Seyssel; (c) Arbois; (d) Etoile; (e) Ripple." (I'm just kidding about the Ripple, of course. The Savoie region would not use Ripple as an insecticide.)

The first event of the evening competition was a blind tasting, where the sommeliers had to identify a mystery wine. We in the audience got to try it, too. It was a wine that I would describe as yellow in color, and everybody at my table agreed it was awful. "Much too woody," said one person. "Heavily oxidized," said another. "Bat urine," I offered. The others felt this was a tad harsh. I was the only one who finished my glass.

Next we got a non-mystery wine, red in color, with a French name, and I thought it was swell, gulped it right down, but one of the wine writers at my table got upset because it was a 1979, and the program said we were supposed to get a 1978. If you can imagine. So we got some 1978, and it was swell, too. "They're both credible," said the wine writer, "but there's a great difference in character." I was the only one who laughed, although I think Mary sort of wanted to.

And so on. It was an easy humor column to write. I honestly don't know how anybody could attend the French Wine Sommelier Contest in America and NOT write a humor column about it. I remember walking, unsteadily, out of the Waldorf-Astoria at the end of the night—my stomach full of fine French fare, my reporter's notebook full of notes ("BAT URINE") written in an increasingly illegible scrawl—thinking, *I cannot believe I am getting paid to do this.*

So that was one part of my job: writing a weekly column on anything I wanted. The other part involved traveling to Miami, usually for a week or two at a time, to write cover stories, like the Orlando-Miami basketball feud story. These were longer and somewhat more coherent than my columns, but still deeply unserious. Often the topics were suggested by

Gene or Tom, who enjoyed pointing me at a target, like a tactical assault clown, and printing whatever I wrote about it.

One of my earliest assignments was an interview with Bob Graham, then governor of Florida. I was granted an appointment—I believe it was for fifteen minutes—and flew to Tallahassee with *Herald* photographer Joe Rimkus. At the appointed time we were sitting in the anteroom to the governor's office, along with a dozen or so other people waiting to see the governor. I was feeling intimidated and nervous. I didn't have any serious journalistic questions to ask, and I didn't know how the governor, obviously a busy man, was going to respond to having his valuable gubernatorial time wasted by some asshole columnist looking for yuks.

As it happened, he responded magnificently. It turns out that in addition to being a Harvard-educated lawyer and an accomplished politician, Graham was a deeply goofy man. Most of the time he hid it. His usual public-speaking style was serious and measured, to the point of being boring. But when the situation called for it—such as when he was being interviewed by a humor columnist—he flipped a switch and went into Zany Mode, as I learned when I walked into his office that day.

Whatever ridiculous question I asked him, he unhesitatingly responded with a vaguely gubernatorial-sounding but equally ridiculous answer. The interview lasted way longer than fifteen minutes; at the end Graham followed me and Joe out of his office, still talking. My cover story ended up being basically a transcript of the interview. Here's an excerpt:

BARRY: What can the state do about harmonica safety? I don't know if you have any idea how many Floridians die every year in harmonica accidents . . .

GRAHAM: Well last year we actually made some substantial improvement. In 1981, there were four people who died of harmonica accidents. Now actually, I think it's only fair to count three of them, because the fourth one was actually, I would say it was more of a swimming-pool accident. He was playing the harmonica in the swimming pool and actually jumped off the shallow end, hit his head, and we don't know whether it was the fact that he swallowed the harmonica, or the brain damage. They counted it as a harmonica accident. Now, this year, or 1982, the last year for which we have statistics, we only had two harmonica accidents. I think it was the result of the public-service ads that I did . . .

BARRY: The Harmonica Safety Day I think was a wonderful . . .

GRAHAM: . . . and we built it around the theme that if you want to play "Dixie," it's fine, but don't do it in front of the air-conditioning duct, because that's where we found that most of the deaths occurred. It was the vacuum that was created.

BARRY: This leads us pretty much directly to toads. I've been staying at a house in Broward County, and there are, every morning out on the patio, toads the size of mailboxes. What can we do?

GRAHAM: I grew up in the town of Pennsuco, and in Pennsuco, in my backyard we had lots of toads, and particularly this time of year, the toads are really out. And the way we dealt with them was with BB guns.

BARRY: The great environmentalist.

GRAHAM: Yeah. I used to go out in the afternoon with my friends and BB guns, and that's how we diminished the toad population.

BARRY: If you were to hit these toads in this Broward County home with a BB gun, they would just get enraged, if they even noticed it. They would barge into the house . . .

GRAHAM: Listen. If you want to just go out there like some ama-
teur, firing away, that's what'll happen to you. But what
you've got to do, you've got to wait until the toad raises
his head above a forty-five-degree angle, you get that
soft . . . have you heard that phrase, the "soft under-
belly"? Winston Churchill was big on soft underbellies,
and he tried it in both World War I and World War II.
But you got to get them right there [gesturing toward
throat].

BARRY: What do you think of the idea of—this is an idea I came up
with . . .

GRAHAM: God, it's about time.

BARRY: What we do is drain the Everglades, kill all the bugs, put
in nice, clean restrooms, fill it back up and have a theme
swamp. What do you think?

GRAHAM: John Kennedy once made the statement that victory has a
hundred parents, but defeat is always an orphan. I want to
tell you, you got a lot of orphan ideas.

In 1986 Graham won election to the US Senate, defeating incumbent
Paula Hawkins. I wrote about that campaign, spending a few days flying
around Florida in a small plane with Graham and some national political reporters from big-time papers. In my story I made a lot of fun of
Graham's speaking style:

We land in Bartow, which apparently consists of a hangar. Inside the
hangar is a smallish agricultural crowd, which Graham, using his
oratorical skills, immediately whips into a stupor. He is not a gifted
speaker. He is the kind of speaker who, if he were not the governor,
people would shoot rubber bands at after a while.

The high point of his Bartow speech comes when he holds up a can of Florida concentrated orange juice, which the crowd applauds, because frankly, and I am not trying to be cruel here, it exudes more charisma than the governor.

"Would you say," I ask, "that spending a lot of time around cows as a child could make a person kind of dull?" Graham grew up on a dairy.

"It could have that potential," he answers, "but on the other hand, some might say—but I am too modest to personally say this—that it brings out a quickness of wit, a sense of ironic humor, an ability to, with a—not a destructive, but a positive uplifting way—with words to bring humor into the world. That's what some people would say. I am too personally modest."

During the Bartow speech, I locate, just outside the hangar, an enormous insect of the type that you would never find in a state such as Ohio. I pick it up, using my notebook, which it spits brown glop on, to test a theory I have about Graham, which is that he will comment on anything. I show it to him, and ask: "Governor, would you comment on this insect?"

"This," he says, picking his words very carefully, as he always does, "is an [here he says a name that sounds like 'Execretius Bolemius,' which he is clearly making up]. It is a Friend to Man. It is a member of the family of Almost-Flying Insects, and one of the many things that it does is that it titillates the toad."

Needless to say, as a humor columnist, I loved Bob Graham. We became friends, to the extent that a humor columnist and a politician can be friends, and we exchanged letters for years. During his Senate career, I occasionally called him to get an official Washington view on major issues of the day, and he never failed me. For example, in 1993 I learned that a technical institute in Winona, Minnesota, was going to eliminate, because of low enrollment, the college's accordion-repair program, which was the last such program in the nation. So I called Bob Graham, and . . .

I had barely got the words "accordion-repair crisis" out of my mouth when he launched into an impassioned oration, from which I got the following quotes, which I swear I am not making up:

"Just last night I ate at an Italian restaurant which, like thousands of other Italian restaurants across America, is now without music, because their accordion is in disrepair and has been returned from Winona, Minn., with postage due."

"We are preparing an anti-dumping order against Liechtenstein, which has become the center of accordion repair on a global basis and has developed some ferociously anti-competitive practices."

For a while, Graham was a rising Democratic star; he was on both Bill Clinton's and Al Gore's short lists for running mate, and he even flirted with running for president in 2004, although health issues ended that plan. Which is a shame. A Bob Graham presidency would have been great for America. Or at least for me.

Graham had fun with the stories I wrote about him; this was not true of all of my profile subjects. I'm thinking here of legendary Miami Dolphins coach Don Shula, whom I profiled in 1988. At that time he was by far the most revered man in Miami, and I include Jesus Christ in that statement.[32] It was Gene's idea for me to profile him, and of course Gene did not want the profile to be worshipful. In fact I believe the whole reason Gene wanted me to do the profile was that he had a profoundly nonreverential concept in mind for the cover photo, which I will get to shortly.

For the story I went out to the Dolphins' practice facility every day for a week and hung out with the sportswriters, watching the football players practice being enormous sweaty human beings. At the end of each practice, Shula, who was sensitive about his potbelly and always trying to lose weight, would jog, alone, multiple times around the perimeter of the practice field. On the spur of the moment, I asked him if I could jog alongside him and interview him as we ran. To my surprise, he agreed;

---

32. Jesus, for all his positive qualities, never won a Super Bowl.

I think it was because (a) jogging is boring, and (b) he knew I wasn't a sportswriter, so I wouldn't ask him a bunch of tedious questions about the nickel defense.

So I kicked off my boat shoes and ran next to him barefoot, holding a tape recorder, the two of us huffing and puffing and sweating as we jogged around and around the field in the South Florida August swelter. I ran with him for two days, and although I was intimidated—Godzilla would have been intimidated by Shula—I actually enjoyed our talks, and I think he did, too. He had more of a sense of humor than I expected (this was a low bar; I expected zero) and he was open to questions on topics he would not normally have discussed with the press. Here's an excerpt:

ME: What kind of music do you listen to?

SHULA: I like the old ballads. I think Nat King Cole had some great songs out, some of the Sinatra songs.

ME: What's your favorite rock song?

SHULA: Got me there. [Pause.] That's not the name of a song, is it?

ME: Do you dance?

SHULA: I used to.

ME: Are you a good dancer?

SHULA: I feel I can handle myself on a dance floor all right, but I'm not what you'd call a good dancer, or have natural rhythm. I think that you'd categorize me, if you've ever heard me try to sing, as tone deaf.

ME: Are you familiar with the Elvis stamp controversy?

SHULA: No, and I'm not going to spend a lot of time getting familiar with it.

ME: OK, briefly, the government wants to put out an Elvis stamp, and the issue is, should it be a picture of the young Elvis, or the late Elvis, who was kind of chunky. Which would you pick?

SHULA: [Pause.] I appreciate his talent. [Pause.] I don't appreciate what happened to him in his final days.

ME: So you'd vote for the younger Elvis?

SHULA: He wouldn't be one of my favorites to talk about. There's a lot of excellent role models out there that I would prefer to talk about.

In the profile I talked about Shula's famous, much feared scowl of disapproval—I called it the Stare—and imagined nightmare scenarios wherein it might be aimed at you:

Nightmare Scenario No. 1: You have a hot date. A very hot date. You have Big Plans. You ring her doorbell. The door opens, and standing there, looking at you, is your date's father: Don Shula.

Nightmare Scenario No. 2: You're in the Express Checkout lane, limit 10 items. You have 11 items. Running the cash register is: Don Shula.

Nightmare Scenario No. 3: "A Mr. Shula called. From the IRS."

Nightmare Scenario No. 4: You die. You're at the Pearly Gates. Blocking your path, holding a clipboard, is . . .

So I poked some fun at Shula. But overall it was a positive and, I think, humanizing profile. I believe that if Shula had read it, he might actually have liked it. But I'm pretty sure he never read it. I doubt he got past the cover of *Tropic*, which I remind you was Gene's idea, and which Gene conceived of, along with the headline to go with it, before I wrote a single word.

The cover was a photo of Shula taken while he was coaching a preseason game against the Bears. I flew to the game to stand on the sideline with photographer Brian Smith, who was given explicit instructions from Gene—*extremely* explicit instructions—about the photo he wanted. Brian, a consummate professional, got the photo, and Gene ran it as the cover. Here it is:

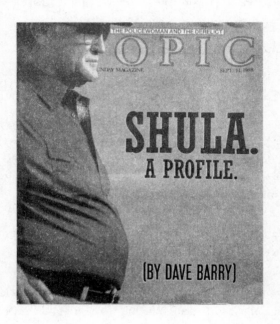

So our cover was essentially Don Shula's stomach, which as I said Shula was sensitive about. Shula did not care for this cover. I know this because a year or so later, I was the MC at a charity event, and Shula was there as a guest. At one point the program called for me to bring him up to the podium to be recognized. As the two of us posed for a picture, smiling at the camera, I said, quietly, "Coach, do you remember me?" Staring straight ahead, smiling at the audience, he said, "Yeah, I remember you." He did not say this in a tone of fond reminiscence. Needless to say we never jogged together again.[33]

---

33. He also never won another Super Bowl, not that I'm suggesting there's a connection.

Another early *Tropic* cover story I wrote that did not please everybody involved Joe's Stone Crab. This is the famous Miami Beach restaurant with the famously succulent stone crabs and the famously long wait times for a table because Joe's, famously, does not take reservations. When you got to Joe's, unless you were a major celebrity such as the Pope—or, even better, Don Shula—you gave your name to the maître d', an imposing tuxedoed man named Roy Garret, who wrote your name in a book the size of the *Oxford English Dictionary.* Then you stood around in a waiting area containing roughly the population of two Canadian provinces, waiting, and waiting, and waiting some more, and then still some more, for Roy to call your name. On a Saturday night you could easily wait two hours, or longer. Such was the desirability of a table at Joe's.

When I started at the *Herald,* savvy locals told me I should go to Joe's, which was viewed as one of South Florida's premier attractions, like the Atlantic Ocean, or Don Shula. Virtually every one of these locals informed me that there was a secret, known only to sophisticates, for skipping the long wait and getting a table quickly. Most of them said the key was to say a certain phrase to Roy when you checked in. Depending on which savvy local was explaining it, the phrase—which you had to say *exactly*—was either:

"I'll take care of you on the way out," or

"I'll see you on the way out," or

"I'll catch you on the way out," or

"I'll punch you on the way out."[34]

Almost all of these sophisticates stressed that you should NOT give Roy money on the way in. That would be a major blunder. Instead, on the way out, you slipped Roy, via a discreet handshake, exactly five dollars. Or exactly ten dollars. Or exactly twenty dollars. It depended on the savvy local.

Other sophisticates said this system worked, but only the *second* time you did it, because then Roy would recognize you.

---

34. Seriously, "punch." There were savvy locals who insisted that this, and only this, was the Secret Passphrase.

Anyway, after hearing numerous savvy locals tell me the secret to getting a table at Joe's, I decided to do some investigative journalism. I enlisted the aid of various people, who went to Joe's on a busy night and tried various approaches to getting a table. The investigation showed that what worked best, at least for us, was to hand Roy money right up front. A $20 bill got a table quickly; a $50 bill got a table instantly.

In other words, as I wrote in my *Tropic* story:

> What we had established, through a grueling undercover investigation, was that, yes, there does appear to be a method for beating the line at Joe's, and it appears to be about as complicated and secret as the method for ordering french fries at Burger King.

My story created quite a stir in Miami. People were shocked, shocked to learn that this had been going on. Paying for tables! All these years they'd believed Joe's was first come, first served. There were letters to the editor about it.

The owners of Joe's were also not crazy about my story. I know this because a little while after it was published I ran into one of them, Steve Sawitz, at a Miami bar. He was cordial, but he told me they'd gotten grief from some of their customers. At the end of our conversation, he told me there were no hard feelings, smiled, and shook my hand.

And slipped me a one-dollar bill.

Years later, at a book event, I ran into Roy Garret, who had retired from maître-d'ing. He said my story had caused him some headaches, but he had long ago gotten over it. We laughed about it and hugged. No money was exchanged.

After a couple of years of traveling from Pennsylvania to Florida to write *Tropic* stories, I had come to realize something: I really liked Miami. It was hot and hectic, and it didn't always feel safe, especially on the highways, where—I have long used this as a joke, but it's actually true—everyone drives according to the laws of his or her individual country of origin. But Miami was by far the most interesting, weird and nonboring place I had ever experienced, including New York City. It was a gushing geyser of humor material.

So by 1986 I was pondering the idea of moving to Miami. But I was also getting approached by other newspapers, most prominently the *Los Angeles Times* and the *Washington Post*. The *Times* flew me out to LA for an interview and offered me a job; it was a good offer, and the folks out there were nice, but I couldn't see myself in California.

The *Post* was a different story. I was interviewed by Mary Hadar, the funny and smart editor of the Style section. Then I had lunch with a group of *Post* people, including the managing editor, Len Downie, and the executive editor, Ben Bradlee. Which was a major thrill for me. For many of us newspaper people who came up in the seventies, Bradlee was a Beatle—the cool, sophisticated yet hard-nosed badass editor who backed Woodward and Bernstein when they were taking down the Nixon administration while I was covering the Downingtown regional sewage authority. And here he was having lunch with *me*, recruiting me for the *Washington* freaking *Post*.

In the end—spoiler alert—I didn't go to the *Post*. That was a tough decision to make; there were people I respected who assured me that I was insane. But the way I saw it, if I went to Washington, I'd inevitably end up writing mainly about politics. I'm sure it would have been OK with the *Post* if I wrote about nonpolitical topics, but I'd have been living in a city, and a media environment, where politics is an obsession. If I worked at the *Post*, that city would have been the audience I was thinking about every time I wrote a column. I didn't want to be in that bubble. I'd come to love the freedom I had at *Tropic* to write about whatever random topic I wanted. And by that point my syndicated column was running in hundreds of newspapers around the country.

So I reluctantly said no to the *Post*, and in July of 1986 I moved from Glen Mills, Pennsylvania, to Miami, where I still live today. (Gene and Tom, on the other hand, long ago left Miami to work for—of course—the *Washington Post*.)

Pretty soon after moving I wrote a *Tropic* cover story about adapting to life in South Florida:

> Our lawn grows like a venereal disease. The Lawn Man comes around regularly and subdues it, after which there is a period of about two hours when you can walk safely on it, but you had damned well better make sure you are standing on the driveway when it regains consciousness and starts lashing out with violent new growth tendrils.
>
> The Lawn Man is named Jorge (pronounced "Jorge") and he speaks virtually no English, but fortunately I took a few Spanish courses in high school, and we were therefore able to have the following conversation:
>
> JORGE (gesturing toward the lawn): Thirty dollars.
>
> ME: Yes.

So some adjustment was required, but the move to Miami turned out to be good for me. I was now living in a target-rich humor environment—not just Miami, but the entire state. Florida, as the world has discovered, abounds with weirdness, and I was within easy driving distance of much of it.

For example: Not long after I moved there, I learned that Kissimmee, a town near Orlando, was home to the world headquarters of the Tupperware company. This interested me, because some years earlier I'd written a blues tune called "The Tupperware Song," which I performed at a Tupperware party back in my *Daily Local News* days.[35] So I sent a tape of my

---

35. It wasn't intended to be a serious Tupperware party; it was basically a keg party, but the two guys who hosted it, Art Howe and Dave Jenny, invited a Tupperware lady because they thought it would be funny. When she got there, she had to be persuaded to stay, since instead of a group of homemakers eager to buy Tupperware, she found a raucous collection of newspaper people, many of them guys, eager to drink more beer. But we talked her into staying, and I performed "The Tupperware Song" with some other people, and it was a major hit. That woman sold a *shitload* of Tupperware. Guys who didn't even have kitchens were buying deviled-egg transporters.

song[36] to Tupperware, and a Tupperware executive named Dick Wilson called me up and invited me to come to world headquarters and perform it to a group of one thousand Tupperware distributors. My big break!

So I recruited a "band"—Tom, Gene and another *Herald* editor, Lou Heldman—and we went up to Kissimmee for our gig. We wore suits and sunglasses, and called ourselves the Urban Professionals. Here's an excerpt from the column I wrote:

> I'm the lead guitar player and singer and also (I'm not bragging here; these are simply facts) the only person in the band who knows when the song has started or ended. The other members of the band just sort of stand around looking nervous until I've been going for a while, and then, after it penetrates their primitive musical consciousnesses that the song has begun, they become startled and lurch into action. Likewise it takes them up to thirty seconds to come to a complete stop after the song is technically over.
>
> The only other normal instrument in the band is a harmonica, played by Gene. Gene has been attempting to play the harmonica for a number of years, and has developed a repertoire of several songs, all of which sound exactly like "Oh Susanna!" "Here's another one!" he'll say, and then he plays "Oh Susanna!" He plays it very rapidly, totally without pauses, as if he's anxious to get back to journalism, so if you tried to sing along, you'd have to go: "Icomefromalabamawithmyban-joonmyknee" etc., and pretty soon you'd run out of oxygen and keel

---

36. Sample verse:
Some folks use waxed paper
Some folks use the Reynolds wrap
Some folks use a plastic baggie
To try to cover up the gap
You can use most anything
To keep your goodies from the air
But nothing works as well
As that good old Tupperware . . .
'Cause it's here
Take a look at what we got
If you don't try some and buy some
Don't blame me if your turnips rot

over onto your face, which Gene wouldn't notice because he'd be too busy trying to finish the song on schedule.

The other two instruments in the band are actually Tupperware products, played rhythmically by Tom and Lou, who also dance. How good are they? Let me put it this way: If you can watch them perform and not wet your pants, then you are legally blind. For one thing, they both are afflicted with severe rhythm impairment, the worst cases I have ever seen, worse even than Republican convention delegates. You ask Lou and Tom to clap along to a song, and not only will they never once hit the beat, but they will also never, no matter how eternally long the song goes on, both clap at the same time.

On top of which you have the fact that they do not have your classic dancer's build, especially Lou, who is, and I say this with all due respect, the same overall shape as a Krispy Kreme jelly doughnut.

We were a hit. The Tupperware distributors gave us a standing ovation. (To be fair, they also gave a standing ovation to a set of ovenware.) This was another one of those times—there have been so many over the years—when I found myself thinking, *I can't believe this is my job.*

That was in 1987, a big year for me. I turned forty, which seemed old at the time. I also wrote some things—the Tupperware column, incredibly, was not one of them—that wound up winning me a Pulitzer Prize.

This was not something I expected ever to happen. I'm not being falsely modest: I loved my job, but it never occurred to me that what I was doing would qualify for a journalism award, let alone a Pulitzer. I honestly did not know I'd been nominated.

The category I won in was Commentary. Tom nominated me (Gene was at Harvard that year on a Nieman Fellowship) and submitted a selection of my columns. He was smart about the ones he chose. One was the column I wrote about my mom's suicide, which I guess showed the judges I could have a serious side. Another column was ostensibly about the major news stories of the day but was actually making fun of journalism awards, especially the Pulitzer Prizes. It began:

The burgeoning Iran-contra scandal is truly an issue about which we, as a nation, need to concern ourselves, because

(Secret Note to Readers: Not really! The hell with the Iran-contra affair! Let it burgeon! I'm just trying to win a journalism prize, here. Don't tell anybody! I'll explain later. Shhhh.)

when we look at the Iran-contra scandal, and for that matter the mounting national health-care crisis, we can see that these are, in total, two issues, each requiring a number of paragraphs in which we will comment, in hopes that

(. . . we can win a journalism prize. Ideally a Pulitzer. That's the object, in journalism. At certain times each year, we journalists do almost nothing except apply for the Pulitzers and several dozen other major prizes. During these times you could walk right into most newsrooms and commit a multiple ax-murder naked, and it wouldn't get reported in the paper, because the reporters and editors would all be too busy filling out prize applications. "Hey!" they'd yell at you. "Watch it! You're getting blood on my application!")

And so on. I proposed that newspapers begin long, boring stories with a warning: "Caution! Journalism Prize Entry! Do Not Read!" I also said that if I won a prize, I'd split the money with the judges.

I'm guessing that column appealed to the Pulitzer judges, who spend many hours slogging through piles of Serious Journalism. They do this over the course of several grueling days at Columbia University, so I suspect they also related to another one of the pieces Tom chose. It was a *Tropic* cover story I wrote about New York City, and it's one of my favorite assignments ever.

The background was, the *New York Times* Sunday magazine had just run a cover story about Miami. The headline was: "CAN MIAMI SAVE ITSELF? A City Beset by Drugs and Violence." It painted a bleak picture of Miami as a hellhole where, in addition to the drugs and crime, there was all this ethnic strife—the Anglos hated the Cubans, the Cubans hated the Anglos, the Black people hated the Cubans AND the Anglos, and so on. The story made a half-hearted effort to present some optimistic voices, but basically the answer to the question CAN MIAMI SAVE ITSELF was a resounding HELL NO.

The *Times* story did not go over well in Miami. The politicians, the business community and the tourism industry all freaked out. This was partly out of defensiveness, because there was of course some truth to the *Times* story. But also a lot of Miamians felt it was old news—yes, Miami had problems, everybody knew that, but things had gotten a lot better since the riots and Mariel boatlift of 1980. To the Miami of 1987, the *Times* story felt dated and condescending.

So a *Herald* photographer named Chuck Fadely came to Tom with an idea: Since the *New York Times* had taken the trouble to come to Miami and point out our problems, maybe it would be nice if the *Herald*, as a gesture of gratitude, visited the fine people of New York City to see if *they* had any problems!

Tom thought that was an excellent idea, so he dispatched me and Chuck to the Big Apple to conduct an investigation. We spent three days there. The story we produced was called "Can New York Save Itself?" As you might imagine, it was extremely nuanced. Here are some excerpts:

We're riding in a cab from La Guardia Airport to our Manhattan hotel, and I want to interview the driver, because this is how we professional journalists take the Pulse of a City, only I can't, because he doesn't speak English. He is not allowed to, under the rules, which are posted right on the seat:

NEW YORK TAXI RULES

1. DRIVER SPEAKS NO ENGLISH.
2. DRIVER JUST GOT HERE TWO DAYS AGO FROM SOMEPLACE LIKE SENEGAL.
3. DRIVER HATES YOU.

Which is just as well, because if he talked to me, he might lose his concentration, which would be very bad because the taxi has some kind of problem with the steering, probably dead pedestrians lodged in the mechanism, the result being that there is a delay of eight to 10 seconds between the time the driver turns the wheel and the time the taxi actually changes direction, a handicap that the driver is compensating for by going 175 miles per hour, at which velocity we are able to remain airborne almost to the far rim of some of the smaller potholes. These are of course maintained by the crack New York Department of Potholes (currently on strike), whose commissioner was recently indicted on corruption charges by the Federal Grand Jury to Indict Every Commissioner in New York.

———

We're staying at a "medium priced" hotel, meaning that the rooms are more than spacious enough for a family of four to stand up in if they are slightly built and hold their arms over their heads, yet the rate is just $135 per night, plus of course your state tax, your city tax, your occupancy tax, your head tax, your body tax, your soap tax, your ice bucket tax, your in-room dirty movies tax and your piece of paper that says your toilet is sanitized for your protection tax, which bring the rate to $367.90 per night, or a flat $4,000 if you use the telephone.

———

And so Chuck and I set off into the streets of Manhattan, where we immediately detect signs of a healthy economy in the form of people squatting on the sidewalk selling realistic jewelry.

———

Although it was constructed in 1536, the New York subway system boasts an annual maintenance budget of nearly $8, currently stolen, and it does a remarkable job of getting New Yorkers from Point A to an indeterminate location somewhere in the tunnel leading to Point B. It's also very easy for the "out-of-towner" to use, thanks to the logical, easy-to-understand system of naming trains after famous letters and numbers. For directions, all you have to do is peer up through the steaming gloom at the informative signs, which look like this:

**A 5 N 7 8 C 6 AA MID-DOWNTOWN 7 3/8
EXPRESS LOCAL ONLY LL 67*
DDD 4* 1 K * AAAA 9 ONLY EXCEPT CERTAIN DAYS**

———

At 3:14 a.m. I am awakened by a loud crashing sound, caused by workers from the city's crack Department of Making Loud Crashing Sounds During the Night, who are just outside my window, breaking in a new taxicab by dropping it repeatedly from a 75-foot crane.

———

A large chunk of my story was devoted to the effort Chuck and I made to track down the Long Island Garbage Barge. It's largely forgotten now, but in 1987 this barge was famous—it was featured (really) on the Phil Donahue show—as a symbol of massive municipal ineptitude. What happened was, New York City ran out of landfill space, so it loaded 3,168 tons of garbage onto a barge, which was towed by a tugboat to North Carolina, where the garbage was supposed to be converted into methane. But after TV news reported that the garbage included medical waste, North Carolina refused to accept it. The barge then continued south, looking for a home for the garbage, but it was rejected by Louisiana, Alabama, the Bahamas and Mexico. It got as far as Belize, which also rejected it, then turned around and came all the way back to New York City. This odyssey was covered extensively in the news media and on the late-night talk shows. By the time the prodigal barge came home, it was a major celebrity, comparable in stature to Harrison Ford.

Chuck wanted to get a good photo of the barge to use as the *Tropic* cover. It was anchored off the coast of Brooklyn, so we took a taxi there, but Chuck, after trying from several locations, couldn't get a good shot, so we had the taxi driver—who thought we were insane—take us to Linden, New Jersey, where we rented a helicopter, piloted by a Vietnam vet named Norman Knodt, who flew us over the barge so Chuck could get his shot. The helicopter rental cost $8,000. Today, in the newspaper business, which is basically going out of business, you cannot spend $8 without prior written authorization from at least three executives. But in 1987 we dropped eight grand on a chopper without even bothering to check with Tom. It was the Golden Age of Journalism Expense Accounts.

When my story ran in *Tropic*—with the barge on the cover—it was a hit. Miamians loved it. Even some New Yorkers were amused by it, although Mayor Ed Koch, when asked about it by a reporter, said he was unimpressed.

But as I said, I think it may have struck a chord with the Pulitzer judges. Apparently something did, because in 1988 I won the prize for Distinguished Commentary. On the day the prizes were announced, I was planning to go to Key West with my son, Rob, who was then seven. He was excited about the trip because I always rented a motorbike down there and we'd ride around for hours, him on the back. He loved that.

That morning as we were preparing to leave I got a call from Gene telling me I had to come to the *Herald* for an important meeting. I resisted—I hate meetings—but Gene said it was mandatory. So I told Rob we had to go to the *Herald* first, and then we'd go to Key West.

The "meeting" was of course a ruse to get me there for the Pulitzer announcements. The *Herald* had won two: mine, and the prize for feature photography, which went to Michel du Cille.[37] The newsroom was

---

37. Michel won for photos he'd done for a *Tropic* story.

packed with people, most of them in on the surprise. I stood cluelessly in the crowd with Rob, awaiting the announcement. About a minute before it came, an editor who apparently had not been let in on the secret came over, shook my hand, and said, "Congratulations."

At that moment, I realized that (a) I was going to win a Pulitzer Prize, and (b) my trip with Rob wasn't going to happen. I looked down at him and said, "Rob, I'm really sorry, but we're not going to Key West."

He looked devastated. I knew at that moment that I had to do something, as a father, to ease my son's pain. So I said, "I'll buy you a Nintendo." At that time Rob really, really wanted a Nintendo game, more than world peace.

"Really?" he said.

"Yes," I said.

Two things happened then: First, Rob, elated by the Nintendo news, jumped into my arms and gave me a huge hug. Second, Janet Chusmir, reading the Associated Press bulletin, announced that I had won a Pulitzer Prize.

The front page of the next day's *Miami Herald* had a story headlined "Two Staffers Win Pulitzer Prizes." With it were two photos. One was of Michel du Cille being congratulated by his colleagues. The other was of me and Rob. I'm beaming; he has his arms wrapped around my neck and looks absolutely ecstatic. Everyone I knew who saw that picture had the same reaction: "It was so great to see how happy Rob was that you won a Pulitzer Prize!" When of course that was not even remotely what Rob was happy about.

But you never know how things will turn out. Rob, ignoring the warnings of his dad, wound up pursuing a career in journalism. He's an investigative journalist at the *Wall Street Journal*, where, among many other projects, he worked on a series of stories about Medicare fraud that, in 2015, was awarded a Pulitzer Prize. I'm thinking maybe the Nintendo helped.

As I say, I truly did not expect to win a Pulitzer. It was a lovely surprise, and an honor for which I'll always be grateful. But it really wasn't life-changing. I already had the best gig in journalism: I was at a newspaper that let me do pretty much whatever I wanted; I had a syndicated

Rob hugging me at the moment my Pulitzer was announced. At left, clapping (nonrhythmically) is Lou Heldman, who performed "The Tupperware Song" with the Urban Professionals.

column that was in something like five hundred newspapers, reaching millions of readers every week.

And a lot of those readers were responding to me. Not all of them liked me. Some of them hated me. But I was definitely getting a reaction, manifested by the massive piles of letters showing up at my *Herald* office. Going through all that mail had become a major part of my job. But it wasn't a chore; in fact, it was often the highlight of my day. Because my readers were wonderful. I loved them, even the ones who hated me. They were all part of this thing I was doing. My column, in a way, had become a collaboration between me and my readers.

So the next chapter's about them.

CHAPTER FIVE

MY READERS

I HAVN'T READ A SINGLE ONE OF YOUR COLUMNS SINCE YOU SHIT ON THE LITTLE DRUMMER BOY AND NEVER WILL.

I **NEVER MET THE VAST MAJORITY OF MY READERS. THIS** was probably a good thing, since a certain segment of my readership—I'm thinking somewhere around 14 percent—consisted of lunatics.

Nevertheless I loved my readers, even the unstable ones, and I had a serious, long-term relationship with them, conducted—this was mostly pre-Internet—via the US Postal Service. Every week I got at minimum dozens, often hundreds, of letters. There were a few times when I'd get over a thousand letters in just a few days, usually because I touched on a highly sensitive topic such as Neil Diamond (more on this later).

At first I tried to answer all the letters myself, but it got to be overwhelming. For a while the *Miami Herald* assigned secretaries from the business side of the newspaper to assist me on a part-time basis. The idea was that I'd dictate responses to my mail and they'd type them up for me to sign. This did not work out. It wasn't the secretaries' fault;

they were intelligent, competent professionals. The problem was that my responses often did not conform to standard business style.

For example, say I got a lengthy letter, multiple pages packed with words, clearly written with a great deal of passion but making absolutely no sense, at least not to me (I got many letters like that). The letter I'd dictate in response would be something like:

> Dear [name]:
> What?
> Sincerely,
> Dave Barry
> PS: Seriously: What?

I routinely dictated one-word replies. Or I'd want certain words capitalized, or underlined, or deliberately misspelled, or circled, or (I had my reasons) typed upside-down. Or I'd use nonstandard punctuation, for example ending a sentence with something like ??!!!(?) Sometimes I wanted the typist to leave room for me to draw a picture of a happy bird,[38] like this:

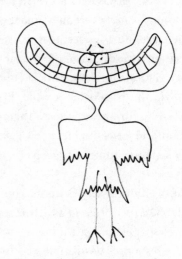

---

38. I've been drawing this bird since middle school. I don't know why.

The professional secretaries, understandably, were thrown by these deviations from normal business style, the result being that I ended up spending a lot of time trying to explain what I wanted ("two question marks, followed by three exclamation marks, then another question mark, but in parentheses, and then leave maybe two inches for a bird"). This defeated the whole purpose of having somebody help me with my ever-growing pile of letters.

Finally, in 1990, the *Herald* agreed to let me hire an assistant, and I knew exactly who I wanted: Judi Smith. She was a school librarian I'd come to know because she wrote me funny letters. Judi was very smart and had a great sense of humor and a high tolerance for my unprofessionalism.[39] She immediately grasped the relationship between me and my readers, and from then on she was my first line of defense against the mail, sorting it into letters I'd want to respond to individually, letters that I'd want to see but that she could answer with a form response, and letters that should immediately be incinerated with a blowtorch.

Judi also coordinated my schedule and answered my office phone. She was extremely good at politely declining invitations from people who wanted me to do things that I didn't want to do. When you write a humor column, your readers tend to think that (a) they know you, and that (b) you're a wacky individual who is always up for some wacky fun. This impression is understandable; it's the persona we present to the world in our columns.

But in real life we humor columnists don't go around being wacky all the time, any more than professional magicians go around pulling quarters out of people's ears. In real life we spend most of our time trying to crank out yet another humor column, which is not as much wacky fun as it sounds. The rest of the time we're engaged in regular boring human activities such as being with our families or buying tires.

Nevertheless I got a lot of phone calls from people wanting to

---

39. When I was writing this chapter, Judi reminded me that she once came to work to find that our computer monitor was messed up. Stuck to the monitor was a Post-it note from me that said, "I did not fuck up this computer with a cow magnet." Which of course was a lie.

connect with Wacky Dave. Sometimes they were visiting Miami and wanted to hang out with me, grab some beers, maybe have dinner, their treat. Sometimes their club or organization or company was having a meeting and they wanted me to be the speaker, give a thirty-minute humorous talk and then take questions, and I'd be their guest for lunch. Sometimes they were having a party and wanted to invite me to meet them and their friends—a really fun group, I'd love them—and maybe I could entertain everybody with some humorous remarks, say fifteen or twenty minutes' worth, and afterward I could stay as long as I wanted.

Most of these callers were perfectly nice people, and it was flattering that they wanted to connect with me. But behind my persona I'm basically a shy and reclusive person. I have enough trouble connecting with my actual friends; I find that being wacky for people I don't know, even nice people, is exhausting.

This is why it was so helpful to have Judi answering my office phone. She had the ability to fend people off without offending them. She was a master fender. She was Mama Bear protective, but she treated everybody with good humor and Midwestern niceness (she was born and raised in Ohio) so that even when she was firmly but politely saying no, people ended up liking her, and thus not hating me. There were occasionally people who tried to bully their way past her, but of course that only guaranteed that I wasn't going to do whatever it was they wanted. If Judi didn't like them, I definitely wasn't going to like them.

But as invaluable as Judi was as a phone wrangler, her most important job was dealing with the letters from my readers, with whom I had a relationship I would describe as "synergistic," by which I mean "involving a lot of news items about toilets." Not to toot my own horn, but I was the only nationally syndicated columnist, and I include George Will in this statement, willing to write consistently about toilet-related issues. My readers appreciated this and were always sending me relevant articles clipped from their local newspapers. If a toilet exploded anywhere in the English-speaking world, or a snake showed up in a toilet—you'd be surprised how often these things happen—there was an excellent chance my readers would alert me.

Readers sent me newspaper articles about many other kinds of weird events as well. Because these events were so weird, and because, as a humor columnist, I lied a lot, I would often feel the need, when I was writing about some ridiculous thing that actually did happen, to tell my readers, "I am not making this up." Obviously I didn't invent that expression, but because I used it so often, it eventually became my trademark, which is why I get paid five dollars any time anybody else uses it.

No, I made that up.

Probably half the columns I wrote, maybe more, were inspired by newspaper articles people mailed to me. In my columns, I always credited these people, referring to them as "alert readers," which became a coveted title. Also everybody who sent me an article, whether or not I wrote about it, received a postcard, signed by me, that read:

> This certifies that [name] is an Alert Reader and should seek some kind of treatment immediately.

We sent out thousands and thousands of these cards. It was time-consuming but totally worth it; my readers alerted me to all kinds of alarming stories I would never otherwise have known about, such as the menace of Rollerblade Barbie.

I found out about Rollerblade Barbie when an alert reader sent me a column in the Jackson, Mississippi, *Clarion-Ledger* called "Ask Jack Sunn," which apparently responded to consumer concerns. One consumer had written:

"Last year, my two daughters received presents of two Rollerblade Barbie dolls by Mattel. On March 8, my 8-year-old daughter was playing beauty shop with her 4-year-old brother. After spraying him with hair spray, the children began to play with the boot to Rollerblade Barbie. My little girl innocently ran the skate across her brother's bottom, which immediately ignited his clothes."

The letter concludes: "There are no warnings concerning fire on these toys . . . I feel the need to warn potential buyers of their danger."

In response to this semi-mysterious letter, Jack Sunn wrote—this was the entirety of the response—"Mattel does not manufacture Rollerblade Barbie any more."

As a nationally syndicated columnist concerned about the issues, I naturally wanted to get to the bottom of this. To do that, I needed to get hold of a Rollerblade Barbie, so at the end of one of my columns I put out a plea, and two of my readers—because that's the kind of readers I had—sent me Rollerblade Barbies, which apparently they swiped from their daughters.

The key feature of Rollerblade Barbie is that she has little yellow Rollerblades with flint wheels, the kind found on Zippo lighters, so that when you roll Barbie along, her booties spew out sparks. So I assumed what happened to the letter-writer's children was that the sparks from the eight-year-old's Barbie ignited the hairspray on the four-year-old's clothes.

But in professional journalism we don't just assume things. In professional journalism, we take a pair of our old underpants out to our driveway one evening and conduct an experiment wherein we apply hairspray to them to determine whether Rollerblade Barbie can set them ablaze.

That's what I did, and I learned that if I sprayed my drawers with hairspray—I got the best results with Rave Extra Hold—the sparks from Rollerblade Barbie's booties did indeed cause them to burst dramatically into flames. While they were burning, a neighbor walked over to see what was going on. And if you think it's easy to explain why you're squatting in your driveway over a pair of burning underpants, while holding a Barbie doll, then you—no offense—know nothing about professional journalism.

I of course wrote a column about this experiment. It came to the attention of one of David Letterman's producers, Dan Kellison, who invited me to re-create the experiment on the show, so that the viewing public would better understand the dangers involved in spraying hair-spray on underwear and running sparking doll booties across it. I of course accepted. I am all about public service.

So I flew to New York and, a few hours before showtime, participated in a dress rehearsal on the stage of the Ed Sullivan Theater. On hand were maybe a dozen Letterman staff people and a very serious representative of the New York Fire Department. We gathered around a large table on which had been placed several pairs of brand-new men's briefs, several brands of hair spray, a brand-new Rollerblade Barbie and—such were the resources of the Letterman show—a Rollerblade Ken.

The rehearsal did not go smoothly. As I later wrote:

The ambience was a lot less casual than it had been in my driveway. Everybody was concerned about the fire danger; everybody was also VERY concerned about how Letterman would react. One guy kept saying things like, "Is this OK with Dave? Is Dave going to be comfortable with this? How close is Dave gonna be? Did we run this by Dave? Maybe we should run this by Dave again."

Many eyes were watching me closely as I spread a pair of men's cotton briefs on a table, then sprayed them with hair spray. Then I picked up a Rollerblade Barbie, put her on the briefs and scooted her forward, sparks flying, and suddenly . . .

. . . and suddenly nothing happened.

"Ha ha!" I said, to add levity to the moment. But it was not a light moment. It was a moment only hours before the taping of a hit national show that was supposed to feature flaming underpants, and here we had a set of what is known in the TV business as Stone Cold Briefs.

So I sprayed more hair spray and tried again. Nothing. I tried a different kind of hair spray. Nothing. I tried a different set of briefs. Nothing. I tried a Rollerblade Ken (which we had on hand as a backup). Nothing.

Pretty soon all the observers had changed from being-concerned-about-too-much-fire mode to being-concerned-that-there-would-not-be-any-fire mode. As I furiously swiped Barbie and Ken across various sets of underwear, people crowded around, offering helpful suggestions, including: "Maybe we should preheat the underwear." At one point, the Fire Department representative, on hand to ensure the public safety, said to me (I swear): "You should use Ken. You're getting more sparks with Ken."

Finally, just as we were about to give up, we got it to work (the secret, discovered by Dan, was to use an ENORMOUS amount of hair spray). As the blue flames flickered on the underwear, Dan and I gave each other triumphant high-fives. I was elated, until suddenly the thought hit me: What if it didn't work on the show?

In the end it did work on the show, thank God. But I was a nervous wreck. And believe it or not, that wasn't the only time I found myself sweating large armpit stains into my sport coat while wondering whether I was going to be able to cause some stupid thing to catch on fire in a stupid way on the Letterman show. On another occasion I went on the show to demonstrate that if you put a Kellogg's strawberry Pop-Tart into a toaster, and you hold the lever down long enough, the Pop-Tart will catch fire and shoot flames several feet into the air.

I became aware of this thanks to an alert reader who sent me an Ohio newspaper article about a house fire caused when a defective toaster failed to eject a Pop-Tart. Following my standard procedure, I reproduced this phenomenon in my driveway, using a sacrificial toaster, then wrote a column about it; the Letterman show flew me to New York to repeat the experiment. I ultimately succeeded, but not before several long, tense minutes during which—try to imagine the pressure—David Letterman and his live audience and presumably millions of viewers stared at the toaster while nothing happened. Again, I was a nervous wreck. "You can't promise an audience you're going to ignite a snack pastry with a small appliance and fail to deliver" is an old show-business maxim, or it should be.

But my point is not that being a humor columnist, while it may appear to be fun and games, is actually a high-stress occupation that requires nerves of steel and the ability to perform under extremely demanding conditions, like test pilot, or neurosurgeon, or omelet-station chef. This is true, but it is not my point. My point is that without my alert readers, I would never have known about the fire hazards posed by strawberry Pop-Tarts or Rollerblade Barbie. Nor would I have known about another product I wrote a column about, thanks to the following letter I received from a person who I would never have guessed was one of my readers:

Supreme Court of the United States
Washington, D. C. 20543

CHAMBERS OF
JUSTICE JOHN PAUL STEVENS

June 24, 1991

Mr. Dave Barry
The Miami Herald
One Herald Plaza
Miami, Florida 33132

Dear Mr. Barry:

Having long been concerned about the problem of exploding cows (I might explain that Mrs. Stevens and I are faithful fans of yours), it seemed imperative to pass on to you the enclosed advertisement the importance of which I am sure will be immediately apparent to you.

Sincerely,

Enclosure

That's right: John Paul Stevens, a US Supreme Court justice, was a faithful fan who wrote to me on his official Supreme Court stationery! Before I tell you about the advertisement he enclosed, I should explain his reference to exploding cows. Starting in the 1980s I had written a number of columns warning the public of the danger of cows exploding because of the amount of methane they produce. I was not 100 percent certain that any cow had ever actually exploded, but in professional journalism we don't take chances with public safety.

As for the advertisement, it was for an anti-flatulence product called Beano, which according to the manufacturer "prevents the gas from beans" and was endorsed by Regis Philbin.[40] I conducted a scientific test of Beano under the most demanding possible field conditions—a Mexican restaurant—and wrote a column concluding that it did appear to reduce a person's tootage.

A lot of readers liked that column, but two newspapers—the Portland *Oregonian* and the *St. Louis Post-Dispatch*—declined to print it on the grounds that it was tasteless and offensive. This made me feel remorseful and determined to be more sensitive to community standards.

I am of course joking. It made me want to yank the chains of the editors of these newspapers. I got my opportunity several weeks later, when I wrote a column about an activist anticircumcision organization called RECAP, which stands for "Recover A Penis," which advocated regrowing the foreskin by taping little weights to the end of the penis.[41]

At the beginning of the column, I noted that both the *Oregonian* and the *Post-Dispatch* had found the Beano column too offensive to publish. I then introduced the topic of circumcision, which I explained thusly:

> This is a common medical procedure that involves—and here, in the interest of tastefulness, I am going to use code names—taking hold of a guy's *Oregonian* and snipping his *Post-Dispatch* right off.

---

40. I am not making this up.

41. I am not making this up, either.

For the remainder of the column I used the papers' names in place of "penis" and "foreskin." Was this juvenile on my part? Yes it was. But it was a deeply satisfying kind of juvenile.

I managed to annoy a number of editors over the years. But what I really excelled at was annoying readers. This resulted in some entertaining hate mail, like the postcard pictured at the beginning of this chapter, sent by a person who strongly disagreed with me on the merits of the much-played Christmas song "The Little Drummer Boy." I dislike that song, and not just because it goes on longer than dental school. As I wrote in a column:

> Oh, sure, "The Little Drummer Boy" is a beautiful song, for maybe the first thirty-five minutes. But eventually it gets on your nerves, those voices shrieking, "Pa-rum-pum-pum-pum!"
>
> For openers, drums do not go "pa-rum-pum-pum-pum." Drums go "rat-a-tat-tat." Also I have issues with the line from "The Little Drummer Boy" that goes: "The ox and lamb kept time."
>
> Really? How? Did they clack their hooves together, castanet-style? Did they dance? Are we supposed to believe that two barnyard animals with legume-level IQs spontaneously started doing the macarena?
>
> I'll tell you this: If I were taking care of a newborn baby, and somebody came around whacking on a drum, that person would find himself at the emergency room having his drumsticks surgically removed from his rum-pum-pum-pum.

Quite a few of my readers disagreed with me on "The Little Drummer Boy." But no column that I wrote on a musical topic generated anything like the level of reader hostility that was directed at me when I made the near-fatal mistake of criticizing Neil Diamond.

What happened was, I wrote a column about songs that, when they come on the radio, make me want to immediately change the station. One of them is "I Am . . . I Said," in which Neil sings, with great intensity and emotion, these lyrics:

"I am," I said
To no one there
And no one heard at all
Not even the chair.

Here's what I said in my column:

Is Neil telling us he's surprised that the chair didn't hear him? Maybe he expected the chair to say, "Whoa, I heard THAT." My guess is that Neil was really desperate to come up with something to rhyme with "there," and he had already rejected "So I ate a pear," "Like Smokey the Bear," and "There were nits in my hair."

Please note that I was not attacking Neil Diamond's entire oeuvre. I think he's a very talented songwriter. I like many of his songs. I was merely pointing out that this one particular lyric is bad.

Well.

This criticism did NOT sit well with the large Neil Diamond fan community, which feels about Neil the way devout Christians feel about Jesus, only more passionately. I got many, many irate letters from these fans, making the following points:

1. You, Mr. Barry, are an idiot.
2. For your information Neil Diamond is a GENIUS.
3. He has written MANY brilliant songs.
4. "Cracklin' Rosie" for example.
5. Also "Sweet Caroline."
6. How many great songs have YOU written, Mr. Barry?
7. NONE, because you have NO TALENT, which is why you are JEALOUS OF NEIL DIAMOND.
8. What about "Song Sung Blue"?
9. WHAT ABOUT "HEARTLIGHT"?
10. YOU STUPID IDIOT.

And so on. My inbox was a seething pile of rage. Needless to say I felt terrible.

No, I am joking again. I felt pretty good. You are no doubt familiar with the saying "When life hands you lemons, make lemonade." The humor-columnist version of that saying is "When readers send you hate mail, they are writing your next column for you."

So I wrote a column about the Neil Diamond fans' reaction to my criticism. This new column generated an even bigger reaction than the first one. There were more letters from Neil Diamond fans, but there were also letters from people who agreed with me about the auditory capabilities of his chair. And many more people wanted to express their hatred, sometimes in vivid language, for other songs, such Bobby Goldsboro's "Honey," which I honestly think would lose to Hitler in a popularity contest.

I had hit a nerve; my readers were deeply passionate about this issue. So in my next column I announced a Bad Song Survey. It got a massive response, thousands of cards and letters. I ended up writing a book about it.[42] To this day, people still tell me about songs they hate. Also there are still Neil Diamond fans who dislike me. But that is the price we sometimes must pay, in journalism, for pointing out inconvenient truths.

Another time I managed to piss off the entire state of North Dakota. What happened was, while scavenging through the newspaper, I came across an article stating that some officials in North Dakota, looking to improve their state's image, were talking about changing its name from "North Dakota" to just "Dakota." I wrote a column making fun of them, saying, in part:

They don't like the word "North," which connotes a certain northness. In the words of North Dakota's former governor Ed Schafer: "Peo-

---

42. The book is *Dave Barry's Book of Bad Songs*. It's out of print, which is probably a good thing because it causes brainworms. The top three most-hated songs in the survey were: 1) "MacArthur Park"; 2) "Yummy Yummy Yummy (I Got Love in My Tummy)"; and 3) "(You're) Having My Baby." Of course the survey was done in 1992; since then many more songs have been recorded, and almost all of them suck.

ple have such an instant thing about how North Dakota is cold and snowy and flat."

We should heed the words of the former governor, and not just because the letters in "Ed Schafer" can be rearranged to spell "Shed Farce."[43] The truth is that when we think about North Dakota, which is not often, we picture it as having the same year-round climate as Uranus.

In contrast, SOUTH Dakota is universally believed to be a tropical paradise with palm trees swaying on surf-kissed beaches. Millions of tourists, lured by the word "South," flock to South Dakota every winter, often wearing nothing but skimpy bathing suits. Within hours, most of them die and become covered with snow, not to be found until spring, when they cause a major headache for South Dakota's farmers by clogging up the cultivating machines. South Dakota put a giant fence around the whole state to keep these tourists out, and STILL they keep coming. That's how powerful a name can be.

So changing names is a sound idea, an idea based on the scientific principle that underlies the field of marketing, which is: People are stupid.

My column also made fun of a North Dakota city that was trying to improve its image:

Are you familiar with Grand Forks, ND? No? It's located just west of East Grand Forks, Minn. According to a letter I received from a Grand Forks resident who asked to remain nameless ("I have to live here," he wrote), these cities decided they needed to improve their image, and the result was—get ready—"the Grand Cities."

The Grand Cities, needless to say, have a website (grandcities. net), where you can read sentences about the Grand Cities written in MarketingSpeak, which is sort of like English, except that it doesn't actually mean anything. Here's an actual quote: "It's the intersection

---

43. I love anagrams. Sue me.

of earth and sky. It's a glimpse of what lies ahead. It's hope, anticipation and curiosity reaching out to you in mysterious ways. Timeless. Endless. Always enriching your soul. Here, where the earth meets the sky, the Grand Cities of Grand Forks, North Dakota and East Grand Forks, Minnesota."

Doesn't that just make you want to cancel that trip to Paris or Rome and head for the Grand Cities? As a resident of Florida ("Where the earth meets the water, and forms mud") I am definitely planning to go to Dakota. I want to know what they're smoking up there.

This column got a strong reaction from North Dakotans, who are a proud people despite living in North Dakota. They sent me dozens of letters defending their state, sometimes including subtle criticisms of mine. "The people are friendly and warm-hearted," stated one writer. "We don't usually shoot tourists like some other states."

The most intriguing letter came from the mayor of Grand Forks, Mike Brown, who made me an offer: If I visited his city, they would name a sewage lifting station after me. This is an honor that is bestowed upon very few journalists. To my knowledge there is no sewage lifting station anywhere named after either Woodward OR Bernstein.

So I flew to Grand Forks in January, arriving on a Tuesday night when the temperature was minus four hundred degrees. And that was inside the terminal!

All kidding aside, it was very cold. But the North Dakotans gave me a warm welcome and invited me to participate in a number of traditional North Dakota wintertime activities, such as driving around for a while and then parking, which was convenient even in downtown Grand Forks because of the numerous available spaces. I also went ice fishing, a popular winter sport, although "sport" probably should be in quotation marks. Here's what I wrote about it:

The idea behind ice fishing is that the northern winter, which typically lasts 43 months, eventually starts to make a guy feel cooped up inside his house. So he goes out to the Great Outdoors, drills a hole in a frozen body of water, drops in a line, and then coops himself up inside a tiny structure called a "fish house" with a heater and some fishing buddies and some cigars and some adult beverages and maybe a TV with a satellite dish. It's basically the same thing as drilling a hole in the floor of your recreation room, the difference being that in your recreation room you'd have a better chance of catching a fish.

I started my ice-fishing trip at the Cabela's outdoor-supply store, which is close to the biggest thing in East Grand Forks, and which has huge tanks inside with fish swimming around. There I met a guy named Steve Gander, who had two snowmobiles running outside in the subzero cold. We hopped on and drove them at a high rate of speed, right through the East Grand Forks traffic. (By "the East Grand Forks traffic," I mean, "a car.")

We snowmobiled down to the Red River, which divides East Grand Forks from Grand Forks, and which gets its name from the fact that the water is brown. There we met Cabela's employee Matt Gindorff, who had drilled some holes in the ice. Matt dropped a fishing line into a hole, and within just 15 minutes—talk about beginner's luck!—nothing happened.

Nothing ever happens in ice fishing, because—this is my theory—there are no fish under the ice. Fish are not rocket scientists, but they are smart enough to spend the winter someplace warm, like Arizona. The only fish anywhere near me and Matt were the ones in the tanks at Cabela's; they were probably looking out the window at us, thinking "What a pair of MORONS."

TRUE FACT: Every January, the Grand Cities hold a day-long ice-fishing tournament called "the Frosty Bobber." The first year it was held, the total number of fish caught was zero. The second year, one person actually did catch something. It was a salamander. So Matt and I sat there, "fishing," until our body temperatures had dropped to about 55 degrees.

Fortunately, Steve had brought along a traditional beverage called "schnapps," which can be used, in a pinch, to fuel your snowmobile.

The people of the Grand Cities also honored me with a potluck supper in the Sacred Heart School gymnasium, to which every family brought one of the three fundamental potluck food substances:

1. A hotdish—one word, not two—which is a dish that is hot.
2. A Jell-O "salad," which is Jell-O with some other kind of food— fruits, vegetables, marshmallows, Peking duck—suspended inside it.
3. Bars, which are handheld rectangular dessert modules, usually made with Rice Krispies.

The potluck supper was nice, but the highlight of my visit was the official ceremony in which the sewage lifting station[44] was named after me. It was very cold, but a crowd of maybe seventy-five people turned out. I was driven there in a limousine, and Mayor Brown made a nice speech, in which he compared my work to the production of human excrement. Then they had me tear down a piece of paper taped to the side of the building, revealing a plaque that read, in large letters:

DAVE BARRY
LIFT STATION
NO. 16

As I later wrote:

Words cannot convey what it feels like to look at a building with your name on it—a building capable of pumping 450,000 gallons of untreated sewage per day—and hear the unmistakable WHUPWHUPWHUP of North Dakotans enthusiastically applauding with heavy gloves.

---

44. I frankly don't know why they lift their sewage. I personally would leave it down there.

So I have fond memories of North Dakota, although I do not plan to go back there, and if I ever do, it will be during summer, which runs from August 17 through 18. But my point is, I believe the North Dakotans no longer have a beef with me.

I'm not so sure about the people of Indiana. I got into trouble with them when I wrote a column about which of the fifty United States is the stupidest. This column was based on a press release from a company that had ranked the states according to intelligence. For the record, I did not say that Indiana was the stupidest state. In fact I objected to the fact that my state, Florida, was ranked only forty-seventh in intelligence. I argued that Florida deserved to be last:

> The three states ranked as stupider than Florida were Mississippi, Louisiana and New Mexico. Granted, these are not gifted states. But stupider than the state that STILL does not really know who it voted for in the 2000 presidential election? Stupider than the state that will issue a driver's license to ANYBODY, including people who steer by leaning out the car window and tapping their canes on the roadway? Don't make me laugh.

I then got into a general discussion of stupid things that states do, such as naming official state crustaceans. I touched briefly upon state nicknames, which is how Indiana came up:

> For nickname stupidity, no state challenges Indiana, which proudly calls itself "the Hoosier State," even though nobody has a clue what "Hoosier" means. It could be a Native American word meaning "Has sex with caribou."

That was all I said about Indiana: two sentences. But I got a LOT of letters from Indiana people taking issue with me about the meaning of their nickname. My favorite was from a man who blew my theory completely out of the water by pointing out that "Indiana has no caribou." Most of the letters—dozens and dozens of them—stated that I was an idiot for claiming that nobody knows what "Hoosier" means. These letters then went on to give me the correct explanation of "Hoosier," which EVERYBODY has always agreed on, which turned out to be: dozens and dozens of different explanations. Really. I wrote a column listing some of them (there were plenty more):

"Hoosier" is a word meaning "highlander" or "hill-dweller."

"Hoosier" is a word referring to anything large of its kind.

"Hoosier" comes from when somebody would knock on a cabin door and Indiana people would say, "Who's there?"

"Hoosier" comes from when Indiana people would stand on the riverbank and shout to people on boats, "Who is ya?"

"Hoosier" comes from when Indiana families would hold big reunions and the mothers, referring to the children, would ask each other, "Who's yours?"

"Hoosier" comes from the aftermath of knife fights in Indiana taverns when somebody would pick up a lump of flesh and say, "Whose ear?"

I concluded the column thusly:

So, when you hear people refer to themselves as "Hoosiers" you'll know exactly what they're referring to: an inquisitive, one-eared, hill-dwelling Ohio River contractor, large for his kind, who has a lot of trouble with pronunciation but does NOT have sex with caribou. Who WOULDN'T be proud!

That column generated still more mail from unhappy Indianans, but I didn't write about them, because of the danger that they might invite me to Indiana and put my name on a large aromatic piece of infrastructure. A man can handle only so many honors.

The Hoosier letters, especially the one about the caribou, fell into a category of mail I got a lot of: "gotcha" letters from readers who believed they had caught me in an error. The tone of these letters was, "Perhaps,

Mr. Barry, before you write your newspaper column, you should do some research, because the lightbulb was NOT invented by Abraham Lincoln."

No matter what wildly inaccurate statement I put in a column, no matter how obvious I thought it was that I was joking, people would be offended and take it upon themselves to set me straight. I once wrote a column about a trip to France, in which I referred to "some of the famous tourist attractions of Paris, such as the Arc de Triomphe, Notre Dame and the Leaning Tower of Pisa." You cannot imagine how many people wrote to inform me that the Leaning Tower of Pisa is not located in Paris, because it is located in Pisa, which is in Italy. So I will tell you: a LOT of people. So many people, in fact, that I created a form-letter response, which I signed and sent to all of them. This letter stated that they were mistaken, because the Leaning Tower of Pisa had been moved to Paris in 1994. Ha ha! Clearly THAT would make it obvious to everyone that I was joking, right?

Wrong. A woman in Kansas wrote an indignant reply to my form letter, stating: "I still don't believe the real original Leaning Tower of Pisa was or ever will be moved to Paris. First, I think Pisa, Italy, would never, never allow such a thing to happen. To move the Pisa, Italy, real Tower of Pisa would require a cost that would be prohibitive. I asked a Travel Agency if they had heard about the Tower having been moved. Of course they hadn't."

That's right: *She asked a travel agency.* She got me!

I loved readers like her.

A column that always generated gotcha letters was when I wrote as Mister Language Person. This is a persona I invented who presented himself as the world's foremost expert on grammar, punctuation and writing in general. Most of the column consisted of Mister Language Person answering questions, which I made up. Some examples:

Q. What is the purpose of the apostrophe?

A. The apostrophe is used mainly in hand-lettered small-business signs to alert the reader that an "s" is coming up at the end of a word, as in: WE DO NOT EXCEPT PERSONAL CHECK'S, or: NOT RESPON-

SIBLE FOR ANY ITEM'S. Another important grammar concept to bear in mind when creating hand-lettered small-business signs is that you should put quotation marks around random words for decoration, as in "TRY" OUR HOT DOG'S, or even TRY "OUR" HOT DOG'S.

Q. What is the proper way to begin a formal letter?

A. The proper beginning, or "salutatorian," for a formal business letter is: "Dear Mr. or Ms. Bob Johnson as the Case May Be." This should be followed by a small dab of imported mustard.

Q. What if the person's name is not "Bob Johnson"?

A. Then he or she will just have to change it.

Q. What is the correct way to conclude a formal business letter to a cable television company?

A. "I Spit on Your Billing Department."

Q. I am a top business executive writing an important memo, and I wish to know if the following wording is correct: "As far as sales, you're figures do not jive with our parameters."

A. You have made the common grammatical error of using the fricative infundibular tense following a third-person corpuscular imprecation. The correct wording is: "As far as sales, your fired."

Q. I, am never sure, when, to use, commas.

A. You should use a comma whenever you have a need to pause in a sentence.

> EXAMPLE: "So me and Tiffany were at the mall and she ate like four of those big fudge squares which is why her butt is the size of a Volkswagen Jetta I don't know WHAT Jason sees in, wait a minute I'm getting another call."

Q. What is the correct spelling of the word "liaison"?

A.   Nobody knows.

Q.   I work in Customer Service, and my co-workers and I are having a big debate about whether we should say that your call is "very" important to us, or "extremely" important to us. We argue about this all day long! My question is, how do we stop these stupid phones from ringing?

A.   Someone will answer your question "momentarily."

Q.   As an attorney, I wish to know the correct legal way to say "I don't know."

A.   There is no legal way for an attorney to say this.

Q.   Thank you.

A.   That will be $400.

Q.   What does "decimate" mean?

A.   This often-misunderstood word is an anterior cruciate predicate that should be used in conjugal phrases, as follows: "Noreen was totally decimated when she found Vern wearing her good pantyhose."

Q.   What is the proper format for a formal wedding invitation?

A   A formal wedding invitation should come in a squarish envelope, inside which should be several increasingly small envelopes accompanied by some sheets of what appears to be Soviet Union toilet paper. Also there should be various cards on which all the numbers are spelled out, as in "at Four O'clock on the Seventeenth of June, Nineteen Hundred Ninety Six" and "Two Hundred Ninety Eight Harbour Oaks Manour Court Drive Terrace, Next To The Seven-Eleven." This information should be written in a high-class style of penmanship so difficult to read that many guests show up in the wrong state.

Q.   What do The Dalai Lama's friends call him in informal social settings?

A. They just call him by his first name.

Q. They call him "The"?

A. Yes. They say, "Hey, The! Don't hog all the Tater Tots!"

Q. As a fourth-year medical student, I am wondering if there is any way to remember the difference between "prostrate" and "prostate."

A. We contacted the Mayo Clinic, which informs us that surgeons there use this simple poem: "If two 'R's are found, it is down on the ground / If one 'R' is on hand, then it is a gland."

Q. What about "transpire" vs. "perspire"?

A. That one still has them stumped.

Q. I am a real-estate developer building a residential subdivision on a former landfill, and I can't decide which name would be more prestigious: "The Oaks at Hampton Chase Manor," or "The Estates of the Falls of the Landings of Hunters Run."

A. How recently was the property used as a landfill?

Q. In some of the yards, you can still see refrigerators sticking out of the dirt.

A. We would recommend "The Knolls at Cheshire Pointe Landings on the Greene."

Most Mister Language Person columns ended with Tips for Writers, such as:

TIP: When writing a résumé, be sure to use "power words" to describe your accomplishments and skills:

Wrong: "I supervised a team of 15 data-entry clerks."

Right: "I can snap your spine like a toothpick."

TIP	In writing a letter of recommendation for an employee, be sure to give it a "positive spin."
Wrong:	Bob occasionally has a problem with his temper.
Right:	Bob took full responsibility for the firebomb in Accounts Receivable.
TIP:	When choosing a title for a novel, try to come up with something that will really "grab" potential readers.
Weak:	*The Death Corpse.*
Strong:	*The Death Corpse* by Stephen King.
TIP:	A good way to "liven up" the plot of a novel is to give the characters some romantic interest.
Wrong:	Doreen entered the room.
Right:	Doreen entered the room and had sex with Roger.

The key attribute of Mister Language Person was that he was always wrong. He was spectacularly wrong. He was wrong about everything. He was often wrong three or four times in a single sentence. Virtually nothing he said was correct.

This is what made the gotcha letters he received from irate readers—people who apparently believed he was supposed to be a real grammar expert—so entertaining. These readers would often enclose the column they were upset about, torn from their local newspaper; many of them had circled, sometimes in red ink, whatever Mister Language had asserted that upset them. Inevitably, this would be: one thing.

That's right: In a column filled with errors, a column that was basically a festering, teeming mass of errors, these readers had discovered: *an error*. And they were irate about it.

"I don't know where you get the nerve to call yourself an expert," was the general tone of their letters, "because for your information the word 'decimate' does NOT mean . . . "

And so on. Mister Language Person got a lot of people upset. I don't know if his relentless incorrectness contributed to the steep decline in the public's respect for the newspaper industry. But I like to think so.

Seriously, though: I enjoyed the mail from Mr. Language Person's critics, just as I enjoyed the mail from the Neil Diamond fans, and the lady who checked with a travel agency about whether the Leaning Tower of Pisa had been moved to Paris, and of course the caribou-loving people of Indiana. I enjoyed almost all the mail I got from people who, for one reason or another, hated me.

But I'm glad that these people didn't make up the majority of my readers, because if they had, my column wouldn't have survived. The majority of my readers, God bless them, got the jokes, not to mention providing me with a steady supply of column fodder in the form of off-beat, often toilet-related, news items.

My readers also enthusiastically responded whenever I called upon them to join me in various crusades, such as the one I led against the telemarketing industry.

This crusade began as a column I wrote in 2003 about the National Do Not Call Registry, a federal program designed to prevent telemarketers from calling people who didn't want to be called. The American people—who in 2003 were really, REALLY tired of being interrupted at dinnertime by callers wanting them to change their long-distance provider—would have preferred a federal program under which telemarketers were wrapped in pig intestines and dropped from helicopters into shark-infested waters. But the Do Not Call Registry was a step in the right direction, and it was very popular with the public.

It was not, however, popular with the telemarketers, who were challenging the registry in court. They claimed they had a constitutional right to call people, even people who did not wish to be called. As I wrote in my column:

Leading the charge for the telemarketing industry is the American Teleservices Association (suggested motto: "Some Day, We Will Get a Dictionary and Look Up 'Services'"). This group argues that, if its members are prohibited from calling people who do not want to be called, then two million telemarketers will lose their jobs. Of course, you could use pretty much the same reasoning to argue that laws against mugging cause unemployment among muggers. But that would be unfair. Muggers rarely intrude into your home.

So what's the answer? Is there a constitutional way that we telephone customers can have our peace, without inconveniencing the people whose livelihoods depend on keeping their legal right to inconvenience us? Maybe we could pay the telemarketing industry not to call us, kind of like paying "protection money" to organized crime. Or maybe we could actually hire organized crime to explain our position to telemarketing industry executives, who would then be given a fair opportunity to respond, while the cement was hardening.

I'm just thinking out loud here. I'm sure you have a better idea for how we can resolve our differences with the telemarketing industry. If you do, call me. No, wait, I have a better idea: Call the folks at the American Teleservices Association, toll-free, at 877-779-3974, and tell them what you think. I'm sure they'd love to hear your constitutionally protected views! Be sure to wipe your mouthpiece afterward.

I had called my readers to action. The question was, would they respond?

Hoo boy.

Here's the Associated Press account:

MIAMI (Sept. 12)—Telemarketers are now screening their calls, instead of the other way around.

The American Teleservices Association isn't laughing at Dave Barry, not after the Pulitzer Prize–winning humor columnist for the *Miami Herald* listed the group's telephone number in his Aug. 31 column and sparked a flood of phone calls to the group's offices.

Barry told his readers to call and "tell them what you think."

"I'm sure they'd love to hear your constitutionally protected views! Be sure to wipe your mouthpiece afterward," Barry wrote.

Thousands of Barry's readers have done as they were told, forcing the association to stop answering its phones. Callers now hear a recording, which says that because of "overwhelming positive response to recent media events, we are unable to take your call at this time."

"It's difficult not to see some malice in Mr. Barry's intent," said Tim Searcy, executive director of the ATA, who said the added calls will be costly to his group because of toll charges and staffing issues.

Barry hardly sounded apologetic.

"I feel just terrible, especially if they were eating or anything," he said.

My telemarketer column got so much reaction that even the *Times*— that's right, the *New York* freaking *Times*—wrote a story about it:

American Teleservices attracted the attention of Dave Barry, a nationally syndicated humorist who writes for the *Miami Herald*. In August, Mr. Barry, reasoning that consumers had the constitutional right to call telemarketers, published the trade group's phone number in his column.

When more than a thousand reader calls clogged the American Teleservices Association's voice mail system, the group disconnected the number.

Tim Searcy, the group's executive director, was quoted in *DM News*, a trade publication, complaining about the disruption Mr. Barry had caused.

Mr. Barry said he was surprised by the reader reaction. "This is the most intense response I've ever gotten," he said in an interview last week. "Even more than low-flow toilets."[45]

It was indeed an amazing reaction from my readers. As I wrote in my follow-up column:

I myself received approximately seven billion phone calls, letters and e-mails on this topic. About 99 percent came from consumers who are wildly enthusiastic about the idea of calling telemarketers. Many of these consumers wanted me to publish more telemarketers' numbers, including residential numbers. As one e-mailer put it: "I think we should call them at home and try to sell them the idea of not calling people at home."

The other 1 percent of the response came from people in the telemarketing industry, who pointed out that I am evil vermin scum, and—even worse—a member of the news media. Their main arguments are that (a) telemarketers are hardworking people, and (b) if they're not allowed to call people who don't want to be called, telemarketing jobs could be lost, and the US economy would suffer.

Tim Searcy of the ATA was quoted in the *Los Angeles Times* as saying that the impact of the Do Not Call Registry would be (I did not make this quote up) "like an asteroid hitting the Earth." Yes. An asteroid!

I don't know if the telemarketing people still hate me. But I like to think they do.

Another column that got an unexpectedly strong reaction was one I wrote in response to a letter I got from two Oregon guys, John Baur and Mark Summers, who had a dream. They believed that the world would

---

45. This is a reference to another crusade I led, against low-flow toilets. Tragically, I lost that one. All I will say about it here is that we once had great toilets in this nation. We had powerful toilets, toilets that could suck down a mature sheep. And now? Don't get me started. (Seriously, don't.)

be a better place if on a certain day each year, everybody—why not?—talked like a pirate. They had settled on September 19, because that was the birthday of one of their ex-wives. In their letter, they told me that for a few years they had been talking like pirates every September 19 except when they forgot, but so far it didn't seem to be catching on. So they were appealing to me to spread the word.

Naturally, as a columnist always on the lookout for issues I could write about without doing any work, I thought this was brilliant. So I wrote a column explaining Baur and Summers's idea and urging my readers to participate:

To prepare for Talk Like a Pirate Day, you should practice incorporating pirate terminology into your everyday speech. For example, let's consider a typical conversation between two co-workers in a business office:

BOB: Hi, Mary.

MARY: Hi, Bob. Have you had a chance to look at the Fennerman contract?

BOB: Yes, and I have some suggestions.

MARY: OK, I'll review them.

Now let's see how this same conversation would sound on Talk Like a Pirate Day:

BOB: Avast, me beauty.

MARY: Avast, Bob. Is that a yardarm in your doubloons, or are you just glad to see me?

BOB: You are giving me the desire to haul some keel.

MARY: Arrrrr.

As you can see, talking like a pirate will infuse your everyday conversations with romance and danger. So join the movement! On Sept. 19, do not answer the phone with "hello." Answer the phone with "Ahoy, me hearty!"

If the caller objects that he is not a hearty, inform him that he is a scurvy dog (or, if the caller is female, a scurvy female dog) who will be walking the plank off the poop deck and winding up in Davy Jones's locker, sleeping with the fishes. No, wait, that would be Talk Like a Pirate in *The Godfather* Day, which is another variation I considered ("I'm gonna make him an offer that will shiver his timbers").

But the point is, this is a great idea, and you, me bucko, should be part of it. Join us on Sept. 19. You HAVE the buckles, darn it: Don't be afraid to swash them!

That column ran in September of 2002, and it turned out that the world, or at least my readership, was indeed ready to swash its buckles. International Talk Like a Pirate Day was an immediate hit, and it has remained popular ever since. Every year on September 19, people—not everybody, but some people—observe it by talking like pirates. Mainly they say, quote, "Arrrr," which turns out to be the only piratical phrase most of us can think of on the spur of the moment.

But my point is that International Talk Like a Pirate Day seems to be here to stay, and although it wasn't my idea, my column played a key role in popularizing it. I believe that long after I've been forgotten—a process, if I'm being honest, that is already well under way—people around the world will carry on this utterly pointless tradition. And that makes me proud, me hearties.

Another cause—this one is actually worthwhile—that I became associated with was (speaking of the poop deck) colonoscopies. I got my first colonoscopy at age sixty-one, more than ten years later than I should have gotten it. As a veteran medical coward, I might never have gotten a colonoscopy if not for the fact that my little brother Sam got one when he turned fifty, and they found that he had colon cancer. They caught it early, and he's fine. But it was a scary wake-up call.

So I got a colonoscopy, and of course I wrote a column about it. One could argue that my entire professional journalism career was a buildup to this column. Here's how it started:

OK. You turned fifty. You know you're supposed to get a colonoscopy. But you haven't. Here are your reasons:

1. You've been busy.
2. You don't have a history of cancer in your family.
3. You haven't noticed any problems.
4. You don't want a doctor to stick a tube 17,000 feet up your butt.

Let's examine these reasons one at a time. No, wait, let's not. Because you and I both know that the only real reason is No. 4.

I talked about my fear of medical procedures, and how Sam's cancer scared me into scheduling a colonoscopy. Then I described the preparation, which in my case involved a laxative called MoviPrep:

Then, in the evening, I took the MoviPrep. You mix two packets of powder together in a one-liter plastic jug, then you fill it with luke-warm water. (For those unfamiliar with the metric system, a liter is about thirty-two gallons.)[46] Then you have to drink the whole jug. This takes about an hour, because MoviPrep tastes—and here I am being kind—like a mixture of goat spit and urinal cleanser, with just a hint of lemon.

The instructions for MoviPrep, clearly written by somebody with a great sense of humor, state that after you drink it, "a loose watery

---

46. You probably will not be surprised to learn that I received emails from irate people informing me that a liter is NOT thirty-two gallons. I'm guessing that at least some of these people were Hoosiers.

bowel movement may result." This is kind of like saying that after you jump off your roof, you may experience contact with the ground.

MoviPrep is a nuclear laxative. I don't want to be too graphic here, but: Have you ever seen a space shuttle launch? This is pretty much the MoviPrep experience, with you as the shuttle. There are times when you wish the commode had a seat belt.

You spend several hours pretty much confined to the bathroom, spurting violently. You eliminate everything. And then, when you figure you must be totally empty, you have to drink another liter of MoviPrep, at which point, as far as I can tell, your bowels travel into the future and start eliminating food that you have not even eaten yet.

I then described the actual colonoscopy experience, which is basically: nothing. In fact it's *better* than nothing, because they give you some kind of extremely relaxing drug. When it's over, you feel great. You're like, "Hey, let's do that *again!*"

I concluded the column by urging people who'd been advised to get colonoscopies but, like me, had not done so, to go ahead and get one. As an inducement, I offered to mail them a cheesy certificate stating that they were a grown-up and got a colonoscopy.

That column got a huge reader response. I think it might be the most viral thing I ever wrote. Usually I try to exercise some control over who reprints my columns, but for that one, I gave permission to pretty much anybody who asked. To this day gastroenterologists and other medical folks give copies of the column to patients. Many websites posted it. It's all over the Internet.

Judi sent out a ton of certificates. Even though she and I are both retired and no longer have an office, I'm *still* getting requests for certificates. People I don't know still approach me in public to tell me about their colonoscopies. On several occasions people have shown me, on their phones, color photographs of the interiors of their colons. Don't get me wrong, these people meant this as a nice gesture, but as the old saying goes, "when you've seen the interior of one stranger's colon, you've seen one too many."

I've heard from people who said that, because of my column, they got colonoscopies, and as a result found out they had serious issues that needed immediate treatment. A few people told me that the column may have saved their lives.[47]

This is, of course, gratifying. But I'm not completely comfortable taking credit, because the truth is, the reason I wrote the colonoscopy column was the same reason I wrote almost everything else: I thought it would be funny.

Over the years I've been told, usually by serious, well-intentioned people, that my column performs an important societal function—that by writing my silly booger jokes, I'm making the world a better place, because laughter is the best medicine, because in troubled times humor is vital, because we all need to laugh at ourselves.

My response to these well-intentioned people has always been: Thanks, but I'd probably be doing this even if it made the world a worse place. It's pretty much the only thing I know how to do. It's in my DNA. I'm a class clown.

And of course a class clown needs a class to entertain. For me, that's been my readers. They've been a wonderful audience. They've laughed at my jokes, alerted me to all kinds of urgent news stories, supported my stupid crusades, bought my books, sent me Rollerblade Barbies. Above all, they've enabled me to go for decades without having anything close to a real job. So to my loyal readers: Thank you.

I also sincerely thank my critics, even the haters. You may not like

---

47. While I was writing this chapter, I got an email from Tom Keogh, a retired Massachusetts pharmacist, who wrote: *When I would dispense the prescribed colonoscopy prep to the patient, I would ask them if this was their first colonoscopy. If so, I would also give them a copy of your column and instruct them to read it before taking their prep product . . . I am happy to report to you that over the years, all of the patients who were in the Most Fearful group reported back to me after the procedure that your column had provided complete relief from their pre-colonoscopy anxiety, without a single side-effect from reading the column! I had no drug in my pharmacy arsenal that could come close to such a success rate!*

me, but you've entertained me, and you've provided me with a lot of material. Believe it or not, you've also helped me, because on those occasions—and there have been some—when you've voiced valid criticisms of me or my work, I have heard you.

Which is more than you can say for the chair.

CHAPTER SIX

POLITICS

I**N FEBRUARY OF 1984 THE *MIAMI HERALD* SENT ME TO**
New Hampshire to write columns about the New Hampshire presidential primary.[48]

Not everybody at the *Herald* thought this was a good idea. I was in Miami when the decision was made, and one of the newsroom editors, an old-school hard-ass, summoned me into his office and, by way of an icebreaker, said: "Are you a flake?"

I asked him what he meant. What he meant was: Could I, a humorist producing a goofy and sometimes wildly nonfactual weekly column for the frequently weird *Tropic* magazine, be relied upon to produce daily columns, on deadline, about a major news story, to be published in the front section—the *serious* section—of the newspaper?

---

48. Of course the *Herald* also sent actual journalists to New Hampshire. The main one was political editor Tom Fiedler, an excellent reporter and writer.

I told him I used to be a real reporter, and I thought I could produce on deadline. He still seemed doubtful, and, as I later learned, he was not alone. But Heath Meriwether, the *Herald*'s executive editor, was in favor of sending me, so I went.

I spent two weeks on the campaign trail in New Hampshire. I stayed on the outskirts of Manchester in an old motel, the kind of place where the instant you open your door, you're outside. I had no guidance on how to cover a primary election, but I had a rental car, a map, and the Manchester *Union-Leader*, which every day published a schedule of candidate appearances. I drove all around the state—it's a small state—usually attending two or three campaign events a day, looking for humor fodder.

At night I went to the Sheraton Wayfarer, a hotel in Bedford, where pretty much the entire national political press corps gathered at the bar. Back then print journalists usually wrote one thing a day, so after they filed their stories or columns they'd go to the Wayfarer to have a cocktail or three, discuss the political situation with other press corps members and—drawing on their vast storehouse of experience and knowledge—formulate the conventional wisdom, which would then appear in various forms in almost every newspaper in the nation, and which quite often was wrong.

Today, because of social media and the twenty-four-hour news cycle and the fact that everybody has the attention span of a gnat, political reporters can never stop reporting, tweeting[49] and retweeting, so they don't get to unwind. They're too busy staring at screens. They don't drink as much as the old press corps did, and they have way more access to all kinds of scientific polling data, but as far as I can tell they're wrong just as often. And they don't have the camaraderie of the Sheraton Wayfarer.[50]

Which is sad for them, because it was pretty great. It was the Oscars for political junkies. You'd see the superstars of punditry holding court, the bigfeet, guys (they were mostly guys) such as R. W. "Johnny" Apple, David Broder, Dan Balz, Jack Germond, Joe Klein, and Curtis Wilkie.

---

49. Or whatever it's called now.

50. Or if they do, they never invite me.

You'd see political reporters from all the big papers, wondrously cynical people who'd been around, it seemed, since Lincoln debated Douglas. You'd also see campaign staffers and hired-gun consultants working the crowd. Sometimes an actual candidate would show up. As Election Day got close you'd see more network TV people; you might see Tom Brokaw—Tom Brokaw!—sitting at the bar like a regular person.

I enjoyed the scene at the Wayfarer. But the real entertainment in New Hampshire was out on the campaign trail, where the candidates and the voters performed a kind of campaign Kabuki.

A typical event would have a candidate showing up at some random venue—a restaurant, a factory, somebody's house, a shopping mall, a bowling alley—where some New Hampshire voters had gathered, motivated by a sincere desire to meet the candidate and/or obtain free food.

Usually the candidate would arrive at the event late, exhausted and hoarse, suffering from some kind of lingering viral infection after too many seventeen-hour days on the campaign trail, but smiling like a lunatic on speed. The candidate would be accompanied by several unsmiling staff people, who were even sicker and more tired than the candidate, and a clot of grumpy press people, also unhealthy from living on a diet of fast food while spending weeks on end attached, remora-like, to the candidate, following him all over the winding roads of New Hampshire—a place they had come to loathe—in crowded vans scented with Egg McMuffin farts en route to yet another campaign event where they must listen to the candidate—whom they had also come to loathe—reiterate, for the seven thousandth time, his six-point plan to revitalize the American economy, after which he'd pretend to give a shit about the questions from the flinty New Hampshire voters, whom everybody—candidate, staff and press corps—had come to loathe. Often, to complete the Kabuki, the candidate would do something visual for the cameras—hold a baby, eat some weird local dish such as "poutine," bowl, put on a hat, flip pancakes or engage in some other demeaning activity utterly unrelated to being chief executive of the United States.

The saddest candidate events were the ones where the voters failed to show up. For example, one of my first columns from New Hampshire was about the campaign of Reubin Askew, a former Florida governor who was one of a half-dozen people seeking the Democratic nomination.[51] He had an excellent résumé and absolutely no chance.

This is a recurring feature of presidential campaigns: politicians who have all kinds of solid qualifications, politicians who could undoubtedly do a competent job of being president, but who for various reasons—such as, in Askew's case, an almost life-threatening lack of charisma—fail to fire up the public. These are confident people, winners, governors and senators who've always succeeded in their endeavors, and they've convinced themselves that if the voters got to see them in person, got to look them in the eye and hear them explain their Vision for the Future, their Blueprint for America, their six-point or seven-point or even eight-point plan, then by God those voters would be won over. There would be a groundswell! Why not? It happened to Jimmy Carter!

And so these successful, confident winners head hopefully to New Hampshire, only to have their presidential aspirations crushed like a bunny rabbit under an anvil. That's what was happening to Askew the day I saw him:

> I caught up with the Reubin Askew campaign in Concord, where he was touring a shopping center and attracting about as much attention as a demonstration of nonstick cooking pots. It was a sad thing to watch: he has this knot of reporters around him, and they keep asking him, in about 700,000 different ways, if he plans to drop out of the race, and he keeps trying to get through them to find a voter or two to shake hands with. I wanted to go up and give him a big hug.

---

51. Ronald Reagan was running for reelection, so there was no real race on the Republican side.

Askew dropped out after finishing last in New Hampshire. Another candidate who did not do well there was John Glenn, a US senator from Ohio and former astronaut. He'd been expected to be a strong challenger for the Democratic nomination, but he was struggling, as I wrote:

> I went to downtown Manchester to watch the John Glenn campaign falter. These days we professional journalists refer to it formally as the Faltering Glenn Campaign, because Glenn is trailing Walter Mondale in the polls.
>
> Don't get me wrong here: I like Glenn fine. It's just that he doesn't electrify the crowd, if you know what I mean. I doubt he could electrify a fish tank if he threw a toaster into it.

My primary coverage—especially the column about Glenn and the toaster—upset some people at the *Herald*. While I was still in New Hampshire I got a call from Heath Meriwether, the *Herald's* executive editor. He wrote a weekly column, and he'd decided to make it about me that week. He'd received a memo from a member of the *Herald's* editorial board who thought my New Hampshire columns did not belong on the news pages next to our serious campaign reporting. Heath read me the memo, which said in part:

"When we treat so prominently such serious business as if it were pratfall comedy, I believe that we demean our reputation as a serious newspaper. I seriously believe that such treatment reassures the public that cynicism about politics is smart. I don't believe that that's what good newspapers should do."

Heath asked for my response, which was, basically: If you think there's nothing comedic about the New Hampshire primary, you really should come up here and see it in person. As for whether it's smart to be cynical about politics, my feeling was, and still is: Nobody could possibly be more cynical about our political system than our politicians.

In any event, the *Herald* let me continue writing political columns, and in the summer of 1984 I went to the national conventions. The Democrats convened in San Francisco, where I filed this report:

> For the benefit of those of you who are just now emerging from comas, the big news here is that Walter Mondale has chosen New York Rep. Geraldine Ferraro, an avowed woman, to be his running mate. This followed a lengthy selection process in which Mondale invited members of every popular minority group to his home, where he would interview them to find out if they were compatible with his views:
>
> MONDALE: So, tell me: Which minority group do you belong to?
>
> INTERVIEWEE: I'm a Black person.
>
> MONDALE: Fine. And how long have you been a member of that particular group?
>
> INTERVIEWEE: Forty-seven years.
>
> MONDALE: Very good. Now as you can see, my aides have arranged a complete set of my views over on the dining table. Do you see any view that you would be incompatible with?
>
> INTERVIEWEE: Let's see . . . that one looks OK, and that one, and . . .
>
> MONDALE: Could you step it up a bit? Because, very frankly, we have minority groups backed out onto the lawn.

I also wrote about the street demonstrations in San Francisco. There are always demonstrations going on outside political conventions, and they never seem to accomplish anything beyond annoying the people who aren't in them:

> Meanwhile, out on the streets, large clots of people continue to barge around with signs demanding that somebody do something about

something. The largest clots to date have consisted of organized labor and the gays, both of whom held huge marches to dramatize their demands. Their demands were:

Organized labor: Ronald Reagan should be placed in a dumpster and then it should be filled with concrete.

The gays: And then it should be dropped from a tremendous height onto the Rev. Jerry Falwell.

The Republicans held their convention in Dallas, where they renominated Ronald Reagan in a climactic extravaganza of red, white and blue Mylar confetti falling onto a horde of wholesome flag-waving youths. As I explained:

The reason for all the Mylar and young people, of course, is that the Republicans want to reclaim the indoor record for Mindless Patriotism Displays, which was taken from them last month in a surprise move by the Democrats in San Francisco. Time was when the Democrats were no competition in terms of patriotism. They were always nominating their presidential candidates at three a.m. amidst clouds of marijuana smoke, and it was always somebody like George McGovern, who would make a speech where he'd call on Cuba to invade the United States, and for the closing ceremony they'd have Eldridge Cleaver spit on a Bible.

But recently, Democratic Party officials detected a new surge of national pride caused by patriotic Olympics-related beer commercials. So at their convention, they distributed thousands of flags to the delegates to wave in a patriotic fashion. It had been a long time since Democrats waved flags, so they were a little rusty at first ("No no NO! You hold it by the STICK end!!"), but eventually they got the hang of it, and they went on to set a record for Mindless Patriotism Displays surpassing anything seen in this country since 1845, when we invaded Mexico solely on the basis that it was a foreign country.

I found the Republican convention delegates to be especially entertaining:

> Those of you who were still awake may have noted that at the end of
> the Republican convention, Ray Charles sang "America the Beautiful." My question is: Does this mean that Ray Charles is a Republican?
> That Ray Charles belongs to the party of Wayne Newton? I raise this
> issue because of the way Republican delegates clap to music.
>
> Let's take, for example, a song like "Hit the Road Jack." A normal
> person or a Democrat would clap to this song as follows:
>
> "Hit the road (clap) Jack . . . "
>
> But a Republican delegate would clap right smack dab on the word
> "road," as in:
>
> "Hit the (clap), Jack . . . "
>
> I suggest you try this a few times in the privacy of your home or apartment, so you'll understand how Republican delegates clap. It is a style of
> clapping that is compatible only with songs from the original cast recording of *The Sound of Music*, and I doubt that all the Republican delegates
> and alternates added together own more than four Ray Charles albums.

I got some angry mail about my political columns. It was pretty
much evenly divided between letters from Republicans who thought
I was an idiot liberal communist Democrat, and letters from Democrats who thought I was an idiot conservative fascist Republican.[52]
But a lot of other readers seemed to enjoy my coverage, and I'd found
that I really enjoyed writing about presidential campaigns. So from
then on, every four years until COVID struck in 2020, I usually went
to the Iowa caucuses, the New Hampshire primary and both national
conventions.

Thus in 1988 I was in Atlanta for the Democratic convention. Since
the ticket—Michael Dukakis and Lloyd Bentsen—had already been

---

52. For the record, I am neither. I am an idiot libertarian.

decided, there was no chance that any actual news would occur. Nevertheless a massive press corps was on hand, which meant that virtually any trivial thing that happened got an absurd amount of coverage.

I personally witnessed this phenomenon one afternoon in the designated protest zone near the convention hall. A young woman was wandering through the area holding a pet rat, and almost immediately she was surrounded by TV camera crews. I counted five of them. That night I saw her on one of the local TV news shows, and not at the end of the broadcast, where they put the fluff. It was one of the top stories from the convention: *Woman with Rat!*

I thought that was ridiculous, so I decided to run an experiment. I enlisted the aid of two of my fellow newspaper columnists, Erik Lacitis of the *Seattle Times* and Bob Morris of the *Orlando Sentinel*. We got some cardboard boxes and cut holes in them for our eyes. Then we went out to the protest zone, put the boxes on our heads, and formed a little triangle, facing outward.

So that was the scene: three guys standing around with boxes on their heads. I later wrote a column about what happened next:

It took seven seconds for the first newspaper photographer to take our picture. Within minutes—I am not making any of this up—we were surrounded by TV people, radio people and various other media people wishing to conduct interviews, which generally went like this:

MEDIA PERSON: Who are you?

DEMONSTRATOR: We're an organization called People with Boxes on Their Heads.

MEDIA PERSON: Why do you wear boxes on your heads?

DEMONSTRATOR: Basically because that's the name of our organization. People with Boxes on Their Heads.

ANOTHER DEMONSTRATOR (helpfully): It's an organization of
people who have boxes on their heads.

And so on. We gave several dozen interviews and were photographed
hundreds of times. I don't know how many interviews got broadcast,
but our pictures were in at least two Georgia newspapers and the
Baltimore Sun, and were included with a nice write-up about the rally
that went out nationwide on the Associated Press wire.

This was true: The People with Boxes on Their Heads were the lead
item in the AP roundup of convention protests. There was also a widely
circulated photo of the three of us in our little triangle, surrounded by a
mob of media people with cameras and microphones.

Erik and Bob also wrote columns about our experiment, so by the
next day we'd received a lot of publicity. Not everybody was amused.
I got phone calls in the press center from maybe a dozen newspaper
people. Some of them, the ones from papers that had printed the box-
head-protest story, were pretty angry; they wanted to know how come
we had hoaxed the media. My position was: We didn't hoax anybody.
We had boxes on our heads, and we *said* we had boxes on our heads.
You're the ones who decided this was a national news story.

Was I wrong? Had we, in fact, crossed an ethical line? Were we making a mockery of the press, an institution vital to our democracy?

Maybe! But it was pretty funny.

One of my favorite political columns from the 1990s didn't come
from a presidential campaign: It came from the 1991 Senate Judiciary
Committee hearing on Clarence Thomas's nomination to the Supreme
Court, after Anita Hill accused Thomas of sexual harassment. This was
a HUGE news story; the entire nation pretty much shut down to watch
the hearings on TV.

It was a serious subject, of course, but it was also highly entertaining, because of the personalities on the committee, including Joe Biden,

who absolutely loved to hear himself talk; Ted Kennedy, who, having had a few scandals of his own, was trying to keep a low profile; Orrin Hatch, who was hilariously prissy; Howell Heflin, who spoke v-e-r-r-r-r-y slowly; and Strom Thurmond, who spoke a language I would call Unintelligible Southern.

This was an easy column to write; it took me maybe an hour. It's technically a parody, but honestly it's not all that different from how the hearings sounded:

Chairman Biden: Judge Thomas, these past few days have been very, very hard for all of us—especially my good friend and colleague Sen. Kennedy, because it is not easy for a man to sit through three full days of hearings with a paper bag over his head—but before we let you go, there is just one more point I want to make, and it is a very, very important point, and I fully intend to make it if I ever get to the end of this sentence, which as you know and I know, Judge, is highly unlikely to occur during the current fiscal year, so . . .

Sen. Hatch: I want to say that I am disgusted. These are disgusting things that we have been talking about here, and I personally am disgusted by them. Pubic hair! Big organs! Disgusting. And yet we must talk about them. We must get to the bottom of this, no matter how disgusted we are, and believe me I am. We must talk about these matters, the pubic hair and the big organs, huge organs, because it just makes us sick, to think that these kinds of matters would come up—I refer here to the organs, and the hairs—that we here in the United States Senate would find ourselves delving deeply into these matters, to be frank, totally disgusts me, both aspects of it, the hair aspect AND the organ . . .

Chairman Biden: Thank you.

Sen. Heflin: Judge Thomas [30-second pause], I certainly appreciate [45-second pause] the fact [20-second pause] that [three-minute-20-second pause] my time is up.

Sen. Thurmond: Soamwhoan ben cudrin' mheah widm tan' bfust drang.

Translator: He says, "Somebody has colored my hair with what appears to be Tang breakfast drink."

Chairman Biden: Thank you. May I just add that the top of my own personal head appears to be an unsuccessful attempt to grow okra. But, Judge, as soon as I make this one final point we're going to let you go, because this has been very, very painful, and believe me I know what pain is, because at one time in my career I was the son of a Welsh coal miner, and let me just say, Judge, that when I do make this point, whatever it is, it will be something that I believe in very, very deeply, because I am the chairman, and I can talk as long as I want, using an infinite number of dependent clauses, and nobody can stop me.

Sen. Hatch: How big an organ? How many pubic hairs? These are the issues that we need to probe deeply into, no matter how much they disgust us! And believe me, nobody is more disgusted than I am! I am revolted that we are thinking about these disgusting things, day and night! Tossing and turning, trying to sleep, writhing and moaning and . . .

Sen. Kennedy (from under his bag): Are the cameras still here?

Chairman Biden: Judge, we know you're tired, and we're going to let
                  you go in just a moment here, just as soon as I make
                  this one point . . .

Sen. Thurmond: Deah wheah etn lonsh yep?

Translator: He says, "Did we eat lunch yet?"

So that was quite a show. But for quality political entertainment, it was hard to beat the presidency of Bill Clinton, which was like a *Mission: Impossible* movie, with Bill starring as a pudgy version of Tom Cruise, relentlessly pursued by powerful forces, trapped time and again in seemingly inescapable predicaments—*He can't possibly get out of this one! His semen is on the dress!*—only to wriggle out of it somehow.

I watched Clinton do this in the 1992 New Hampshire primary. He had been considered the front-runner for the Democratic nomination, but then he got hit with accusations of draft-dodging and philandering, and the overwhelming consensus emanating from the Sheraton Wayfarer bar was that he was toast. That was the theme of my first column from that primary:

MANCHESTER, NH—And so, once again, we in the professional news media have descended upon this bitter-cold, windswept, snow-covered state in an effort to answer the question that, every four years, burns in the mind of every American who cares about the democratic process, namely: Can we charge thermal underwear to our expense accounts?

Also we're interested in the presidential primary, which is coming up next week and should be very exciting because every single candidate involved, for both parties, is now seen by the press as a pathetic loser.

Our biggest loser right now is Bill Clinton, who was declared the front-runner several weeks ago despite the fact that nobody has the vaguest idea where he stands on any issues and his nose always seems to be stopped up. But we in the press always need a front-runner, because we need to have somebody who we can declare is faltering, and so we gave the job to Bill.

If you voters feel it's high-handed of us to make this kind of decision before any actual voter has actually voted, all I can say, by way of thoughtful explanation, is: Shut up. This is an ELECTION CAMPAIGN we're talking about. The public has NOTHING TO DO with it. If you voters want to have a say in it, you should get press credentials like everybody else.

So anyway, Bill was the front-runner for 15 or 20 minutes, after which we declared him to be in Falter Mode because of all these disgusting unsubstantiated rumors, which I will not dignify by repeating here, concerning Bill and Gennifer Flowers and Tammy Wynette and Donna Rice and the Brazilian national gymnastics team and draft evasion and an unsolved string of 17 convenience store robberies.

Bill's poll ratings are now dropping like a pig thrown out of a helicopter, and so we in the press have selected a new front-runner. We apparently were drinking heavily when we did this, because the choice we came up with is—get ready—Paul E. Tsongas. Really. This is a man so low-key that he may be capable of photosynthesis, a man who makes Michael Dukakis seem like James Brown.

Nevertheless he is our front-runner, and I'm sure he holds many important views on the issues. But right now the important thing for you, the voters, to bear in mind when considering him as a potential president is that the letters in "Paul E. Tsongas" can be rearranged to spell "Gaseous Plant."

A few days after I wrote that column, I caught up with Tsongas as he was leaving a campaign event. I asked him: "How do you respond to published reports that the letters in your name can be rearranged to spell 'gaseous plant'?" He paused thoughtfully, then said: "I see no scientific evidence that that's the case."

Tsongas was a smart guy. And he did in fact win New Hampshire. But Clinton, defying the Wayfarer wisdom, did well enough to stay in the race, and the rest is history. He was really, really good at politics. He was to nineties politics what Michael Jordan was to nineties basketball.

The night before the '92 New Hampshire primary, I went to dinner with a group of reporters and columnists. There were maybe ten of us, and we agreed we were all sick of New Hampshire and did not want to see or hear anything remotely connected to the primary. So we picked an out-of-the-way Italian restaurant in Manchester, not in the downtown area, nowhere near anybody's campaign headquarters.

We ate late, and by the time we were finishing we were the only diners in the restaurant. Toward the end of our meal, as the restaurant staff was closing up, the front door opened, and in walked three people: Dee Dee Myers, who was Clinton's press spokesperson; Gwen Ifill, who was covering Clinton for the *New York Times*; and Bill Clinton. Dee Dee and Gwen both looked exhausted; they rolled their eyes at our table, conveying the message *Can you believe this guy is still going?*

Clinton looked like he was having a great time, as if the most fun thing a person could do after a zillion soul-sucking days on the campaign trail was drive around Manchester late at night stopping wherever there might be a live voter. He smiled and waved at our table, then went into the kitchen, where he went around shaking hands with the staff. Then he came over to our group and—I will never forget this—walked around the table shaking everybody's hand, smiling and joking and saying something to every single one of us in such a way as to leave the distinct impression that he knew exactly who we all were. Which I still believe he did. In some cases, that made sense; some of us were well-known national political journalists. But some of us were humor columnists specializing in booger jokes. And I swear he knew us all.

Clinton then left, trailed, unhappily, by Dee Dee and Gwen, off to do more campaigning, leaving our table to marvel at what we'd just witnessed. We were a group of people who'd spent the past week or so trashing this guy's campaign, and he'd acted like we were all great pals, and even though we knew that he didn't *really* like us, he managed—this was his gift—to make us cynical ink-stained wretches feel, at least for a few nanoseconds, as though he did.

As he left the restaurant, somebody at our table said: "Goddammit, now *I* want to vote for him!"

Somebody else said: "Vote for him? I want to quit my job and campaign for him!"

Somebody else said: "Campaign for him? I want to have sex with him!"

We were kidding, of course. Sort of.

The story on the Republican side of the 1992 primary was that President George H. W. Bush, who as the incumbent was originally expected to have his renomination locked up, was facing an unexpectedly strong challenge from Patrick Buchanan. So Bush went to New Hampshire, bringing with him the massive bloated horde of security, staff and media that engulfs American presidents whenever they attempt to interact with the outside world. I caught up with the horde at a mall in Bedford:

> The big campaign news is that President Bush has announced that he has an Agenda and would like to be re-elected.
>
> Within seconds his campaign began to falter, so he came up here to make an appearance at a shopping mall, the idea being that he'll get in touch with ordinary citizens going about their ordinary lives in an ordinary way except that they cannot move because they are being controlled by enough police and security personnel to subdue North Korea. There was so much security that a lot of people couldn't even get into the mall, including some people who were actually attempting to shop.
>
> "But I'm not here for Bush," a woman with two small children was saying to a police officer guarding a mall entrance. "I'm just trying to get to a store."
>
> But he wouldn't let her in. It is against security regulations to ad-

mit ordinary citizens to a mall when the president is inside getting in touch with ordinary citizens.

"I'm voting for somebody else," said the woman, stomping off into the parking lot.

On a different day I caught up with First Lady Barbara Bush, who was campaigning for her husband:

In these difficult times, the No. 1 issue troubling American voters, on the eve of the crucial New Hampshire primary, is: hair care. That's why Barbara Bush came here over the weekend to visit the Continental Academie of Hair Design, which trains people to become hair technicians.

Before Mrs. Bush arrived, I spoke to one of the instructors, Earl Titus, who told me that the trainees received 1,500 hours of instruction in hair-related issues, including ethics. I asked him to give me an example of a hair ethic, and he said, "You don't lie to your client or steal from your client." So it's just like law school, only with more emphasis on conditioners.

Mrs. Bush arrived right on time with a festive entourage of Secret Service agents, who all decided on the spur of the moment to get their hair dyed purple and have nicknames like "Mojo" carved into their scalps.

I'm kidding, of course. The agents did what they always do, which is stare directly at you with an expression that makes it clear that they believe that you keep human body parts in your refrigerator. Mrs. Bush, on the other hand, went around to all the hair technicians and the women getting haircuts and smiled relentlessly at them and said how happy she was to see everybody. Being happy to see everybody is her job, and she's extremely good at it. Nothing disconcerts her. She could be going through a crowded room, greeting everybody, and suddenly she could encounter an eight-foot-tall rutabaga wearing a BUSH button, and she'd be happy to see it.

Barbara Bush looked like the world's kindliest grandmother, but she was a tough lady, and she had an edge to her. Sometimes, when she was making yet another campaign stop, dutifully smiling at whatever person or place or thing or haircut she was supposed to be admiring, you could see it in her eyes, a look that said, *Well this is ridiculous, but here we are.*

I know this because I experienced being on the receiving end of Mrs. Bush's looks. She was appearing at a reception in a donor's home; I was there as part of the press corps that had been traveling around New Hampshire in her motorcade. For some reason her photographer wanted a photo of us journalists, so he arranged us in a group around Mrs. Bush. I wound up right next to her, the two of us half-facing each other.

Maybe you've been in a situation like this. You're standing in close proximity to somebody famous. This person has no idea who you are. There is no reason for you to say anything, and anyway you have nothing to say. You know this in the part of your brain that is intelligent. But somewhere in one of your more primitive brain sectors, a clump of cells—the kind of cells responsible for basic, noncerebral bodily functions such as burping—have an idea.

Wow! they think. *We are standing RIGHT NEXT TO A FAMOUS PERSON! We must SAY SOMETHING!*

And so the burp cells hastily form what they believe to be a meaningful thought, and before one of the smarter lobes can stop them, they transmit it to your mouth, which, being one of the least intelligent organs in your body, immediately blurts it out.

That's what happened to me in the New Hampshire donor's house. As we stood posing for our photo, I announced to Barbara Bush, out of the blue, in an unnaturally perky voice: "I shop in the same supermarket as your son Jeb."

This was a true statement. Several times, while shopping at my Publix supermarket, I had seen Jeb Bush in the deli section. But clearly this was not a fact that Mrs. Bush would find interesting. This was not a fact that anybody on the planet would find interesting. *I* didn't find it particularly interesting. Yet I announced it to the First Lady of the United States.

Since we were standing maybe a foot apart, she had to respond. She turned toward me, and in her eyes I could clearly see what she was thinking, which was: *Why on earth would you tell me that?* But what she said to me was: "We saw Jeb recently. He just turned thirty-nine." Then she turned back to the photographer.

This was a gracious response from Mrs. Bush. Instead of pointing out that I had just made a ridiculously inane statement, she had created the illusion that we were having a conversation. We weren't, of course. We had made two statements that were unrelated except for the fact that they both contained the word "Jeb." But Mrs. Bush, a pro at handling these situations, had smoothly moved us past what could have been an embarrassing moment for me. She had bailed me out.

The intelligent part of my brain immediately recognized this and was grateful. *Thank you, Barbara Bush,* it was thinking.

Unfortunately my burp cells completely misread the situation.

Wow! they were thinking. *We are really hitting it off with First Lady Barbara Bush! We need to TELL HER SOMETHING ELSE!*

And so I heard my mouth—following up on the fascinating fact that I shopped at the same supermarket as Jeb—make the following statement to Mrs. Bush, regarding her son: "He's very tall."

Which was true. Jeb Bush was (and still is) quite tall. He had been for years. But we can safely assume Mrs. Bush was already aware of that fact. She turned toward me again, and now there was no mistaking the look in her eyes, which conveyed the message: *What is* wrong *with you?* Of course she was too classy to say that. What she said was: "He didn't just grow this year."

Then she turned back to the camera, and the photographer took the picture, and my conversation with the First Lady was over, which was good because God only knows what my burp cells would have come up with next.

Years later, I was one of the authors invited to speak at a fundraiser for Mrs. Bush's adult-literacy foundation. The Bushes held a luncheon for the authors at their home in Houston; when Michelle and I arrived,

George Bush met us at the front door and led us into the living room, where he started telling us an involved story about the rug. As he was talking, Barbara entered the room.

"George," she said to the former president of the United States, "they don't care about the rug."

"Right," he said, and that was the end of the rug talk.

Mrs. Bush turned out to be quite funny when she wasn't required to beam First Lady smiles at everything all the time. After a while I felt comfortable enough to tell her about my humiliating effort to converse with her in New Hampshire years before. She of course didn't remember that incident, but she assured me that I was by no means the only person who had turned into a blithering idiot in her presence. Which made me feel a little better.

But getting back to 1992: Barbara Bush's rival for the First Ladyship in that election was Hillary Clinton. She was smart and ambitious, and she envisioned herself as a different kind of First Lady, less focused on traditional ribbon-cutting-type activities and more involved with policy. But the polls showed that the public was uncomfortable with the idea of an assertive First Lady, so when the Democrats held their convention that summer in New York City, there was an effort to soften Hillary's image. Part of this effort involved having her host a tea for congressional wives, which I attended:

I finally caught up with the New Hillary Clinton. She has replaced the Old Hillary Clinton, who was unpopular with the public because she was going around discussing the issues and acting forceful and just generally appearing to have opinions.

This is, of course, unacceptable to the American public, which prefers its political wives to have a stay-in-the-background, stand-by-your-man, worshipful-gaze type of personality, as epitomized by Pat Nixon and most Labrador retrievers.

So a few months ago, when the Clinton campaign was faltering, party officials had Hillary abducted and taken to the top-secret Housewife Indoctrination Clinic, operated by Betty Crocker, where

Hillary was subjected to thousands of hours of *Ozzie and Harriet* reruns and was given massive intravenous doses of Lemon Pledge.

When she emerged she looked like the Old Hillary, but she was no longer shooting her mouth off about matters that frankly do not concern persons of the gal gender, such as the US government.

When I caught up with the New Hillary, she was talking about cookies. This took place in the Waldorf-Astoria Hotel, where Hillary was host to a tea for the wives of Democratic congresspersons.

She told the congressional wives that *Family Circle* magazine has gotten her into a contest against Barbara Bush to see who has the best chocolate-chip-cookie recipe. I am not making this campaign development up. Hillary told the wives to please vote for her cookie recipe, and they all applauded some more.

Then Hillary started talking about the Clinton-Gore ticket, and her voice started getting forceful, and it appeared as though she was just about to bring up some actual issues when her Democratic Party handlers, standing just out of sight, hit her with a tranquilizing dart, and the moment of danger was past.

As it happened, Hillary won the cookie-recipe contest, and she and Bill beat Barbara and George in the election.

The Clinton administration got off to a rocky start. Their big issue was healthcare reform, with Hillary heading the task force developing the legislation. Their initiative quickly became mired in the partisan bog that so often prevents Congress from actually doing anything. (As a libertarian, I approve of this system.)

By 1994, while the rest of the nation was obsessed with the O. J. Simpson trial, Washington was consumed by the healthcare issue. So the *Herald* sent me up there to see if I could make any sense of it, which—spoiler alert—I could not. Here's how I began my story:

For more than a year now, the Clinton administration, the Congress and scores of special-interest groups have debated the health-care issue with such intense passion that their photocopying machines routinely burst into flames.

This debate, although bitter at times, has resulted in a broad national consensus on two fundamental conclusions:

1. The United States has the best system of health care in the world.
2. Something needs to be done about this.

I spent a couple of days with the White House press corps, which, as I wrote, was in a state of open warfare with the Clinton administration:

> This hostility has always existed, of course, but it's especially intense now. The Clinton administration feels that the press has been extremely unfair, always focusing on negative stories, such as the allegation by Paula Jones that she was sexually harassed by Bill Clinton, while ignoring the positive stories, such as all the women—and there are literally dozens of them—who have NOT alleged that Bill Clinton sexually harassed them, as of yet. For its part, the press hates the Clinton administration because it's whiny and never wants to talk about anything except health care, which the press has been sick of since the 1992 New Hampshire primary.

I watched Dee Dee Myers, whom I'd last seen in the Italian restaurant in New Hampshire, give the daily press briefing, which was fascinating. It was like watching a tennis match between two players who can't stand each other, don't agree on the rules and sometimes aren't even using the same ball:

> Myers is the White House press secretary, which means her primary responsibility in the briefing is to never reveal anything remotely newsworthy to the press. The press, for its part, is responsible for repeatedly badgering Myers with questions that she has already refused to answer, until the hostility level in the room reaches the point where the smoke detectors go off. It's a ritualistic, decades-old dispute car-

ried on by whoever happens to be the White House press secretary and whoever happens to be in the press corps. It reminds you of an elderly married couple that's still arguing about a remark one of them made at a cocktail party in 1953.

The major topic of discussion at the press briefing was—brace yourself—health care. Specifically, the press wanted to know what "universal coverage" means. Myers said it means coverage for every American. This did not satisfy the press, which immediately demanded to know what "every American" means. Clearly this discussion had gone on before, because Myers immediately became a little testy and said, "I am not going to be drawn into a debate about numbers." This was followed by a lengthy effort on the part of the press to draw her into a debate about numbers, involving all kinds of hypothetical questions ("Dee Dee, IF the Congress passes a health-care bill covering 96 percent of all Americans, and IF it has a triggering mechanism mandating total coverage by the year 2002 contingent on certain conditions, and IF Train A leaves Cody, Wyo., traveling east at 47 miles per hour . . . ").

But Myers did not budge. I liked her. I sensed that, underneath her tough-gal exterior, she's a fun person, the kind of person you could go to a bar and have a few beers with and maybe, late at night, if you got lucky, draw into a debate about numbers.

Eventually the reporters gave up on defining "every American" and asked about the dollar. Myers, however, was not going to be tricked into saying anything about that, either.

"All comment on the dollar will be coming out of the Treasury Department," she said. This irritated the reporters. One of them told me, angrily, that the Treasury Department was also refusing to say anything about the dollar. I feigned disgust, although the embarrassing truth was that up to that moment I had not realized that there was anything going on with the dollar. There had been no mention of it in the O. J. Simpson hearings.

This was followed by some more testy questioning about the meaning of "every American," which in turn was followed by a sequence of questions from various reporters on President Clinton's recent trips to Camp David. Here, to the best of my ability to reconstruct it from my hastily scribbled notes, is the exchange:

VOICE: What is he doing up there? Can you tell us?

ANOTHER VOICE: Does he fish?

YET ANOTHER VOICE: Has he been doing any fishing?

MYERS: He has not been doing any fishing to my knowledge.

VOICE: Does he smoke?

MYERS: He has been known to chew on one.

VOICE: But he doesn't inhale!

[Laughter]

MYERS: So many creative minds in such a little room.

After a couple of days at the White House, during which I learned virtually nothing about healthcare reform, I went over to the Capitol to try to understand what Congress was doing about it. This turned out to be impossible:

On this day, two of the key rooms were in the Capitol, where the Democratic and Republican senators were separately holding their weekly caucuses.

A crowd of several dozen reporters had gathered in the corridor outside the caucus rooms; these reporters were, in a word, desperate. They were attempting to cover a story that would be stupendously complex even if there were only one health-care plan, and if all the major players would tell them honestly what was happening. But there were a number of plans, with new ones being formed at that moment; and different players were secretly making different deals regarding different parts of these different plans in different rooms all over town. So none of the reporters really knew what was going on, although they would all be expected to write authoritative stories for the next day's papers. Hence their desperation.

As senators emerged, one by one, from the caucuses, the reporters would instantly form dense clots around them, pressing close, trying to get them to reveal the latest health-care developments. The first senator I saw was John Breaux of Louisiana, who announced—I'm pretty sure I got this right—that he was rejecting his own health-care plan. Several reporters explained to me that Breaux and other Democrats were now waiting for a new plan, from Sen. Patrick Moynihan, chairman of the powerful Senate Finance Committee. They said Moynihan was introducing this plan with the specific intent of having it voted down by his committee.

"Why?" I asked.

"Because he wants to show that it can't pass," the reporters answered, as if that explained everything.

While I was trying to comprehend this, Sen. Bob Dole (R-Raptor) emerged from the caucus room, and it turned out that he had a new health-care plan.

"Tell us about your plan," said a reporter.

"It's very nice," said Dole.

(You think I'm making all this up, right?)

More senators emerged and were pounced on by reporters with health-care questions. I found myself getting swept up in the spirit, pressing forward toward the center of the clot, writing down incomprehensible notes like "EMPLOYER MANDATE TRIGGER." It was a media frenzy. If Lee Harvey Oswald had suddenly appeared in our midst, we would have asked him about health care.

One of the last senators to emerge was majority leader George Mitchell; the clot pounced on him for comments about Moynihan's plan, the one that everybody was eagerly awaiting because it was going to get voted down.

"I haven't seen the details, but I commend the chairman for his leadership," said Mitchell, in a fine demonstration of the veteran political leader's ability to say absolutely nothing on a moment's notice.

As Mitchell was leaving, somebody asked him about the Red Sox.

"As of seven days ago," he said, "they're five and two."

I wrote that down; it was the only solid information I got that day.

Ultimately the Clinton healthcare initiative went nowhere, and in the 1994 midterm elections the Republicans, led by Newt "Newt" Gingrich, gained control of Congress.

In 1996 the Republicans nominated Bob Dole, a war hero and skillful legislator who could be likable and funny in small-group situations. His problem was that when he made speeches, he tended to come across as old and cranky, like a guy complaining that somebody stole his egg-salad sandwich from the office refrigerator. He had no chance against Clinton, who easily won the 1996 election.

The dominant story during Clinton's second term was the impassioned yet remarkably inept effort by the Republican Congress to remove him from office on the constitutional grounds that he was a hound dog. This effort of course failed, because the American public already knew Clinton was a hound dog and generally liked him anyway, especially compared to, say, "Newt" Gingrich.

In 2000 the Republicans nominated George W. Bush in Philadelphia. During that convention I had a semi-intimate encounter with the Extremely Rev. Jerry Falwell, founder of the Moral Majority. He and I had both been booked on MSNBC as guests of Tom Brokaw and Tim Russert, who were broadcasting from the convention hall. As I explained in a column:

The Rev. Falwell was on the show to talk about gay people, whom, as a Christian, he sincerely and deeply loves, which is why he wants to inform them that they are degenerate perverts going to hell. I have no earthly idea why I was on the show. All I know is that, when the Rev. Falwell was done with his segment, a technician removed the earpiece from his ear, and, with the Rev. Falwell standing right next to me, our hips practically touching, the technician inserted the SAME EARPIECE, which was still warm, into MY ear.

Yes, there was penetration. Yes, there was probably an exchange of earwax. No, neither one of us was (as far as I know) wearing a condom. But so what? This is the year 2000, darn it! If two consenting male adults choose to share an earpiece, then it is nobody's business but their own. That is my view, and I am sure it is the Rev. Falwell's view, although I have not discussed this with him personally. (Jerry, if you're reading this, call me! I miss you, you big lug!)

The 2000 Democratic convention was held in Los Angeles, where the Democrats nominated Al Gore. Their convention was a lot more glamorous than the Republicans', because the Democrats attracted a glittering galaxy of A-list Hollywood stars, whereas the Republican galaxy was pretty much Bo Derek.

So there were some glitzy, exclusive parties happening in LA during the convention, and needless to say the press was not invited to any of them. Nevertheless I managed to get into one of the more exclusive parties, one that everybody was talking about, being thrown by the influential lobbying firm Patton Boggs. The way I got in was by posing, along with a group of cartoonists, as the security detail for the mayor of Los Angeles. Really.

This happened because of a friend of mine, Ted Habte-Gabr, who lives in Los Angeles. Ted is easily the most outgoing human being on the planet—a combination of schmoozer, entrepreneur,[53] cheerleader and lunatic, a man who will confidently ask anybody for anything, and usually gets whatever it is.

I met Ted in 1991 when I gave a speech at the University of Iowa, where he was a student and head of the lecture committee. At the time

---

53. Ted started and runs *Live Talks Los Angeles*, a popular series of onstage conversations involving writers, actors, musicians and others.

I was running for president of the United States. This is something I'd been doing as a joke every four years since the early eighties, strictly so I could write columns about it. I never did any actual campaigning, although I did have bumper stickers printed up with a variety of slogans, including:

DAVE BARRY FOR PRESIDENT
Yes, of the United States

DAVE BARRY FOR PRESIDENT
A Catchy Slogan Should Appear Here

DAVE BARRY FOR PRESIDENT
It's Time We Demanded Less

Ted promoted my Iowa speech as a "State of the Union Address and Presidential Debate." I actually got some national press coverage in the form of Adam Nagourney, a usually serious political reporter who then worked for *USA Today* and later went to the *New York Times*. He was doing a semi-tongue-in-cheek story about my campaign, and after my speech he joined me, Ted and some other students at a bar called Fitzpatrick's. In his *USA Today* story, Nagourney stated that I drank four beers that night. I responded to this allegation in a column:

> I was accompanied to Iowa by—this is still true—a reporter from *USA Today* (motto: "If You Didn't Read It in *USA Today*, It Probably Contained More Than 50 Words"). He wrote a story stating that, while at Fitzpatrick's, I consumed four beers and promised to appoint every student in the bar to the US Supreme Court. This is yet another example of the media's frenzied desire to dig up sensationalized "dirt." I want to set the record straight by presenting some facts that were "conveniently" left out of the *USA Today* story:

1. The *USA Today* reporter had AT LEAST three vodka–and–cranberry juices.[54]
2. The Supreme Court might benefit greatly by the addition of several hundred college students. ("WASHINGTON—In a landmark decision yesterday, the Supreme Court ruled 356–9 that the Constitution contains WAY too many big words.")

Anyway, at some point during the evening at Fitzpatrick's I appointed Ted as my campaign's field coordinator, and he has held that title ever since. He has done a far more diligent job of coordinating the field than I have of running for president. He once talked an Iowa farmer named Daryl Neitderhiser into letting me hold a baby pig for a photo op intended show my concern for agriculture. (This was tricky because Mr. Neitderhiser was seriously concerned that I would give his pig a disease.)

Ted has also persuaded many famous people to pose for photographs holding a "Dave Barry for President" bumper sticker. Among the people who've agreed, at Ted's request, to show their support for my candidacy (I have the photos to prove it) are Kurt Vonnegut, Steve Allen, Frank McCourt, Barry White, Jules Feiffer, Robert Goulet, Jane Smiley, Steve Martin, Magic Johnson, Charlton Heston, Christopher Hitchens, Al Roker, Hugh Hefner, Donny Osmond, several Playboy Playmates and Elmo.

But getting back to the 2000 Democratic convention: The mayor of Los Angeles at that time was Richard "Dick" Riordan, a very successful Republican businessman. Since I was in LA to cover the convention, Ted, as my field coordinator, asked the mayor if he would formally endorse my candidacy for president. Mayor Riordan, who had a quirky sense of humor, agreed.

And so a meeting was arranged. The site was the Pantry, a legendary Los Angeles coffee shop, which at the time Mayor Riordan owned. He was going to be there with his people; I was to join him for breakfast

---

54. This is true. It could easily have been four.

with my people. The problem was, the only people I had was Ted. So I recruited a group of cartoonists. I often hung around with cartoonists at the conventions, because they were usually looking for the same kinds of angles I was looking for, namely, stupid angles.

Five cartoonists—who among them have won roughly three hundred Pulitzer Prizes—accompanied me to the meeting: Mike Luckovich, Walt Handelsman, Dan Perkins, Rob Rogers and Chip Bok. We had a nice breakfast consisting of fried cholesterol, and the mayor, as promised, endorsed me for president. Then he happened to mention that he was going to be attending the exclusive Patton Boggs party that night. We immediately asked if we could accompany him as his security detail. To our surprise, as well as the surprise of his people, he said yes.

That night at nine p.m. the cartoonists, Ted and I gathered in the parking lot of the party venue, the Sunset Room in Hollywood. We had carefully prepared for our mission:

- We wore dark suits (I bought mine that afternoon).

- We wore sunglasses, despite the fact that it was nighttime.

- For security purposes we had given ourselves Secret Code Names, including "Kitchen Magician," "Thrusting Rod" and "Pocket Fisherman." I was "Magenta Eagle."

- We had cords plugged into our ears. These were coiled cords that we had removed from our hotel telephones. We stuck the other end of the cord into our suits, connected to nothing. This was our communications system.

Finally the mayor—we had assigned him the Secret Code Name "Sourdough"—arrived with his wife ("Pork Chop"). The mayor also had a real security detail from the Los Angeles Police Department, whose members did not appear thrilled to see us.

With the mayor leading the way, we all went up to the venue entrance, which was manned by Patton Boggs people, there to keep the riffraff out. They clearly did not want to let us in. This was understandable, since we were a group of idiots wearing sunglasses at night and pretending to talk in code ("Pocket Fisherman, this is Magenta Eagle, do you copy?") into hotel phone cords stuck into our ears. But before they could say anything, Mayor Riordan—leadership like this comes along once in a generation—pointed to us and said, "They're with me." And the gatekeepers had no choice but to let us pass.

Thus we got into the exclusive Patton Boggs party that everybody was talking about. Which, to be honest, was nothing special. I mean, it was nice, but as is so often the case with exclusive parties, it was basically a bunch of people standing around.

For a little while we provided security for the Riordans, mainly by being assholes. At one point some distinguished-looking people—my vague recollection is that they had something to do with a foreign government, possibly Spain—wanted to talk to the mayor, and we blocked their path, informing them that, for security reasons, they had to keep back. And they did!

Fortunately before we could create an international incident we found the bar, which needless to say was an open bar. We remained there for the duration, leaving Sourdough and Pork Chop to handle their own security.

That evening was definitely the highlight of the 2000 presidential race, as far as I was concerned. The lowlight was the actual election, specifically the performance of my state, Florida. For the life of us, we Floridians could not figure out which candidate we had voted for. Was it George W. Bush? Al Gore? Maybe William Shatner? We had no idea!

For weeks the nation was treated to the spectacle of Florida election officials squinting at ballots that appeared to have been attacked by rabid weasels, trying to figure out what the voters who turned these ballots in might have been thinking, if "thinking" is the right word. That election was what cemented Florida's reputation as the Stupid State (Official motto: "Florida—You Can't Spell It Without Duh"). Florida still has this reputation, although people keep moving here from states such as New York that are allegedly smarter and more likely to remain above sea level, so go figure.

In the end, Bush was declared the winner. Pretty soon after that we had 9/11, and then the Iraq War. So in the 2004 election the big issue was the War on Terror. At the time it was widely believed that another major attack on US soil was imminent, and we were all vigilantly defending the homeland by taking such measures as not boarding commercial aircraft carrying more than 3.4 ounces of shampoo. (We're still not doing this, but now we think it's stupid.)

Mainly what I remember about the 2004 political conventions was the massive security, and the general vibe of paranoia. Knight Ridder, the company that owned the *Miami Herald*, ordered all reporters and photographers who were going to the conventions or the Olympics (I did both) to attend special terrorism training classes. These were taught by a pair of badass British paramilitary dudes who basically scared the crap out of us, telling us what we should do if we saw a radioactive cloud (run away) or if one of our colleagues was spurting blood from an important artery (faint).[55]

Knight Ridder also issued each of us emergency supplies, which I wrote about:

> I've been issued an Anti-Terrorist Kit. Really. It consists of an "evacu-ation hood" that you put over your head in case of gas attack; a flash-light that you shine in the terrorists' eyes to temporarily blind them; and a whistle you use to scare them (or yourself, if you blow it inside your evacuation hood).

We were told to carry our Anti-Terrorist Kit everywhere, but this proved to be a problem when I tried to take mine through the security checkpoint for the Democratic convention at the FleetCenter in Boston:

---

55. No, seriously, you're supposed to apply pressure. But I would definitely faint.

Three security people examined my kit; one of them held up the flashlight and asked me (I swear) if it was an approved Democratic National Committee flashlight. When I said I didn't know, they told me they had to confiscate it. So I said: "How am I supposed to fight terrorism without a flashlight? Ha ha!" I used a jocular tone to indicate that I was a trained humor professional making a joke, but the security personnel did not seem at all amused, so I strode away quickly, before they decided to take my whistle.

I ended up just leaving my Anti-Terrorist Kit at the hotel, which is also what most of my colleagues did. Fortunately the terrorists, apparently unaware of how vulnerable we were, did not attack.

The Democrats nominated John Kerry and John Edwards; the Republicans renominated George W. Bush and Dick Cheney. The Bush-Cheney ticket won a second term, of which the unquestioned highlight, from the perspective of a person working in the humor industry, was when Vice President Cheney, while attempting to bring down a quail with a shotgun, shot a prominent attorney. As Wikipedia notes: "It was the first time someone had been shot by a sitting vice-president since Alexander Hamilton was shot in a duel by Aaron Burr in 1804."

Fortunately the attorney recovered, and the vice president was not charged. In my Year in Review for 2006, I explained: "Local authorities ruled the shooting was an accident, noting that if the vice president were going to intentionally shoot somebody, it would be Nancy Pelosi."

The theme of the 2008 presidential race, after eight years of Bush-Cheney, was Change. As I wrote from New Hampshire:

Everybody in this race, Democrat and Republican, is now officially for Change. They get more fervent about Change every day; it's only a matter of time before they start calling for tactical air strikes on Washington.

The big story on the Democratic side was that Hillary Clinton, who was on record as being in favor of Change and who had been heavily favored to win the nomination, was all of a sudden being seriously challenged by this newcomer Barack Obama. When he got to New Hampshire Obama was drawing huge, enthusiastic crowds to his rallies, as I reported:

> I drove to Derry to attend a jam-packed event for Barack Obama, who is surging ahead in the polls and is now basically a rock star. People were cheering, chanting and throwing their underwear at him. And those were the journalists.
>
> Just kidding! Sort of.
>
> Anyway, Obama noted that he is for Change, and that he was for Change before Change was cool. He is unchanged in his commitment to Change. He did not mention his arch-rival, Hillary Clinton, by name, although he made several subtly veiled references to "my opponent, the screeching harpy."
>
> Just kidding! Sort of.

The Obama-Clinton competition got pretty testy, and there was still antagonism between the two factions when the Democrats convened in Denver to nominate the Obama-Biden ticket:

> Already there has been sporadic gunfire between the Barack Obama and Hillary Clinton delegates. Political observers see this as indication that there is still some underlying tension between the two sides. Yes, Clinton has been making speeches urging her supporters to work for Obama; but at the same time she has also been using what one Obama adviser described as "a lot of air quotes."
>
> It's hard to blame Sen. Clinton for being bitter. Here she is, the smartest human ever, PLUS she spent all those years standing loyally behind Bill Clinton wearing uncomfortable pantyhose (I mean Hillary was, not Bill) (although there are rumors), PLUS she went to the trouble and expense of acquiring a legal residence in New York State so she could be a senator from there, PLUS she assembled a

team of nuclear-physicist-grade genius political advisors, PLUS she spent years going around to every dirtbag community in America explaining in detail her 23-point policy solutions for every single problem facing the nation including soybean blight. And after all that, she loses the nomination to a guy who has roughly the same amount of executive governmental experience as Hannah Montana. Hillary is like: "Are you KIDDING me?"

The Republicans nominated John McCain, who shocked the political world by selecting, as his running mate, Alaska governor Sarah Palin, a person almost nobody outside of Alaska had heard of. She was THE topic of conversation when Republicans convened in St. Paul, Minnesota:

As the Republican convention nears its conclusion and John McCain prepares to make his acceptance speech, we in the news media, having finally grown weary of the endless speculation and gossip about Sarah Palin, are turning our attention, at long last, to additional speculation and gossip about Sarah Palin.

This seems to be all anybody talks about at this convention. It is Palin-Palooza. Critics continue to ask how much McCain really knew about Palin before he selected her as his running mate, especially in light of the fact that he keeps referring to her, in speeches, as "whatshername." But McCain's staff insists that it conducted a thorough investigation of Palin, which included not only inspecting her driver's license, but also, according to a campaign spokesperson, "reading almost her entire Wikipedia article."

Still, questions remain. Right now there are reporters swarming all over Wasilla, Alaska, digging up information about Palin's past. So far, this is what they have learned:

- Wasilla is not a hotbed of luxury hotels.

- Likewise, restaurants.

In the general election the Obama-Biden ticket won easily, which meant that on Inauguration Day, January 20, 2009, two historic things happened:

1. Barack Obama became our first Black president.

2. I marched in his inaugural parade.

Yes. I happen to be a member of the World Famous Lawn Rangers, an elite, exclusive marching unit whose membership is strictly limited to anybody who wants to join. The Rangers, who perform precision parade maneuvers with lawnmowers and brooms, are based in the small central Illinois town of Arcola, which proudly bills itself as the Broomcorn Capital of the World, because it once was a major producer of the corn used to make old-fashioned brooms. Every September Arcola holds the Broomcorn Festival, featuring a parade, the highlight of which is the World Famous Lawn Rangers.

In 1992 Pat Monahan, one of the founding Rangers, invited me to march with them in the parade, and of course as a professional humor columnist I had no choice but to accept. I traveled to Arcola, where I was issued a broom, a lawnmower, a cowboy hat and a black Lone Ranger–style mask to protect my secret identity. Before I could march, I had to go through Rookie Orientation, a grueling ordeal lasting nearly ten minutes, during which I learned the Rangers' two elite precision marching maneuvers:

- "Walk the Dog," in which you push your mower around in a small clockwise circle with one hand while holding your broom aloft with the other;

- "Cross and Toss," in which you and the Ranger marching next to you (we march in two columns) exchange sides, then toss your brooms to each other and catch them, unless you drank too much beer during Rookie Orientation.

I'll never forget that first parade, marching down Arcola's main street with my fellow Rangers, pushing our mowers, performing our maneuvers and seeing the looks on the faces of the people in the crowd, some of whom were so overwhelmed by our elite precision that they could barely remain standing. On that day I became a proud Ranger, and I've marched in a number of Broomcorn parades since.

The Rangers also sometimes march in other parades; they will march in any parade that will have them. In 2003, they were marching in the St. Patrick's Day parade in Chicago when they had a fateful encounter with an ambitious young politician campaigning for the US Senate. That politician, as you have no doubt guessed, was Abraham Lincoln.

No, seriously, it was Barack Obama. The Rangers got him to pose for a photo with them, in which he is grinning broadly and triumphantly holding aloft a toilet plunger. (When the Rangers march, the column leaders use toilet plungers to signal which precision maneuver we're supposed to perform.)

In 2008, when Obama won the election, Pat Monahan remembered that photo, and he submitted an application to the inauguration organizers to have the Rangers march in the parade. When he told me this, I assured him that he was insane. Inaugural parades traditionally feature highly disciplined military units and bands that practice for countless hours, wear matching uniforms and almost never have to urinate in mid-parade because of overconsumption of beer. There was absolutely no way, I assured Pat, that the Rangers would be allowed to march.

But I was wrong. Maybe the organizers wanted to incorporate some humor into the parade. Maybe they just happened to be fans of the broom industry. But for whatever reason, the Rangers were accepted.

And so on that cold January day in Washington, with night falling, fifty-six of us Lawn Rangers stepped out onto the parade route, holding brooms and pushing lawnmowers that had been trucked in from Arcola, one of which displayed the Obama plunger photo. We'd been waiting for hours, and we were very cold. I later wrote a column describing the scene:

By now it is dark, and the parade crowd is sparse, consisting largely of police officers on hand to control the nonexistent parade crowd. But we put on a show anyway, executing our two precision lawnmower maneuvers. Since we have not practiced, our first few efforts are rusty, but the spectators are clearly impressed, as indicated by their laughter.

As we move up Pennsylvania Avenue, the crowd picks up a little, but we can still see basically every face. Every now and then my column partner, Bernie Casella, shouts to a spectator, "Thanks for coming!"

Finally we turn a corner onto a brilliantly illuminated street. Ahead we can see the reviewing stands set up in front of the White House, and the special enclosed area for the presidential party. This is it.

With renewed energy, we push our mowers forward, and suddenly there they are, looking at us from just a few feet away: President and Mrs. Obama, and Vice President Biden. The president is pointing to the mower with his plunger picture, and saying something to the First Lady. And they are laughing. Whew.

We perform a precision lawnmower maneuver for the presidential party. In a few seconds it's over, and we're moving on, back into the darkness, and the cold.

But we're feeling good. Because we have made a statement here tonight. Our statement is: Yes, an inauguration is a serious event; but it is also a time to celebrate the diversity of this great nation, which includes all kinds of people, some of whom are clowns.

The president seemed to get that. On behalf of all the Rangers, I say to him: Sir, we wish you the best in dealing with the many huge challenges you face. And if you ever want to march with us again, we will keep your plunger warm.

For the record, Obama—I'm sure he had his reasons—did not march with the World Famous Lawn Rangers after being elected president. Nevertheless the Democrats renominated him in 2012, when his Republican opponent was Mitt Romney.

Romney's biggest challenge, as I noted in a column from the GOP convention in Tampa, was to appear relatable to ordinary people:

> The Republican convention finally got going Tuesday with a parade of speakers taking the stage to express the official theme of the evening, "Mitt Romney: You're Darned Tooting He's Human!"
>
> This theme is intended to counteract what the Republicans see as their candidate's biggest weakness, which is that when many voters look at Mitt, they do not see a regular person like themselves. They see this tall, fit, handsome, rich Mormon with a square jaw and perfect hair and a blond wife and at least 23 tall handsome clone sons; a man who appears to be calculating and reserved; a man who has never once, even at a wedding reception, gotten hammered and danced the Funky Chicken and then passed out face-down in the prime rib.
>
> Voters see this, and they say to themselves: "This man can't possibly relate to me and my everyday problems, such as my financial woes, my hemorrhoids, and this tendency I have to talk to myself."
>
> So the Republicans brought out a parade of humanizers, with the star being Mitt's wife, Ann. She talked, movingly, about a completely different Mitt Romney, a Mitt Romney whom most people have never seen, a Mitt Romney who is funny, spontaneous, tender, laid-back, five feet tall, overweight, bald and—in some states—Jewish.

Despite receiving the endorsement of his wife, Romney lost to Obama. That was the last election we had that was relatively drama-free, especially compared to what came next.

If the 2016 election proved anything, it's that smart, highly educated, impressively credentialed people—people who consider themselves to be far more informed than the average citizen—sometimes have no clue what is actually going on. As it happens my profession, journalism, is full of such people.

During the 2016 Republican convention I went to a dinner with a group of journalists and political professionals. It was a private, off-the-record gathering, so I won't name names, but trust me when I tell you that this was an impressive group—famous, successful, respected people. And they all knew with 100 percent certainty that Hillary Clinton was going to defeat Donald Trump in the general election. *Everybody* in the political world knew this.

I certainly knew it. I'd been making fun of Donald Trump in books and columns for literally decades. I'd even made fun of his presidential aspirations, way back in 1999, when he flew to Miami on what was billed as a trip to explore the possibility of a candidacy. I followed him around that day and wrote a column, which said in part:

Potential presidential timber Donald Trump, who, by his own admission, is "the very definition of the American success story," came to Miami Monday on an exploratory mission to find out whether he is hugely popular or what. He arrived at Miami International Airport (motto: "You Expect to Get Your Luggage BACK?") shortly after 10 a.m. in a private 727 jet, which was easy to spot because of the big gleaming gold letters on the side, spelling out the name "RYDER."

No, seriously, they spelled "TRUMP," the name that appears on all of Trump's casinos, hotels, condos, ex-wives, etc. On the Trump plane with Trump was the Trump entourage, which included a number of Trump employees, a Trump bodyguard who looked like a UPS truck wearing a suit, and the official Trump girlfriend, Melania Knauss, who, it goes without saying, is a supermodel.

Trump and his entourage then motorcaded, with a police escort, to the Bay of Pigs veterans library and museum in the heart of Little Havana. There, Trump told the standing-room-only crowd that "Fidel Castro actually has done some good things."

No, I'm kidding again. He said that Castro is bad. This courageous stance was a big hit with the crowd.

Next, everybody motorcaded over to the Radisson Mart Plaza Hotel for a press conference, where Trump, speaking frankly, revealed, "I've done very well at everything I've ever done." He said that he has taken a look at the other candidates, specifically Al Gore and George W. Bush, and he has not been impressed.

"Let me ask you," he said, in a quote that I am not making up. "Did they make billions of dollars in a short period of time? No. Could they make billions of dollars in a short period of time? I don't think so."

It's hard to argue with that. For too long this country has been run by losers who never once made a billion dollars in a short period of time. Abraham Lincoln is only one example.

That was only one of a bunch of columns I've written over the decades making fun of Trump and his rampant blowhardiness. So in 2016 I, along with all the smart people, viewed his candidacy as basically a joke. Everybody assumed Hillary Clinton would win.

One problem with that assumption was that the Democrats were not super-unified. Clinton had an unexpectedly tough time beating Bernie Sanders in a fight for the Democratic nomination that got pretty nasty. When the Democrats held their convention in Philadelphia, there was a lot of hostility between the Clinton and Sanders delegates; my impression was they hated each other more than either side hated Trump. I wrote about this in a column from the opening session:

The gaveling and the Boyz II Men portions of the Democratic convention went smoothly, but right after that there was a major outbreak of non-unity. This happened during—I am not making this up—the invocation. It was delivered by the Rev. Cynthia Hale, who was basically asking God to bless the Democratic Party. It went OK until she said the words "Hillary Rodham Clinton."

At that point the hall erupted, with the Bernie Sanders delegates shouting "BERNIE!" and the Clinton delegates shouting "HILLARY!" It was so loud that for a while the Rev. Hale was unable to say anything else to God, who at this point, having presumably also monitored the Republican convention, was up there rolling His eyeballs and thinking about going third party, or maybe even creating a new planet.

The Rev. Hale finally got through the invocation, after which they had the Pledge of Allegiance, which went smoothly, but only because it does not mention Hillary Clinton.

There continued to be sporadic outbreaks of disunity throughout the day, but by evening things had calmed down. The most anticipated speaker of the night was Sanders, who issued a heartfelt appeal to his followers to support Clinton on the grounds that "otherwise they will shoot my dog."

No, seriously, Sanders gave Clinton a strong endorsement. Granted, he had a pained expression when he did so, but he always has a pained expression. Even when he's saying something upbeat he looks like a man passing a kidney stone the size of a box turtle.

The Republicans held their convention in Cleveland. Many high-level Republicans—who also expected Trump to lose—didn't attend, as I noted in my first column from there:

As the old saying goes, "You can't spell 'fun' without using some of the letters in 'Republican.'" So it looks like Cleveland is in for a rollicking good time, because the GOP convention is in town, and the whole gang is here!

OK, not the whole gang. A large sector of the Republican Party establishment had to bow out of the convention at the last minute when it remembered that it had a haircut appointment. Currently the highest-ranking elected Republican official here is Arthur A. "Bud" Klampf, deputy vice mayor of Ant Mound, Arkansas, who is scheduled to deliver what has been billed as "a major prime-time address, assuming he can locate his dentures."

But there will still be plenty of excitement, with the highlight expected to come Tuesday, when the Republican delegates, barring a last-minute commando assault led by George Will in a camouflage bow tie, are expected to nominate Donald J. Trump, who according to recent polls actually has a chance to defeat Hillary Clinton and become president of the United WAIT WHAT ARE YOU SERIOUS??

Oops! I allowed my mask of professional-journalism objectivity to slip there. We professional journalists are freaking out over the fact that no matter how hard we try to explain to the public that Trump is unqualified, a lot of the public keeps right on liking him and his bold vision for America consisting of whatever happens to cross his mind at a given moment. We journalists are like, "What is WRONG with you people? Why aren't you LISTENING to us?!? We're PROFESSIONAL JOURNALISTS WITH VERIFIED TWITTER ACCOUNTS!!!"

Sorry, I had to get that out of my system.

When I wrote that column, I was kidding about Trump's chances of winning—I genuinely didn't think he had any—but I wasn't really kidding about the news media's loss of objectivity. It's no secret that reporters generally tend to be more liberal than conservative. But the political reporters I've known and worked with over the decades, whatever their leanings, genuinely tried to be balanced and professional in their coverage. I believe the mainstream media did a pretty good job of covering politics fairly. Until Trump.

For the record: I can't stand Trump. He's a narcissistic jerk and a liar, and his behavior on January 6 was despicable. I'd never vote for him.

But I don't think anybody can credibly deny that much of the established national news media, the big papers and networks, leaned anti-Trump in their coverage, in big ways and small.

The argument I've heard from some of my colleagues for unbalanced coverage—for going after Trump more aggressively than we go after his opponents, and for downplaying news that might benefit him—is that he is uniquely corrupt and dangerous, an existential threat of Hitlerian magnitude, and therefore we journalists should—in fact must—abandon our neutrality.

The problem with this argument is that when the public sees us taking sides—and the public definitely sees it—we lose the only reason we had any influence with the public in the first place: our credibility. We become just another partisan voice in a cacophonous chorus, one more basement blogger.

As I write these words, public confidence in the news media has sunk to a dismally low level. Way too many people simply no longer trust us to be fair and truthful. And I hate to say this, but I don't know if we can win them back. I do know we won't win them back by insisting that the problem is not that we've made mistakes, but that people are too stupid to agree with us.

For the record: I have friends—smart people, people I respect—who think that I'm completely wrong about this issue. They believe that the media coverage of Trump has been, if anything, too forgiving; that in trying to be fair, the media have allowed him to get away with a level of dishonesty that wouldn't be tolerated from any other politician.

So maybe I'm wrong. I don't think so. But maybe.

Anyway, getting back to the 2016 election: Trump won, and politics has been a shitstorm ever since. I haven't been on the campaign trail since then, partly because of COVID, partly because I'm old, and partly because it doesn't seem to be as much fun as it used to be.

Speaking of fun: This chapter has become way too serious. Let's move on to happier topics.

CHAPTER SEVEN

BOOKS, MUSIC
AND MOVIES

IN JUNE OF 1984 I GOT A PHONE CALL, OUT OF THE BLUE, from a woman in Los Angeles named Shirley Wood. She told me she was a talent coordinator for *The Tonight Show*, and she was thinking about booking me as a guest to be interviewed by JOHNNY FREAK-ING CARSON.

She didn't actually shout in capital letters, but that's how it sounded in my brain. Because in 1984 the Carson show was huge. Everybody watched it, and all the big stars were guests on it. An appearance on *The Tonight Show* could make a comedian's career.

Carson also sometimes had authors on, but usually they were big-name bestsellers like Truman Capote. I was an extremely small name, with two published books. The first was a collection of my early newspaper columns called *Bad Habits*, which had reached a nationwide readership of my mom. My second book was *The Taming of the Screw*, a modest little paperback published in 1983 by Rodale Press. It was a parody of do-it-yourself manuals for homeowners, full of terrible advice. For example, I said that the best way to fix a clogged commode was to discharge a firearm at it. In fact I'd wanted the book to be titled *Shoot Your Toilet*, but somebody at Rodale Press thought that was too crude.

My publicity campaign for *The Taming of the Screw* consisted of going on one local morning talk show on a Philadelphia TV station. This appearance did not cause sales to soar. As far as I could tell, nobody watched it. I'm not sure the cameraman watched it. But somehow, nearly a year later, a tape of that appearance made its way into the hands of Shirley Wood. She auditioned me over the phone by asking me questions about sections of the book, then listening to my attempts to give funny answers. After each answer I gave, she would say either "No" or "OK." She did not laugh once. But somehow she decided I was *Tonight*-worthy, and she booked me on the show.

So that was my second TV appearance. I went from a local show nobody watched to a national show millions of people watched. *The Tonight Show* flew me from Philadelphia to Los Angeles and picked me up in a limo—I had never been in a limo—that took me to the studio, where I was ushered to a dressing room with my name on the door. I didn't have to dress—I had flown in the clothes I'd wear on the show—so I just sat around my personal dressing room being nervous until Shirley Wood came in and went over the questions Carson would ask. Then she walked me to the backstage bar and got me a tall glass filled with wine, which she ordered me to drink, which I did. Then I stood around continuing to be nervous for an hour or so. And then I was on *The Tonight Show*.

Me on the Tonight Show with Johnny Freaking Carson.

It went great. It turned out that Johnny Carson—prepare for an insight—was really good at interviewing. As I later wrote about my experience:

What everybody asked me later was: "What's Carson like?" The answer is: How the hell would I know? In the entire seven minutes during which I sat next to him on national television, he did not once lean over and confide in me what he is like. But he was wonderfully professional, I will tell you that. He set me up for all the jokes, and he let me have the laughs. He didn't get the least bit annoyed when, in my eagerness to answer him, I kept interrupting his questions. I mean, he could have said: "Dave, I know that you know these questions, inasmuch as you and Shirley Wood discussed them for an hour today, but it's conceivable that some members of the audience may not know them." But he didn't. So after the first minute I realized I was in good hands and it was going to be fine, and by the end of the show I was actually enjoying myself, right up until I threw up on Dick Cavett.

That was a joke, of course; I did not throw up on Dick Cavett. But I could have: I sat right between him and Johnny Carson. I even had a tiny private moment with Carson, in which he joked about the premise of my book. When the segment was done and the red camera light went off, he lit a cigarette, turned to me, and said, "I used to try to do it yourself. [Pause.] You can't do shit yourself."

Less than three hours later, I was sitting in the coach section of a red-eye flight on the way back to Philadelphia, wide awake, surrounded by dozing non-celebrities who were unaware that in their midst was a person who had just been interviewed by JOHNNY FREAKING CARSON.

Many people saw the broadcast of that interview, which definitely sold some books and opened some doors. Although not all of these were doors I should have gone through. For example, I was contacted by a nice couple who owned a hardware store on Cape Cod. They thought my Carson appearance was hilarious, and they wanted me to come to their store and do a book-signing event. They were very enthusiastic about this idea. Their theory was that since my book was about home repair, their hardware-store customers would love it. It was a perfect fit! I'd sell a lot of books! And if I paid for my transportation up there, they'd pay for part of the cost of the motel!

For some reason—most likely because I was an idiot—this sounded like a solid plan to me. So on a Friday I drove up to Cape Cod, which is not all that close to suburban Philadelphia, and on Saturday I did an event at the nice couple's hardware store. They had ordered more than a hundred copies of my book, and they had promoted my appearance by taping up a little sign in the store window. They had scheduled me to be there for four hours.

To the best of my recollection, and I believe I'm being generous, I sold five books. It may have been fewer. It turned out that the primary reason why people go to a hardware store is to buy hardware. They're not really in the market for a humor book, even if the author has been on national TV.

At first, when customers entered the store, the nice couple would drag them over to me and tell them how hilarious I was on Carson and point out that I had a book for sale. This announcement was inevitably followed by several seconds of awkward silence, which is the sound people make when they're trying to figure out how they can edge away without buying your book.

After going through this excruciating experience several times, I asked the nice couple to please stop trying to get random customers to buy my book. I spent the rest of the four hours wandering around the store looking at hardware. After a while I was familiar enough with the stock that when customers mistook me for an employee (this happened several times) I was able to help them find what they were looking for.

That's the nature of author celebrity for most authors who aren't Stephen King. There are times when you can actually feel sort of famous, such as when you're being interviewed by Johnny Carson. But there are many more times when you are reminded how far down authors rank in the celebrity ecosystem, as we see in this list:

Top 30 Celebrity Occupations

1. Taylor Swift
2. Major movie star such as Tom Cruise
3. Musical superstar other than Taylor Swift
4. Star athlete
5. Kardashian
6. President of the United States
7. Major TV star
8. Elon Musk
9. Whoever is currently dating Taylor Swift
10. Stephen King
11. Celebrity DJ
12. Major Internet influencer you've never heard of but your kids have
13. Supermodel
14. (Tie) The GEICO Gecko and "Flo" of Progressive Insurance
15. Celebrity chef
16. Celebrity fashion designer
17. Celebrity billionaire other than Elon Musk
18. Person doing some idiot thing in a viral video
19. The Pope
20. Stand-up comedian with a Netflix special
21. Member of the British royal family
22. "Reality" TV show star
23. The Dalai Lama
24. Minor movie star such as that guy, whatshisname, in that movie
25. Whoever was previously dating Taylor Swift
26. Vice president of the United States
27. TV weatherperson
28. Nobel Prize winner
29. Author other than Stephen King
30. Member of Congress

As we see, authors rank, celebrity-wise, below everybody except Congress. That's because, compared to other forms of popular entertainment, including professional cornhole, the book industry is small potatoes.

How small? Let's look at the numbers. In the book business, it's considered a big deal for a book to make one of the various *New York Times* bestseller lists. Even if a book barely manages to make it to the bottom of a list and remains on it for only a single week, every piece of publicity associated with that book forever after will declare that it's a *New York Times* bestseller. I know this because some of my books fall into that category.

Guess how many copies a book has to sell in a week to make it onto a *Times* list. Never mind, I'll tell you: a thousand books, give or take. That's right: If, in a given week, the number of people in the entire world who buy your book is slightly less than the average attendance at *a single game* of the Central California minor league baseball team the Modesto Nuts,[56] then your book could be a *New York Times* bestseller.

So every book you sell matters. This is why most authors spend a lot of time and energy promoting their books at the retail level. This is why they go to bookstores—or even, if they are stupid, hardware stores—and do book-signing events, despite the risk that few people, or even no people, will show up. This is why authors obsessively check their rankings on Amazon, and become inordinately excited when their book skyrockets from number 63,981 all the way up to 47,828. (To be fair, some authors say they never check their Amazon rankings. These authors are lying.)

This is also why authors go on book tours, where they will do anything to sell copies of their book. At least I did.

For example, in 1996 I was in St. Louis on a book tour when I got a call from a producer on *The Oprah Winfrey Show*. This was a very exciting call for me, ranking up there with the *Tonight Show* call, because Oprah sold a ton of books. Any book she chose for her book club instantly became a bestseller. I wasn't being considered for that honor, of course; Oprah's club was for serious, important books that did not

---

56. According to Wikipedia, the average attendance at a Modesto Nuts game in 2023 was 1,259.

contain booger jokes. But just having a book mentioned by Oprah on her show was a big deal for an author.

The producer said she was interested in having me be part of the guest panel for a show the following day. The theme of the show was "Things We Do in Secret." We guests would each confess to something we had done wrong, and then do something, on air, to make it right. The producer wanted to know if I had something I could confess to.

Of course I said yes. To get on Oprah's show, I would have claimed sole responsibility for the JFK assassination. But the crime I came up with was theft. Some years earlier, I'd stayed at a Hyatt hotel that had a plastic sign in bathroom, which read:

> Our towels are 100 percent cotton. Should you wish to purchase a set, they are available in the gift store. Should you prefer the set in your bathroom, a $75 charge will automatically be added to your bill.

This was Hyatt's polite way of saying: If you steal our towels, we'll charge you seventy-five bucks.

So I stole the sign. I took it home and put it in our guest bathroom, where it amused guests for several years.

When I told this story to the Oprah producer, she said it was perfect. She said I'd tell my story on air, then drop the sign into a "give-back" box, where they'd be collecting things that people had stolen. The producer said it was "essential" that I return the sign on the air.

"OK!" I said. "No problem!"

Except there was a problem: I was in St. Louis, the show was in Chicago the next day, and the sign was in Miami. I called Michelle and told her to FedEx the sign to Chicago the fastest possible way, but I wasn't sure it would get there in time. If it didn't, I wasn't sure I'd be on the Oprah show. I was seriously worried about this.

Then a realization struck me: I was staying at a Hyatt hotel in St. Louis, *and my room had a plastic sign.* This one explained the hotel's no-smoking policy, but from a distance there would be no way to tell.

So I stole that sign.

In the end, the original sign made it to Chicago on time, and I returned it on air, under the approving gaze of Oprah and her studio audience. But my point is, in order to appear in a show about correcting past wrongdoings, I was perfectly willing to steal again *and* lie. To Oprah!

You do what you have to on a book tour. Several times I went on Bill Maher's show, back when it was called *Politically Incorrect*, to be on panels debating the serious issues of the day. The entire reason I went on those shows was that they promised to mention my books. I had no special expertise, or even strong feelings, concerning the issues we discussed.

Nevertheless I went on and debated heatedly, *passionately*, about issues I did not in fact care much about. I clashed aggressively with the other panelists. At one point I got into it so much with Vicki Lawrence, the actress and comedienne from *The Carol Burnett Show* who sang the hit song "The Night the Lights Went Out in Georgia,"[57] that she leaped to her feet and yelled at me because of something I said—I don't remember what—regarding the death penalty. On another *Politically Incorrect*, former Monkees member Micky Dolenz and I got into a vehement disagreement about something. Again, I don't remember what, only that at the time I felt strongly that it was my job, as an author promoting a book, to stand up for my beliefs, whatever they were.

But mostly what you do on book tours is talk about the book you're trying to sell. You do many interviews, in which you say the same things over and over and over, trying to sound enthusiastic even though deep down inside you're starting to hate your book.

Sometimes the people interviewing you have read your book, but much more often they have not. This isn't necessarily their fault. If it's a morning-drive radio show where they're squeezing you in with the music, traffic and weather, or a local TV news broadcast where they're doing nineteen other segments, they don't have time to read your book. Sometimes they don't

---

57. This song has a complex plot, which I have never really understood. So before the Maher show, in the greenroom, I asked Vicki Lawrence what it was about. She replied: "I have absolutely no idea."

really have time to even talk about your book. I did many interviews with midday TV-news anchorpersons that went basically like this:

> ANCHORPERSON: With us now is humor author Dave Barry, who has a new book out. Welcome, Dave!
>
> ME: Thank you!
>
> CO-ANCHORPERSON: So, Dave, what's this book about?
>
> ME: Computers.
>
> CO-ANCHORPERSON: Ha ha!
>
> ANCHORPERSON: Funny stuff! Thank you, Dave Barry! On a more tragic note, a kennel fire has claimed the lives of fifty-three puppies. For more on that story, we go to . . .

All authors have stories about awkward book-tour interviews. My favorite is one that was told to me by the late historian David McCullough. He was on a TV show discussing his book about the Panama Canal, *The Path Between the Seas,* and the host asked him how he felt about the United States handing the canal over to Panama. David's answer was that regardless of the canal's legal status, it would always, in a sense, belong to the United States, "like Normandy Beach."

According to David, the interviewer looked puzzled, paused, then said: "I don't understand. Who is Norman D. Beach?"

The best part about book tours is meeting the readers, the people who, instead of staying home and watching TV, go to bookstores to see you, pay actual money for your books, stand in line to have you sign them, and almost always act as though you're doing *them* a favor. Sometimes they even bring gifts. My readers have brought me, among many other things, T-shirts, whoopee cushions, cakes, cookies, Pop-Tarts, Pez dispensers, a coconut brassiere, beer—a *lot* of beer—Slim Jims, Cheez-Its, regular brownies and some highly irregular brownies, if you catch my drift.

In forty years of book-touring I've signed I don't know how many thousands of copies of my books. I've also signed books by other authors, as well as photos, newspaper clippings, CDs, tapes, Kindles, laptops, shirts, hats, shoes, casts, arms, legs, chests, foreheads and the diapers of multiple babies.

Usually people want me to personalize the books, for either themselves or somebody else. Sometimes they also want me to write a special message for the person they're giving the book to, such as "Happy Birthday!" or "Keep laughing!" or "You're an idiot!" Occasionally, they want me to write some inspirational message that I would never actually say to anybody, like "Keep striving and you will achieve your dreams!"

I'll write pretty much anything people want. Hey, it's their book. If they don't care what I write, I'll write *For [name], with best wishes,* or a deeply insincere inscription such as:

For [name], my absolute closest personal friend

For [name], my idol

For [name], without whom I would never have written this book

For [name], the mother of my children

I enjoyed—I still enjoy—getting out and meeting readers. But the era of the multicity, in-person book tour is coming to an end, replaced by social media and virtual events. I'm not sure that book tours have ever been a particularly effective way to sell books anyway. What really sells books is word of mouth, by which I mean women.

Women read more books, especially novels, than men. Women also are better at sharing their feelings than men, who—I'm generalizing here, but you know I'm right—usually are reluctant to say how they really feel about anything other than pass interference. When women like a book, they let people know. That's how books become bestsellers.

I've witnessed this process firsthand. Remember the hugely successful novel *The Kite Runner*, by Khaled Hosseini? That book sold seven million copies, and I would conservatively estimate that five million of those sales were the direct result of pressure from my wife, Michelle, who is a woman. She loved *The Kite Runner*, and for a period of roughly a year after reading it she insisted that every human being she encountered—in bookstores, on airplanes, in elevators and public restrooms, on the Small World ride at Disney World—had to buy it.

This is a true story: When our daughter, Sophie, was four, her preschool class had a Mother's Day lunch. The teachers had asked the children to describe their moms, then wrote the descriptions on posters taped to the wall. The other moms' posters said things like "My mom bakes cookies," "My mom plays with me" and "My mom is pretty." Michelle's poster—I swear I did not set Sophie up to do this—said: "My mom tells everyone to read *The Kite Runner*."

I have met Khaled Hosseini. He's a nice guy and a fine writer. But he is not, to the best of my knowledge, married to my wife. Whereas I am. Multiple times during Michelle's intensive yearlong promotional campaign for *The Kite Runner*, I asked her if maybe she could, if she had a few spare minutes, make one of *my* books into a bestseller. Each time she laughed and assured me that she loves my books, too. Then she resumed promoting *The Kite Runner*.

Despite the lack of support from my wife, most of my books have done OK. A couple of them did well enough that a TV producer bought the rights to be used as the basis of the TV sitcom *Dave's World*, which ran on CBS for four seasons in the early nineties. It starred the late Harry Anderson as Dave Barry, a newspaper columnist.

That was a weird experience, because many people assumed that (a) I wrote the show, and (b) it resembled my actual life. Neither of these assumptions was correct. The show was written by professional TV writers in Los Angeles, and the plots involved Dave getting into wacky sitcom situations with his family, friends and colleagues such as Kenny Beckett, played by Shadoe Stevens, who was Dave's editor at his newspaper, the *Miami Record-Dispatch*. Often at the end of an episode Dave would learn a life lesson.

My real life was nothing like that. My real life, at that time, consisted of sitting in a room with two dogs and zero other humans, hour after hour, day after day, staring at a computer screen and thinking: *This is not funny*. This experience did not teach me any life lessons, other than that dogs fart a lot. Also my real newspaper was the *Miami Herald* and my editor was Tom Shroder, who is far more journalistically qualified than Shadoe Stevens but has way less hair.

I don't mean to be whiny here. I got paid for the book rights, and the *Dave's World* people were always nice to me. They even flew me out to California in the first season to meet everybody and appear in a cameo role. It was a scene set in an appliance store where two guys are competing to buy the last air conditioner during a heat wave. Harry Anderson played me, and I played a person with no acting ability.

I really enjoyed hanging out with Harry; he was a funny, smart, very unpretentious guy. He knew I'd played in rock bands, and he had this idea for a bit we'd do together at the end of the episode in which he and I would play "Wild Thing" on guitars. Harry didn't play guitar. He'd practiced the chords for maybe fifteen minutes, but even for "Wild Thing" that's not really enough.

In the episode, as the end credits are rolling, Harry and I play a verse and a chorus together on our guitars. Then I stop playing and say, "Take it!" Harry then takes a solo, which is unquestionably the worst rendition of "Wild Thing" ever recorded. After maybe ten seconds, I stop him and say, "OK, give it back."

So that was fun. But I was relieved when *Dave's World* ended its run, because as I say it was awkward, having this network TV show about a guy with my name living this life that was theoretically based on mine but wasn't really much like it.

A few years after *Dave's World* ended I wrote my first novel. This came about because of an idea of Tom Shroder's. He wanted to showcase the many writers with connections to South Florida, so he got thirteen of us[58] to collaborate on a serial story published weekly in the *Herald*'s Sun-

---

58. Brian Antoni, Edna Buchanan, Tananarive Due, John Dufresne, James Hall, Vicki Hendricks, Carl Hiaasen, Carolina Hospital, Elmore Leonard, Paul Levine, Evelyn Mayerson, Les Standiford and me.

day *Tropic* magazine, with each of us writing a chapter, then handing the story off to the next writer.

I wrote the first chapter, which involved a manatee named Booger. Elmore "Dutch" Leonard wrote the second-to-last chapter, and Carl Hiaasen heroically wrapped it up. We called it *Naked Came the Manatee*, in tribute to *Naked Came the Stranger*, the 1969 parody sex novel written by a group of *Newsday* staffers.

Naked Came the Manatee was not a great work of literature. It had a convoluted and wildly improbable plot, involving not one, but two, severed heads, both allegedly belonging to Fidel Castro. Also as the story progressed Booger became increasingly assertive and intelligent—traits not normally associated with manatees—and wound up performing heroic deeds, like some kind of big fat aquatic Lassie.

Nevertheless the project was popular with *Tropic* readers, and to our astonishment Neil Nyren, who'd been Carl Hiaasen's editor at Putnam, liked it enough to buy it and publish it as an actual book. Carl, Dutch and I spent a week in New York doing publicity, which was as much fun as I've ever had promoting a book, because we didn't have to take it seriously.

The highlight occurred on the Charlie Rose show, when Rose, noticing that Dutch was giving vague answers to his questions, finally asked him point-blank: "Have you read this book?" At which point Dutch, Carl and I collapsed into uncontrollable giggles, because Dutch had not, in fact, read the book. He had delegated that chore to his research assistant, who'd given him enough information so that he could write a standalone chapter, thereby passing all responsibility for the plot along to Carl. Dutch Leonard was nobody's fool.

Whatever its merits, *Naked Came the Manatee* actually sold reasonably well (all proceeds went to charity). And Neil Nyren liked my opening chapter enough that he asked me if I'd be interested in writing a novel. Until then I'd never thought of myself as a novelist. I thought of myself as a joke writer. My columns were basically bunches of jokes; my books were basically larger bunches of jokes. I'd never written anything with what you would call a plot.

But Neil was offering me actual money to give it a try, so I wrote *Big Trouble*. The plot elements included municipal corruption, Russian gangsters selling Soviet military weapons out of a Miami bar, a runaway herd of Santeria sacrificial goats and people getting high on a psychedelic substance secreted by a toad. I wish I could say these elements sprang from my fertile imagination, but in fact all of them sprang directly from news stories published in the *Miami Herald*.

Big Trouble came out in 1999. It got pretty good reviews and became a *New York Times* bestseller (a real one, not a Modesto Nuts one). Then it got made into a movie, which is basically the dream scenario for a first-time novelist, although in my case there was an unexpected twist.

The movie was a big-budget, major-studio project. It was directed by Barry Sonnenfeld, and it had a big cast of name actors, including Tim Allen, Rene Russo, Sofia Vergara, Stanley Tucci, Zooey Deschanel, Omar Epps, Dennis Farina, Ben Foster, Janeane Garofalo, Johnny Knoxville, Jason Lee, Heavy D, Tom Sizemore and Patrick Warburton. The screenplay was by Robert Ramsey and Matthew Stone.

It was filmed in Miami, which was a surreal experience for me—watching my words get converted, at tremendous effort and expense, into movie sets. For example, in the book I'd written a scene set in a treehouse. Filming that scene required an army of movie people, who descended with a vast fleet of vehicles and tons of equipment on an unsuspecting tree for several long, intense, sometimes frantic days. It was like the Normandy invasion, but with much better catering.

And that was just for one scene, which in the movie lasts maybe a minute or two. This process was repeated all over Miami during the summer and fall of 2000. At one point the production took over a concourse of Miami International Airport for a week, filming a scene wherein a pair of spectacularly incompetent crooks board an airplane carrying a suitcase that they believe contains jewels, but which actually contains a nuclear bomb.

The studio spent $40 million making *Big Trouble*, and another $6 million promoting it. Before the planned Hollywood premiere they held

206

a special advance screening in Miami, which I attended with my family and friends. I went to bed that night feeling pretty excited.

The next morning I awoke to the sound of Michelle urgently calling me to come see what they were showing on TV.

It was September 11, 2001.

Not a good time to release a wacky movie comedy, especially one with a suitcase nuke on an airplane.

So the release of *Big Trouble* was postponed. It finally came out, quietly, in April 2002, with a subdued Hollywood premiere and very minimal publicity. It got mixed-to-crappy reviews and disappeared from theaters quickly. So it bombed at the box office, though in time it developed a bit of a cult following in cable reruns. There are some people who think it's actually quite good.

I think it's fine, but in my mind it's connected with 9/11. This feeling is irrational, but it makes the movie less fun for me to watch. In fact after the 2002 premiere, I didn't watch it again until twelve years later, when I presented it to an audience in St. Petersburg, Russia. To explain how that came about, I'm going to backtrack a bit, because the story involves my friend and sometime collaborator Ridley Pearson.

I met Ridley when we became original members of the Rock Bottom Remainders, a rock band of authors founded in 1992 by Kathi Goldmark. Members have come and gone, but over the years the band, in addition to Ridley and me, has included Mitch Albom, Sam Barry, Tad Bartimus, Roy Blount Jr., Robert Fulghum, Matt Groening, Carl Hiaasen, Greg Iles, Mary Karr, Stephen King, Barbara Kingsolver, Greil Marcus, Dave Marsh, James McBride, Frank McCourt, Joel Selvin, Amy Tan, Scott Turow and Alan Zweibel.[59]

These are excellent writers. Some of them are even good musicians.

---

59. We've been greatly helped by two professional ringers: drummer Josh Kelly and saxophonist Erasmo Paolo, both great musicians and great guys. Also we have a superb professional sound man, Gary Hirstius, who has been forced to listen to us at close range and still loves us. And for many years we've been managed—this is basically an impossible job—by Ted Habte-Gabr, who's also field coordinator of the Dave Barry for President juggernaut.

But the Remainders are not a good band. We don't really even rise to the level of mediocre. Our genre, as Roy Blount put it, is "hard-listening music." At one time we had T-shirts that said "This Band Plays Music as Well as Metallica Writes Novels."

Nevertheless being in the Remainders has been—I say this without shame—one of the highlights of my life. I love the camaraderie, hanging out with other writers, talking about everything except our Writing Process, happily making fools of ourselves onstage. But I also love making music, however ineptly, with other people; I'd been missing that experience since my Federal Duck days.

And as bad as we are, we've gotten to play with some pretty great musicians, starting with rock legend Al Kooper, who courageously agreed to be our musical director in our early days. I'll never forget the pep talk he gave us after our first rehearsal: "When we started this morning, we stunk. But by this afternoon, we stunk much better. Maybe eventually we can be just a faint odor."

Another rock legend, the great Roger McGuinn, has played with the Remainders, off and on, for years; he's so good that he somehow manages to make us sound almost like the Byrds, especially when the rest of us turn our amps down to zero or below. The late Warren Zevon, who was a buddy of Carl Hiaasen's, loved hanging out with the Remainders and joined us for many gigs. Lesley Gore got up with us once and sang "It's My Party." We also backed up Judy Collins on "Both Sides Now," Darlene Love on "He's a Rebel" and Gloria Gaynor on "I Will Survive."

And then there was the night in Los Angeles in 1994 when we were playing for a booksellers convention. We were down to our last song when we got word that a special guest was in the house, and he was willing to get onstage with us. He wasn't an author, but we let him perform anyway, because he was Bruce Springsteen.

He strolled out in jeans, T-shirt and a baseball cap, and the place went nuts. I handed him my guitar, thereby ensuring that I would forever after be able to claim I owned a guitar that had been played by Bruce Springsteen. Then we launched into our last song, which was "Gloria."

As it happens, I sing lead on that song. So when we get to the chorus, I spell out "G-L-O-R-I-A!" and the backup singers respond "GLOOOOR-I-A!" What I'm saying, in case you haven't figured it out, is that *Bruce Springsteen sang backup for me.* And that was the moment when his career really took off.

Seriously though, that was a very cool moment, one of many I've had thanks to the Remainders. But for me the best thing about the band has been the friendships. Which brings me back to Ridley Pearson. He and I bonded right away. He's the bass player, and an excellent musician. I always stand next to him, because I can rely on him to know important technical information, such as what specific song we're supposed to be playing.

So Ridley and I became close friends, and in 2004, we became coauthors. The way that came about was, Ridley was reading J. M. Barrie's *Peter Pan* to his daughter, Paige, when she stopped him and asked: How did Peter Pan meet Captain Hook in the first place? Ridley thought that was an excellent question; in fact, he thought the answer could be a book. He asked me if I'd be interested in working with him on a prequel to *Peter Pan.* I said yes, because it sounded like a quick, fun little project.

And it *was* fun. But it was not quick or little. In fact it wound up dominating my writing life for the next half-dozen years. We thought we were going to write a short children's book; we ended up writing a 450-page YA novel, *Peter and the Starcatchers.* It did really well. It even became a Broadway play, adapted by Rick Elice as *Peter and the Starcatcher* (without the final "s"), which won five Tony awards.

Peter and the Starcatchers was published by Disney, which meant Ridley and I did some very Disneyfied promotional events. For a big book signing at the Walt Disney World Contemporary Resort, they built a mock pirate ship to serve as our backdrop, complete with a cannon that actually went BOOM. Also on hand were Disney people dressed as Peter Pan and Captain Hook.

While we were waiting for the event to start, Ridley and I hung out in a tiny room with Peter Pan for about fifteen minutes, just the three of us. That was awkward because, as a Disney cast member in costume, he was required to remain in character at all times. I was unaware of this policy, so I attempted to make small talk with him. It did not go well:

ME: So how do you like working at Disney?

PETER PAN (*placing hands on hips*): It's a beautiful day in Never Land!

ME: Huh.

(*Fifteen seconds of awkward silence*)

PETER PAN: Have you seen Wendy?

If you want to experience a *long* fifteen minutes, try hanging out in a small confined space with Peter Pan.

Ridley and I wound up writing five books in the *Starcatchers* series. We also wrote a standalone YA novel called *Science Fair*, which resulted in one of my favorite fan letters ever, from two elementary-school boys:

Dear Mr. Barry and Mr. Pearson:
Both of us think that your book "Science Fair" is one of the awesomest books out there. Just to warn you, two authors that our book club has written to have died. We hope that the curse skips you so that you can make a sequel as soon as possible.
Sincerely,
[Names]
P.S. for most of the letter we alternated writing three words at a time.

Ridley and I went on many book tours together, but the most memorable was in 2014, when we traveled to Russia. We were part of the US State Department's American Writers Series program, under which authors are sent over there to improve relations between the two nations. Clearly this program did not work; as I write these words, the United States and Russia are practically at war. But I don't think it's fair to blame me. It was Ridley's fault.

Seriously, though: Ridley and I did our best over there, despite challenging circumstances. And by "challenging circumstances," I mean, in my case, "a world-class case of the trots."

On our second night in Moscow, I stupidly did the one thing you should never, ever do in Russia: I ate at a Mexican restaurant. It was operated by Russians, and Mexican food is not their forte. (If I'm being honest, they're not that great at Russian food either.)

At this Russian Mexican restaurant I ate what I later realized must have been a weaponized chimichanga. We should all pray, for the sake of humanity, that the Russians never unleash this thing on the rest of the world, because it caused me to develop a severe case of what gastroenterologists call CBS, or Chernobyl Bowel Syndrome.

But aside from that experience, I enjoyed touring Russia, at least those parts of Russia that were within sprinting distance of a bathroom. Ridley and I did a bunch of presentations for Russian audiences, talking about our careers and how we wrote the *Starcatchers* books. We had a slide show, which included a picture of me, in my newspaper-columnist days, embarrassing my son, Rob, by picking him up at his middle school in the Oscar Mayer Wienermobile.

The Russian audiences would look at this photo—they don't have the Wienermobile over there—and I could tell they were thinking: *How the hell did we lose the Cold War to these people?*

The groups we spoke to were generally polite and receptive. At the end of each talk I asked them what stereotypical views they thought Americans held about Russians. Inevitably they brought up two stereotypes, both of which they thought were unfair: that they drink vodka all the time, and that they're all gangsters.

This brings me, finally, back to *Big Trouble*, which as you may recall (though I doubt it) is what started me on this digression about my friendship with Ridley. At the end of our Russia tour, I was asked to do a special event for the American consulate in St. Petersburg. Each month they held a movie night in the consul general's residence, with the Russian public invited to screenings of American films. Since I'd had a book made into a movie, they thought it'd be fun to show *Big Trouble*, and have me introduce it to the audience.

I hadn't seen the movie since I attended the premiere way back in 2002, so on the day of the screening, to prepare my introduction, I reviewed the plot. That's when I realized that I was going to standing in front of an audience of Russians—who resent the fact that Americans stereotype them as gangsters—to introduce a movie that actually has some Russian characters in it, and . . .

. . . and they're gangsters!

So that was a lot of fun, by which I mean not fun at all. In my introduction I pointed out that while the Russian characters in *Big Trouble* were, in fact, criminals, they were at least *intelligent* criminals, whereas many of the American characters were both criminal *and* stupid. But I don't think this mollified the audience. It's possible that, contrary to the entire purpose of the American Writers Series program, I actually worsened relations between the United States and Russia; I might, after all, be partly responsible for the fact that we're currently almost at war. If so, allow me to state, in all sincerity: My bad.

Not long after *Big Trouble* was originally released, I had another adventure in the movie industry. It began when I got this email:

Hi Dave, it's Steve Martin.

I'm hosting the Oscars this year [2003] and am trying to put together a team of geniuses to help me write it. Here's my question: do you know any? HA!

I'm wondering if the idea appeals to you at all. You, me, Rita Rudner and a few others. Best Oscar monologue ever. California. Tickets to the show. Fame.

I know you won't do it, so go fuck yourself.

Steve

Of course I said yes. For one thing, I had long been a huge Steve Martin fan. For another thing, if I'd said no Michelle would have divorced *and* killed me. She immediately started assembling her Oscars outfit. Literally within hours of when I received Steve's email she had purchased uncomfortable shoes.

A few months later I flew to Los Angeles for the first writers' meeting. I was terrified. I'd never been part of anything like that, while the rest of the writers—Beth Armogida, Dave Boone, Andy Breckman, Jon Macks, Rita Rudner, Robert Shapiro and Bruce Vilanch—were experienced showbiz comedy pros.

We met in a hotel conference room. I later wrote about that first meeting:

Steve Martin was to my immediate left, taking notes on his laptop computer as the other writers tossed out idea after idea. This group process was unfamiliar and intimidating to me; I've always written alone. I tried to have an idea, but my brain had frozen into a cold, hard mass of lifeless tissue. For about an hour, the only coherent thought it could form was: *I'm sitting right next to Steve Martin!*

But gradually my brain began to thaw, as I realized a surprising thing: These people were all remarkably generous. I'd assumed that they'd be competitive—lobbying for their own jokes, maybe even criticizing other people's.

But it wasn't like that at all. In fact, it was the opposite: If somebody came up with something good, the laughter around the table was instant and genuine; if somebody came up with a joke that needed help, everyone tried to think of ways to improve it. Many jokes mutated through a number of forms, with various people coming up with various elements, until eventually there was no way to tell whose joke it was.

This is the way it works in Hollywood; almost everything is collaborative. All of these people had spent many hours sitting in writer-filled rooms just like this, dreaming up stuff.

By the second meeting, we were comfortable with each other and with the way Martin liked to work. There was a clear pattern to the way he reacted to ideas. When somebody tossed out a joke, Martin would, most of the time, nod and say, "Ya, ya, ya." This meant: "No." He almost never actually said no, because he's a genuinely nice guy, and he wanted to let the joke-tosser know he appreciated the effort. But "ya" definitely meant "no."

When Martin liked an idea enough to at least consider using it, you could tell because he typed it into his computer. The taptaptap of his keyboard was kind of like applause. If he really liked the joke, he'd perform it, trying different wordings and deliveries; sometimes he'd even stand up to do this, giving it the full stand-up–comedian treatment. And if it was your idea, you'd think—at least I did—*Steve Martin is performing MY joke.*

I ended up greatly enjoying the whole Oscars experience, especially getting to know Steve. He is, as you'd expect, very smart and very funny, but he's also serious, meticulous and intensely analytical in his approach to his craft. He spent hours rehearsing the opening monologue, constantly adding, cutting and tweaking jokes right up until the day of the show.

On Oscars night we writers, clad in formal attire, watched from a small room just offstage equipped with monitors and a direct phone line to the teleprompter operator. After each of his segments Steve would join us to review how it was going and discuss possible changes to upcoming material. He was remarkably calm and focused, always looking for ways to make the show better, even as the show was going on.

At one point Michael Moore, who won the Oscar for Best Documentary Feature, launched into an angry speech ripping President George W. Bush and the second Gulf War. It was the first overtly political moment of the show, and it definitely changed the vibe in the theater. There was some booing.

Moore's speech was followed by a commercial break, after which Steve was due back onstage. In the writers' room, we felt he needed to address the situation. We had maybe three minutes, during which we somehow—I was there, but I can't really explain what happened—came up with a joke. When Steve went back out, he said, "It's so sweet backstage, you should have seen it. The Teamsters are helping Michael Moore into the trunk of his limo." That got a big laugh, and the show went on.

Backstage at the Oscars: Steve Martin, me, Bruce Vilanch and Rita Rudner

So that was a thrilling way to experience the Oscars. Michelle, who was in the audience, also had an exciting time. She had an excellent seat, directly in front of Bono—that's right, Michelle had a better seat than Bono—and in the same row as Julie Andrews, who is one of Michelle's absolute favorite people, ranking just below our daughter but well above me.

After the show we sat at Steve's table at the Governors Ball, where we met a cavalcade of movie stars and discovered that many of them—Julia Roberts, for example—are minuscule humans who apparently never eat any meal more substantial than a Tic Tac. It was a fantastic, memorable night, although by the end of it Michelle's feet were in critical condition and I was carrying her shoes.

I wrote for Steve again in 2010, when he cohosted the Oscars with Alec Baldwin. I haven't done the Oscars since then, although I have remained involved in the movie industry, in the sense that I've had screenplays in development.

In case you're unfamiliar with the movie industry, I should explain what we mean by the term "a screenplay in development." We mean "a screenplay that will never become an actual movie." At least that has been my experience.

Writing for the movies turns out to be very different from the kind of writing I've done for most of my career. When you write for print—newspapers, magazines, books—this is the process:

1. You write something.
2. You submit it to an editor.
3. The editor edits it.
4. It gets published.

Some of these steps may take a little time; for example, the editor might want to make some changes, which you and the editor might discuss. But these four steps are essentially the process for print.

Now here, based on my experience, is the process for writing for the movie industry:

1. You write a screenplay.

2. You submit it to your agent.

3. Six months pass.

4. Your agent calls with exciting news: A company you've never heard of that is somehow connected with the movie industry has optioned your script! They want to schedule a conference call ASAP!

5. Six more months pass, during which the conference call is rescheduled four times because everybody in the movie industry is very, very busy.

6. The call finally happens. There are somewhere between three and eight people on the other end; there is no way to tell. But they're excited about your screenplay. They love it! In fact they're thinking of it as a project for Tom Cruise! With whom they are somehow vaguely connected! Also there's a director whose name you don't recognize but they say he's very hot and he might become attached! Whatever that means! So while they're thrilled with the screenplay, they'd like you to make a few tweaks. Specifically they want you to reimagine the setting, characters, plot and overall concept. But they love it! They're eager to move forward!

7. You completely rewrite the screenplay and send it to the movie people.

8. Absolutely nothing happens for eleven months.

9. Your agent calls with good news: The movie people love the rewrite and want to have another conference call ASAP.

10. Eight more months pass, during which the follow-up conference call is rescheduled nine times.

11. You have the call. It sounds as though some, maybe most, of the movie people on this call are different from the ones who were on the first call. But whoever they are, they love the screenplay. It's perfect! However now they're thinking of it as more of an Adam Sandler vehicle. They're wondering if you can make it less Tom Cruise–y and more Adam Sandler–y.

12. You completely rewrite the screenplay.

13. A year passes, during which the follow-up conference call is re-scheduled twenty-nine times.

14. You have the call. You're certain that this time you're talking to a completely different group of people. Nevertheless they love the rewrite. Here's the thing, though: They're now seeing it as more of an Emma Stone vehicle, or possibly Joe Pesci, or—thinking outside the box—a musical featuring the pig from *Babe*. They'd like you to have another go at it with this in mind. You try to ask "With *what* in mind?" But before you can speak everyone has left the call. They're extremely busy out there.

15. You completely rewrite the screenplay with an Emma Stone/Joe Pesci—type protagonist and a subplot involving a pig that sporadi-cally bursts into song.

16. Two to five years later you have another call. This time there's only one person on the other end. His name is Liam, and he is at most twenty years old. You can hear video game noises in the back-ground. Liam is a senior executive in a company that bought the company that originally optioned your screenplay. He loves your screenplay, or at least the title, which is the only part he has read. He's wondering how you would feel about adapting it as an episode of a series they're developing for Hulu about competing gangs of transgender Amish flamingo breeders.

17. You completely rewrite the script.

And so on. And on. And on.

You think I'm exaggerating, right? That's because, no offense, you've never had a screenplay in development. What I've described is, in fact, the process. You will keep rewriting your screenplay until not a single molecule of the original version remains. Why do you do this? *Because they pay you.* They pay you quite well, in the movie business, to crank out revisions of screenplays for movies that they are never going to make.

How are they able to do this? What is the business model? Where does the money come from, if there's no movie? My best guess is that many of the people in the movie industry are also in some *other* industry—bathroom renovation, maybe—that is actually profitable. They're paying you to rewrite your screenplay with money they make from renovating bathrooms, which is time-consuming, which is why it's so hard to get them on the phone.

I speak with authority here. I have a screenplay that has been in development long enough that if it were a human being, it would be dating Leonardo DiCaprio. My collaborator in this project is Alan Zweibel, a good friend and veteran comedy pro. He was one of the original *Saturday Night Live* writers and was the cocreator, with Garry Shandling, of *It's Garry Shandling's Show*. He has worked with everybody in the business, and everybody loves him, which is quite an achievement. He also has a very large head, a head that would not look out of place on Easter Island, but he's sensitive about it, so I plan to delete this sentence later.

A while back Alan and I cowrote a novel titled *Lunatics*, about two suburban dads who get into a dispute over an offsides call at a children's soccer game and wind up, purely by accident, overthrowing the governments of both Cuba and China, bringing peace to the Middle East and running against each other for president of the United States.

So it's not a work of gritty realism. It's a Wacky Romp. We sold the movie rights, under a deal that had us write the screenplay. That was in 2012. We are still, as I type these words, rewriting the screenplay. We have done this multiple times over the years, each time tweaking the plot a bit more. Currently it's a story about transgender Amish flamingo breeders.

Not really. Although we may get there before we're done.

Despite the seeming endlessness of the process, I've enjoyed working with Alan, a very funny guy who's easy to work with once you get used to the size of his head, about which I will say no more.[60] In fact

---

60. Seriously, it's enormous.

after we wrote *Lunatics*, Alan and I combined on two other books with a third collaborator, Adam Mansbach, who's the author of a heartwarming book of gentle, soothing poems for parents to read to their young children at bedtime, *Go the Fuck to Sleep*.

Together Alan, Adam and I wrote *For This We Left Egypt?* and *A Field Guide to the Jewish People*. These are humor books about Judaism. Our qualifications for writing them are that Alan and Adam are Jewish, and I am circumcised. We did some fun publicity tours for those books; the events consisted almost entirely of the three of us telling Jewish jokes[61] and two of us making fun of Alan's head.[62]

Which brings me back to book tours, which have been a big part of my life going back to my insanely improbable guest appearance on *The Tonight Show*. That was the beginning of what turned out to be a wild and wonderful ride for me as an author.

I may not be a literary giant; I'll never have the critical acclaim of, say, Marcel Proust. But was Marcel Proust ever on Carson? Did he ever steal a hotel sign for Oprah? Does he currently have a screenplay in development? Did he write jokes for Steve Martin to deliver before an Oscars audience in which his (meaning Marcel Proust's) wife was sitting in the same row as Julie Andrews? Can Marcel Proust claim that books of his were made into a network sitcom, a Broadway play *and* a major motion picture featuring both Zooey Deschanel and Sofia Vergara? Did Marcel Proust ever sing "Gloria" with Bruce Springsteen singing backup? Was he (meaning Marcel Proust) even circumcised?

The answer is no, to the best of my knowledge. I know for sure he was never in the Remainders.

My point is this: For a person who started out writing columns for the West Chester, Pennsylvania, *Daily Local News* in between obituaries and meetings of the regional sewage authority, I've had a damn good

---

61. For example: Two Jewish men are standing on the deck of the *Titanic* as it sinks into the cold, dark sea. One of them starts sobbing. The other says, "Why are you crying? It's not *your* boat."

62. Because it's so big.

run. In fact it's been a *great* run. I've had a charmed career, far beyond anything I could have dreamed of.

Of course nothing goes on forever. There comes a time, inevitably, when you have to accept that, no matter how much fun it has been, you've reached the end. And I regret to say that, for me, that time has come. It's over.

I'm referring to this chapter.

CHAPTER EIGHT

THE END

O N JANUARY 2, 2005, MY SUNDAY COLUMN IN THE
Miami Herald began:

> There comes a time in the life of every writer when he asks himself—as
> Shakespeare, Tolstoy and Hemingway all surely asked themselves—if
> he has any booger jokes left in him.

I then announced that I was ending my weekly column. I gave two
reasons. The first was:

> I want to stop before I join the horde of people who think I used to
> be funnier.

To be clear: I still thought I was funny. My column was syndicated
in something like five hundred newspapers, and nobody was pressuring
me to quit writing it. I had the best job in American newspapers.

But here's the thing about doing humor for a living: You always wonder if you still have it. There's a good reason for this: There are always
people eager to inform you that you do not, in fact, still have it. Or that
you never did have it.

My favorite quotation about humor writing—it hangs, framed, on my office wall—is from a review in the *New York Times Book Review* written by the great Dorothy Parker about *The Road to Miltown*, by S. J. Perelman:

> The author's lot is a hard one, and yet there are those who deliberately set out to make it harder for themselves. There are those who, in their pride and their innocence, dedicate their careers to writing humorous pieces. Poor dears, the world is stacked against them from the start, for everybody in it has the right to look at their work and say, "I don't think that's funny."

Dorothy Parker was, as usual, correct. If you're a Serious Opinion Columnist, most people who read your column either agree with you or disagree with you. Or they don't care. But however they feel about your column, they implicitly accept the idea that you performed your basic function as a columnist, which is to express an opinion.

If, however, you're billed as a humor columnist, the readers' expectation is that you will entertain them, just as people who go to comedy clubs expect to be entertained by the comedians. If your readers are offended, or simply not amused, they can declare—it's their right!—that you suck at your job.

Before I start to sound whiny—and I will, in a second—I want to stress that the response I've gotten from readers over the years has been overwhelmingly positive, even loving, occasionally verging—a little scarily—on worshipful. I've been blessed with wonderful, loyal readers, and I am deeply grateful to them.

But as Dorothy Parker noted, an occupational hazard of this job is that anybody can judge you to be a failure. I've been told countless times—in letters, in emails, in reviews, in the comments section and in person—that I'm not funny, or that I used to be funnier. People have been telling me that I used to be funnier since I was columnizing for the *Daily Local News*. If I believed all those people, I'd have to accept that my writing has declined to the point where it's less amusing than the federal tax code.[63]

I don't believe that. I do believe that some people don't like my writing. But that doesn't mean I'm not funny. It means those people are assholes.

Ha ha! Not really!

OK, in some cases, really.

But my point is that humor is subjective, and my humor doesn't work for everybody. Fortunately for me it resonated with enough people that I had a good career as a columnist, which as of January 2005 was still going strong.

But.

But I was fifty-seven years old, and had been writing a humor column for about thirty years. More and more I'd find myself thinking things like, *Have I used this joke before? Have I in fact sort of written this entire column before?*

I worked hard to make sure each column was genuinely new. But I could see a time coming when I'd get tired of that effort, and I didn't want to get to the point where I was phoning it in. So, as I wrote in my farewell column, I decided to quit before I became one of the people who thought I used to be funnier.

That was one of the two reasons I gave. The other one was:

I want to work on some other stuff.

By that I meant stuff like this book, and screenplays for movies that will never get made—things that don't have a deadline perpetually looming. I wanted to get away from always thinking, whenever I went anywhere or did anything, including playing dolls with my four-year-old daughter: *Maybe I can use this for a column.*

Deadlines are the columnist's curse. No matter what else they're doing, columnists are always—*always*—thinking about their next column. I'd spent much of my adult life thinking about mine. I didn't want to spend any more time thinking about it. Because you only get so much time.

---

63. Although to be fair, the federal tax code can be pretty funny.

I'd had a stark reminder of that fact a few years before I retired, when Jeff MacNelly, the brilliant cartoonist—he won *three* Pulitzer Prizes for editorial cartooning and created the *Shoe* comic strip—died at age fifty-two, after a rough battle with lymphoma. Jeff was my friend and collaborator; he illustrated my column for thirteen years. He drew my all-time favorite drawing of me, when I, improbably, won the Pulitzer Prize for Distinguished Commentary:

Jeff and I talked a lot, because when I was running late with a column he'd call to find out what it was about so he could illustrate it. I'd say something like, "I think it's gonna be about how Zippy[64] pooped on the only nice rug we have. It's a small rug. It had to be intentional." And Jeff would say, "Got it." And with only that to go on, he'd draw a cartoon that was much funnier than my column.

Jeff's death—he was a big, full-of-life guy with a booming laugh—

---

64. At that time Zippy was my small emergency backup dog. My large main dog was named Earnest.

shook me. It led to a conversation that, for me, was life-changing. I wrote about this conversation at length in my book *Lessons from Lucy*; I'll summarize it here.

A few months after Jeff's funeral, I was aboard a sailboat with Jeff's widow, Sue, and others who'd gathered to honor Jeff's memory by shooting his ashes from a cannon into the waters off Key West. After the ceremony I got to talking with the cartoonist Mike Peters, who was Jeff's closest friend, and who'd been at the hospital when Jeff died. Mike told me he'd been struck by the fact that the hospital staff had no idea who Jeff was. They didn't know he was a famous cartoonist with many accolades: To them, he was just Mr. MacNelly, the patient in room whatever.

What Mike realized then, as I wrote in *Lessons from Lucy*, was this:

> In the end, your professional achievements don't matter. In the end, all that really matters—all you really have—is the people you love. Not your job, not your career, not your awards, not your money, not your stuff. Just your people.

Which is not to say wealth and fame aren't nice; just that they're nothing compared to family and friends.

I've thought about that conversation a lot; I still think about it almost every day. It was very much on my mind when I decided to quit my column. I wanted to be able to spend less time fretting over deadlines, and more time focusing on the people I love. Which, the occasional deadline notwithstanding, I've mostly been able to do for the past twenty years.

I've been asked many times if I miss writing a weekly column. I don't. I still occasionally write columns, and every year I produce a longish Year in Review for the *Herald* and some other papers. Some readers look forward to it; others view it as an opportunity to inform me that I used to be funnier. I like it because it keeps me connected with the newspaper business, which I still love.

But it's not the same business anymore. The Internet exploded the revenue model that once made newspapers so profitable, forcing many papers to cut back, lay off people or shut down altogether. And the toxic nature of our political discourse has made what's left of the news business a lot less fun.

Which brings me to Art Buchwald.

In the mid-1980s, when my column was starting to gain traction nationally, I got a letter from Art. That was a big deal for me. When I was growing up, Art Buchwald was literally a household name in the Barry family. Both of my parents were fans, but my mom absolutely loved him; she sometimes read his columns aloud from the *Herald Tribune*.

The reason for Art's letter was to invite me to become a member of the prestigious American Academy of Humor Columnists. In the letter, which was written on official academy stationery, Art informed me that the other members were Russell Baker, Erma Bombeck and *San Francisco Chronicle* columnist Art Hoppe.

I of course was elated to accept the invitation. My elation was in no way diminished by the fact that the prestigious American Academy of Humor Columnists did not actually exist, except in Art's imagination, and on his official stationery.

But I was genuinely honored that he'd reached out to me, an upstart whippersnapper in the genre he had long dominated. We exchanged letters, then phone calls, and we became friends. Whenever he came to Miami, we'd go to lunch or dinner. He was excellent company, funny as hell, and always generous with encouragement and advice.

In 2005 Art's health worsened badly. One of his lower legs had to be amputated, and his kidneys failed. His doctors told him he had to have dialysis, but he decided the hell with that, he'd rather die. So in February of 2006 he went to a hospice to die.

Except he didn't die. He was definitely supposed to; his doctors assured him he would. But he didn't. His friends—he had a million friends—came around to say goodbye, and they ended up laughing with Art at the absurdity of the situation.

I called him at the hospice, expecting to have a sad goodbye talk. Instead he was in great spirits, thoroughly enjoying hospice life.

"I love it!" he said. "I eat well, and everybody treats me like a million dollars."

I asked him what the doctors were telling him.

"A week or two," he said. "I could do dialysis, probably for the rest of my life, or I could just go happily into the sunset.

"I'm gonna go to heaven," he assured me.

I told him the world missed his column.

"We need you," I said. "The vice president is shooting people."

He laughed, then we said goodbye. I figured that was it.

But Art kept on not dying. In June, having not died for more than four months, he left the hospice and started writing again. In July Ridley Pearson and I went to see him at his house on Martha's Vineyard (we were on the island for a book event). Art's son, Joel, ushered us into the room where Art had been receiving a steady stream of visitors.

Art, who was seated, greeted us, then gestured toward an artificial limb lying on an ottoman a few feet away.

"That's my leg," he said. He was not fond of it.

We stayed for about an hour, during which Art recounted his medical saga, which sounds like a grim topic but, take my word, it was hilarious. We hugged goodbye, and that was the last time I saw Art.

He continued not dying until January of 2007, when he finally proved the doctors correct. In March there was a celebration of his life at the Kennedy Center. It drew over five hundred people, among them Bob Woodward, Andy Rooney, Russell Baker, Sam Donaldson, Nancy Pelosi and John Glenn. I was given the honor of being one of the speakers, along with Ben Bradlee, Tom Brokaw, Ethel Kennedy, Mike Wallace and members of Art's family.

In my eulogy, I recalled the first time Art and I spoke on the phone:

"We talked about column-writing, and I remember thinking: 'Here I am, a rookie columnist, getting advice from one of the all-time greats. If only I could understand what he was saying.' As you know, Art spoke as though he had a family of hamsters living in his mouth."

Which was true.

Art also spoke at his celebration, in a video. It showed him in 1981, delivering a monologue at the Kennedy Center to a black-tie audience. Sitting in the front row, roaring with laughter at Art's jokes about him, was President Ronald Reagan.

Think about that: We were celebrating a guy who got laughs from both Ronald Reagan and Nancy Pelosi. Art was definitely a Democrat, but he made fun of whoever was in power, and he was beloved by people on both sides. Art, like Johnny Carson, epitomized an era when it was still OK to make political jokes without worrying about which party was the target of the joke.

That era is over. We're now in an era when many people insist that politics is Not a Joking Matter—the stakes are too high!—and humor is viewed not as entertainment, but as a tactical weapon to be used exclusively for attacking the other side. Some people are really good at tactical political humor. Some of it is very funny. But I wouldn't call it fun.

Man, I'm sounding old here.

Anyway, Art has gone to the Big Syndicate in the Sky. So have Russell Baker, Erma Bombeck and Art Hoppe. That leaves me as the sole surviving member of the prestigious American Academy of Humor Columnists. Although I have not performed any official acts, because Art had all the stationery.

But I'm still around. Apparently there's some question about this. If you start a Google search with the phrase "Is Dave Barry," the words immediately suggested by Google autocomplete are "still alive."

For the record, I am in fact still alive, and I'm in reasonably good

health for a man of seventy-seven. And when I say, "I'm in reasonably good health for a man of seventy-seven," I mean, "every single organ in my body is disintegrating." At least that's my understanding, as a layperson, of what my doctors tell me.

Like most old people, I have nearly enough doctors to form a softball team. I have a heart doctor; a second heart doctor that the first heart doctor regularly sends me to for additional consultation; a kidney doctor whom I was referred to by the second heart doctor to determine whether my kidneys were able to handle a certain test, which they were, but now I have to keep seeing the kidney doctor throughout all eternity because apparently that is a rule; another kidney doctor who's the brother of the first kidney doctor and sees me when his brother is busy; an eye doctor; a second eye doctor whom the first eye doctor sent me to for a procedure that the first eye doctor doesn't perform which needless to say requires many follow-up visits; and of course a doctor who examines my prostate gland using what I know, on an intellectual level, is merely his forefinger, although in the moment—which seems to last as long as the Super Bowl halftime show—it feels as though he's rooting around in there with a Louisville Slugger.

I like all of my doctors as human beings. I am less crazy about them as doctors, because they have a tendency—I suspect it's a habit they picked up in medical school—to deliberately look for medical problems.

I do my best to discourage them. I approach visits to my doctors' offices much the way a Mafia boss approaches a congressional hearing: I give them nothing. I answer "no" to all the questions on the Patient Health History Questionnaire, including "What is your address?" I *never* admit to having symptoms. If I were to notice something amiss— if, for example, I started finding live tadpoles in my underpants[65]—I would not disclose this to my doctors.

But that doesn't stop them from finding things that could be cause

---

65. Is that normal? Asking for a friend.

for alarm. Every time I see a doctor, I have an unsettling conversation like this:

DOCTOR (*frowning at computer screen*): Your HDP level is up.

ME   My what?

DOCTOR: Your hyperbolic dissimulation parameter. Last time you were at 53.7, but now you're at 61.2.

ME: Is that bad?

DOCTOR: It depends. It could mean your frenulum is having trouble extrapolating plenary acids.

ME: Is that bad?

DOCTOR: It depends. It can lead to CDFV.

ME: To what?

DOCTOR: Catastrophic devolution of the fiduciary viaduct.

ME: Is that bad?

DOCTOR: In 30 percent of the cases it's fatal.

ME: What about the other 70 percent?

DOCTOR: They're also fatal.

ME: So I'm going to die?

DOCTOR: It depends.

The result of these conversations is always that I need more tests, which always turn up more things for the doctor to be concerned about, and possibly a new doctor for me to add to the team. No doctor ever says "Everything looks great, Dave! See you in five to ten years!"

Of course my situation isn't unique: Most people my age are in declining health. Sadly, the sun is setting on the Baby Boomers—the generation that survived the Great Depression, won World War II and landed a man on the moon.

No, wait, that wasn't us. We're the generation that went to Woodstock and partied naked for three solid days on a diet consisting entirely of LSD and mud. We were young then, full of life and fearless; now we read the ingredients on bottled water. Assuming we can find our reading glasses.

So we Boomers are old. Our race is almost run. The time has come for us to pass the baton to the younger generations, along with all the precious nuggets of timeless wisdom that we have acquired over the years.

Unfortunately, the younger generations are not interested in receiving our wisdom. In fact the one thing that Gen X, the Millennials and Gen Z all agree on is that the Boomers should shut up.

This is understandable. A lot of the precious wisdom nuggets that we Boomers like to pass along to younger people sound like this:

"Your music sucks."

"Why are you always staring at your cell phone?"

"There's no melody! It's just people shouting!"

"When I was your age we didn't even have cell phones!"

"Someday you're going to regret getting those tattoos."

"We didn't have Instagram OR TikTok!"

"You'd be so much prettier if you didn't have that stupid ring in your nose."

"We didn't have influencers!"

"If you didn't waste your money on Starbucks, you could afford to buy a house."

"We didn't have blah!"

"Blah blah blah!"

And so on. A lot of Boomer wisdom is simply complaining, the senescent spewing of a generation that has turned into old farts, just as the generations before us did.

I am definitely guilty of this behavior. If my daughter happens to mention to me that she was at a concert that had a celebrity DJ, I will reflexively—I can't help myself—launch into a rant about how stupid I find the concept of "celebrity DJ" to be, because we're talking about a person who is *playing records*, which requires no more musical talent than operating a toaster oven, so why for the love of God do people carry on as though this person is some kind of Jimi Hendrix–level virtuoso when HE'S JUST A HEADPHONE-WEARING DWEEB MAKING EMO FACES WHILE HE FIDDLES WITH SOME KNOBS?

Even as I say these things I'm aware of how pathetically old I sound. I can see the pity in the eyes of my daughter, who has heard this rant many times before. But I repeat it anyway. *I must speak my Boomer truth, consarn it!*

So the question I'm asking myself, as the duly elected spokesperson for my entire generation, is: Do I have any *real* wisdom to impart? Have I learned *anything* worth passing along?

Maybe.

Long ago, when I turned fifty, I created a list of twenty-five things I'd learned to that point. Some of these things were basically jokes. For example:

- If you had to identify, in one word, the reason why the human race has not achieved, and never will achieve, its full potential, that word would be: "meetings."

- You should never say anything to a woman that even remotely suggests you think she's pregnant unless you can see an actual baby emerging from her at that moment.

- The one thing that unites all human beings, regardless of age, gender, religion, economic status or ethnic background, is that, deep down inside, we all believe that we are above-average drivers.

- There is a very fine line between "hobby" and "mental illness."

But some of my twenty-five things were sincere attempts to express life lessons. Five of those things still strike me as fundamentally true, and worth passing along:

1. You should not confuse your career with your life.
2. A person who is nice to you, but rude to the waiter, is not a nice person.
3. No matter what happens, somebody will find a way to take it too seriously.
4. Your friends love you anyway.
5. Nobody cares if you can't dance well. Just get up and dance.

I hereby pass those five nuggets along to any members of future generations willing to heed the words of a DJ-dissing old fart.

There's one more wisdom nugget I'd like to add, something that seems truer to me the older I get:

It's gonna be OK.

Here's what I mean by that:

All my life I've been told that some Very Bad Thing or another was going to happen. I've been told that there was going to be nuclear war. I've been told that the planet would become an uninhabitable wasteland because of global cooling, and also because of global warming. I've been told that we were going to run out of food, and oil, and water. I've been told that civilization would collapse because of a pandemic. I've been told multiple times that a worldwide economic catastrophe is imminent. I've been told that the United States government was going to be taken over by communists, and also by fascists. I've been told that someday breakdancing would be an Olympic sport.

OK, that last one happened. But the others did not. My point is, I've been hearing apocalyptic predictions, often from people considered to be authorities, for going on eighty years. If I'd believed all of these predictions, I'd have lived my entire life in a state of abject quivering terror.

Fortunately, I didn't. Most of us didn't. Most of us lived our lives as if we expected life to go on. We had careers and kids, and now our kids are having kids, because they also expect life to go on, because that's what life does.

Does that mean no catastrophically bad thing can ever happen? No. Does it mean you shouldn't educate yourself about issues like climate change? Again, no. What it means is that if you spend all your days worrying about some horrible catastrophe that never actually happens, you're wasting the only days you get.

There will always be people telling you to be afraid, because sowing fear is profitable. There are whole industries devoted to scaring you; it's the business model of most major world religions. Both major political parties raise millions of dollars by telling you that if the other party wins, we're doomed. We journalists *love* to explain why you should be terrified.

Yet life goes on. It did for my generation; it will for yours. So when the next Very Bad Thing comes along, and the winds of panic start to swirl around you, try to remember: *It's gonna be OK.*

Anyway, that's the wisdom, such as it is, that I have accumulated over the course of my life, which as you may recall is the subject of this book. The book is almost over, although my life, as I type these words, is still going on. And despite the concerns of my softball team of doctors, I like to think it will go on for a while.

But in the end everybody dies, with the possible exception of Keith Richards. So it's only natural, when you get to be my age, to think about your own death. When will it happen? How will it happen? Will you die with dignity, wearing clean pajamas, or will you keel over on the toilet Elvis-style, in midpoop? Will your last words to your loved ones be memorable and wise, or something along the lines of "Glurg"? What will your obituary say? Will it mention any of your life accomplishments other than International Talk Like a Pirate Day, which wasn't even your idea?

I don't have the answers to these questions. I do, however, have an inkling of what it might feel like to be dead. That's right: I've had first-hand experience as a corpse.

This happened because of a column I wrote in 1994, in which I argued that listening to opera could be fatal to humans:

> I base this statement on an Associated Press article, sent in by many
> alert readers, concerning an alarming incident in Denmark involving

an okapi, which is a rare African mammal related to the giraffe. The article states that this okapi—I am not making this quotation up—"died from stress apparently triggered by opera singers."

The okapi was not actually attending an opera when this happened. It was in a zoo located 300 yards from a park where opera singers were rehearsing. A zoo spokesperson was quoted as saying that okapis "can be severely affected by unusual sounds."

So here are the essential facts:

1. An okapi, minding its own business, was killed by opera music being sung three football fields away.
2. Okapis are members of the mammal family.
3. Most human beings, not counting Congress, are also members of the mammal family.

When I consider these facts together, a very disturbing question comes to my mind, as I'm sure it does yours: What were three football fields doing in Denmark?

Another question is: Could opera, in sufficient dosages, also be fatal to human beings?

I concluded by saying that the federal government might, as a public-health measure, have to ban opera altogether. I was of course joking, but some opera-lovers *really* took offense. That column resulted in some of the most strongly worded hate mail I ever got. Here's an actual quote from one letter, referring to one of my many inaccurate statements about opera: "*Così Fan Tutte* is Italian and not Spanish, you cocksucker. Fuck you."

I got one nice letter in response to that column. It was from Janice Mackey, who was the general manager of Eugene Opera in Eugene, Oregon. She invited me to go out there and play the part of a corpse in a performance of the Puccini opera *Gianni Schicchi*.

Of course I said yes. As I wrote in a follow-up column, "I am always looking for new ways to get paid for being motionless."

So I went to Eugene, which, if you're traveling from Miami, is not an easy voyage:

> To get there, you have to take a series of "commuter" airplanes, each one smaller than the last, until finally there isn't room for both you and the pilot, and you have to fly yourself. "Eugene is that way!" the airline personnel tell you, gesturing vaguely. "Just look for the rain cloud!"

The Eugene Opera people were great. The experience of being a corpse was not so great. They made me wear itchy tights, an itchy old-man nightshirt and an itchy wig, and they put a ton of itchy makeup on my face. Then I had to lie in a bed onstage under bright lights and hold absolutely still—dead men don't scratch—while a squadron of professional opera singers armed with vocal cords like tram cables bellowed in a foreign language for forty-five solid minutes at extremely close range without once pausing to inhale.

Based on my stint as a corpse, I would describe the experience of death as loud. Also, itchy. It was, frankly, unpleasant. I don't plan to die again unless I absolutely have to.

———

So that's my memoir. Thanks for reading it. You now know where I got my ideas (Costco) and you're up to date on my life, as of age seventy-seven. If anything major happens to me in the future, I believe I'd be legally required to write another memoir, which I am hoping to avoid. So my plan from now on is to lead a quiet, event-free life—to take it easy as I drift, at a leisurely pace, toward age eighty, and whatever lies beyond.

Whatever it is, I think it's gonna be OK.

APPENDIX

A GOOD NAME FOR
A ROCK BAND

WHEN I WROTE MY WEEKLY COLUMN, I HAD A RUN-
ning gag: I'd use a phrase, then observe, after the fact, that it
would be a good name for a rock band—or, for short, WBAGNFARB.
For example, in a column about trying to learn how to windsurf, I wrote:

> This involves standing on a surfboard with a sail attached to it, and
> then, by shifting your weight and pointing the sail in a certain direc-
> tion relative to the wind, falling into the water like a sack of gravel.
> I estimate that I got up on the surfboard, and immediately fell back
> off, 50 times, in the process traveling forward a total of 11 feet. I was
> the source of much entertainment for the people on the beach. Even
> the reef was emitting billions of tiny but hearty polyp chuckles, which
> would be a good name for a rock band.

So "Hearty Polyp Chuckles" WBAGNFARB.
I often got rock-band names from news stories:

> But you should be aware of an alarming Associated Press news story,
> sent in by alert reader Brian Kinney, concerning a tragic incident that
> occurred in Thailand because of gangs fighting over—I swear I am

not making this up—bat dung. According to the article, some villagers in an area northeast of Bangkok had been "gathering bat dung in a mountain cave," and when they emerged from the cave "with seven sacks of valuable dung," somebody threw a grenade at them. The story states that Thai police "believe rival dung gatherers were behind the attack."

Obviously, "Rival Bat Dung Gatherers" WBAGNFARB.
Here are some of the other band names that found their way into my columns over the years:

The Flaming Salmonella Units
Excessive Deer Doots
The Fecal Pellets
The Wood Tick Snorkels
Heave
Squatting Turnips
The Bones of Contention
Pinot Noir and His Nuances of
    Toast
The Fabulous Snake Doots
Shy Fruiter and the Saplings
Weasel Nostrils
Three Fatty Acid Radicals
The Flaming Booty Moths
Earl Piedmont and the
    Diphthongs
Slippery Spleens
Sheep Eyeballs
The Flaming Croutons
Rodent Passion
Flaming Squirrels
Balky Charcoal

St. Vincent and the Grenadines
The Biscuit Whackers
Gaseous Worms
Raymond Burr's Legs
Shark Puke
Jimmy Music and the Stomach
    Contents
Little Heed
Short Shrift
Gastric Contents
The Phlegmtones
Crotch
Effluent
The Postal Patrons
The Vestigial Organs
Decomposing Tubers
Diminished Penile Sensation
Bill and the Bracts
The Foliage Eaters
Crab Shrapnel
DeWayne Hurlmont and the
    Compunctions of Soul

APPENDIX

Contaminated Tumbleweed

Varlet and the Squeaking Codpieces

Violently Fracturing Water Closets

The Flying Shards

The Fierce Prune-Eating Hamsters from Space

Duane Ketter and His Wildlife Technicians

Paint-Peeling Puffs of Flatulence

Mosquito Hunter and the Unreliable Pollinators

The Mighty Shaking Wattles

Bleeding Nipples

Rapid Sucking Action

Nuclear Underpants

Marcel and the Turpitudes

The Groin Whappers

Thrusting Balloon Puppies

Drastic Toilet Air

The Eerie Groin Legumes

Drawers Full of Slugs

Groping for Elmo

The Pig-Stinging Jellyfish

Fugitive Squirrel and the Clearly Disturbed Beavers

The Moos of Derision

IMAGE CREDITS

5, 6, 12, 13, 16, 17, 21, 22, 34, 37, 45, 59: Courtesy of the Barry Family

89, 100: Courtesy of the *Miami Herald*

113: Courtesy of Brian Smith

115, 116, 123, 149, 211: Courtesy of the author

194: Courtesy of Carson Entertainment Group

215: Copyright © 2014, *Los Angeles Times*. All rights reserved.

226: Courtesy of Gallery on Greene

ACKNOWLEDGMENTS

I'll start by thanking two wise women who encouraged me to write this book: my agent, Amy Berkower of Writers House, and my editor at Simon & Schuster, Priscilla Painton. Thanks also to associate editor Johanna Li for painstakingly shepherding the manuscript through the production process, and to Larry Hughes, a patient and unflappable publicist.

Thanks, as always, to Judi Smith, whom I would describe as my right hand, but I'm left-handed, and it sounds weird to describe her as my left hand, so I'll just say she's my invaluable assistant.

Thanks to my brothers, Phil and Sam, for helping me recall our Armonk days, both the good and the not-so-good. I love you, little bros.

Thanks to Joe DiGiacinto, my oldest friend as well as the Barry family *consigliere*, who started kindergarten with me and who remembers everything, though he would never tell.

Thanks to Gene Weingarten and Tom Shroder for their help with the chapter on *Tropic* magazine, and for making *Tropic* the most fun place to work in all of journalism, if not the entire world.

Thanks, again, to all my readers, even the ones who wanted me to be fired. And thanks to all the editors who had to deal with readers calling the newspaper to complain that my column made an inaccurate statement such as that Abraham Lincoln invented the light bulb, when everyone knows it was Benjamin Franklin.

ACKNOWLEDGMENTS

Thanks to my beloved bandmates in the Rock Bottom Remainders, because writing is a lonely job, but it feels less lonely when you're onstage with other writers mangling the lyrics, such as they are, to "Wild Thing."

Finally, thanks, for their love and support, to my wonderful family: Sophie Barry; Rob, Laura, Dylan, and Kyle Barry; and Celia Kaufman. Above all, thanks to Michelle Kaufman, my wife, best friend, and officemate, for her steadfast assurance that this would turn out to be a good book, despite the fact that it is not *The Kite Runner*.